ALL GLORY TO ŚRĪ GURU AND GAURĀṄGA

ŚRĪMAD BHĀGAVATAM

of

KṚṢṆA-DVAIPĀYANA VYĀSA

स वै मनः कृष्णपदारविन्दयो-
वचांसि वैकुण्ठगुणानुवर्णने ।
करौ हरेर्मन्दिरमार्जनादिषु
श्रुतिं चकाराच्युतसत्कथोदये ॥

sa vai manaḥ kṛṣṇa-padāravindayor
vacāṁsi vaikuṇṭha-guṇānuvarṇane
karau harer mandira-mārjanādiṣu
śrutiṁ cakārācyuta-sat-kathodaye

(pp.97–98)

BOOKS by
His Divine Grace A. C. Bhaktivedanta Swami Prabhupāda

Bhagavad-gītā As It Is
Śrīmad-Bhāgavatam, Cantos 1–9 (27 Vols.)
Śrī Caitanya-caritāmṛta (17 Vols.)
Teachings of Lord Caitanya
The Nectar of Devotion
The Nectar of Instruction
Śrī Īśopaniṣad
Easy Journey to Other Planets
Kṛṣṇa Consciousness: The Topmost Yoga System
Kṛṣṇa, the Supreme Personality of Godhead (3 Vols.)
Perfect Questions, Perfect Answers
Dialectic Spiritualism—A Vedic View of Western Philosophy
Transcendental Teachings of Prahlād Mahārāja
Kṛṣṇa, the Reservoir of Pleasure
Life Comes from Life
The Perfection of Yoga
Beyond Birth and Death
On the Way to Kṛṣṇa
Geetār-gan (Bengali)
Rāja-vidyā: The King of Knowledge
Elevation to Kṛṣṇa Consciousness
Kṛṣṇa Consciousness: The Matchless Gift
Back to Godhead Magazine (Founder)

A complete catalog is available upon request

The Bhaktivedanta Book Trust
3764 Watseka Avenue
Los Angeles, California 90034

ŚRĪMAD BHĀGAVATAM

Ninth Canto

"Liberation"

(Part One—Chapters 1-8)

With the Original Sanskrit Text,
Its Roman Transliteration, Synonyms,
Translation and Elaborate Purports

by

His Divine Grace
A.C. Bhaktivedanta Swami Prabhupāda
Founder-*Ācārya* of the International Society for Krishna Consciousness

THE BHAKTIVEDANTA BOOK TRUST
New York · Los Angeles · London · Bombay

Readers interested in the subject matter of this book are invited by the International Society for Krishna Consciousness to correspond with its Secretary.

International Society for Krishna Consciousness
3764 Watseka Avenue
Los Angeles, California 90034

First Printing, 1977: 20,000 copies

Printed in the United States of America

Library of Congress Cataloging in Publication Data (Revised)

Puranas. Bhāgavatapurāna.
Śrīmad-Bhāgavatam.

Includes bibliographical references and indexes.
CONTENTS: Canto 1. Creation. 3 v.—Canto 2. The cosmic manifestation. 2 v.—Canto 3. The status quo. 4 v.—Canto 4. The creation of the Fourth Order. 4 v.—Canto 5. The creative impetus. 2 v.
1. Chaitanya, 1486-1534. I. Bhaktivedanta Swami, A. C., 1896- II. Title.
BL1135.P7A22 1972 73-169353
ISBN 0-912776-94-3

Table of Contents

Preface

We must know the present need of human society. And what is that need? Human society is no longer bounded by geographical limits to particular countries or communities. Human society is broader than in the Middle Ages, and the world tendency is toward one state or one human society. The ideals of spiritual communism, according to *Śrīmad-Bhāgavatam,* are based more or less on the oneness of the entire human society, nay, of the entire energy of living beings. The need is felt by great thinkers to make this a successful ideology. *Śrīmad-Bhāgavatam* will fill this need in human society. It begins, therefore, with the aphorism of Vedānta philosophy *janmādy asya yataḥ* to establish the ideal of a common cause.

Human society, at the present moment, is not in the darkness of oblivion. It has made rapid progress in the field of material comforts, education and economic development throughout the entire world. But there is a pinprick somewhere in the social body at large, and therefore there are large-scale quarrels, even over less important issues. There is need of a clue as to how humanity can become one in peace, friendship and prosperity with a common cause. *Śrīmad-Bhāgavatam* will fill this need, for it is a cultural presentation for the re-spiritualization of the entire human society.

Śrīmad-Bhāgavatam should be introduced also in the schools and colleges, for it is recommended by the great student-devotee Prahlāda Mahārāja in order to change the demoniac face of society.

kaumāra ācaret prājño
dharmān bhāgavatān iha
durlabhaṁ mānuṣaṁ janma
tad apy adhruvam arthadam
(*Bhāg.* 7.6.1)

Disparity in human society is due to lack of principles in a godless civilization. There is God, or the Almighty One, from whom everything emanates, by whom everything is maintained and in whom everything is merged to rest. Material science has tried to find the ultimate source of creation very insufficiently, but it is a fact that there is one ultimate source of everything that be. This ultimate source is explained rationally and authoritatively in the beautiful *Bhāgavatam* or *Śrīmad-Bhāgavatam.*

Śrīmad-Bhāgavatam is the transcendental science not only for knowing the ultimate source of everything but also for knowing our relation with Him and our duty towards perfection of the human society on the basis of this perfect knowledge. It is powerful reading matter in the Sanskrit language, and it is now rendered into English elaborately so that simply by a careful reading one will know God perfectly well, so much so that the reader will be sufficiently educated to defend himself from the onslaught of atheists. Over and above this, the reader will be able to convert others to accepting God as a concrete principle.

Śrīmad-Bhāgavatam begins with the definition of the ultimate source. It is a bona fide commentary on the *Vedānta-sūtra* by the same author, Śrīla Vyāsadeva, and gradually it develops into nine cantos up to the highest state of God realization. The only qualification one needs to study this great book of transcendental knowledge is to proceed step by step cautiously and not jump forward haphazardly like with an ordinary book. It should be gone through chapter by chapter, one after another. The reading matter is so arranged with its original Sanskrit text, its English transliteration, synonyms, translation and purports so that one is sure to become a God-realized soul at the end of finishing the first nine cantos.

The Tenth Canto is distinct from the first nine cantos because it deals directly with the transcendental activities of the Personality of Godhead Śrī Kṛṣṇa. One will be unable to capture the effects of the Tenth Canto without going through the first nine cantos. The book is complete in twelve cantos, each independent, but it is good for all to read them in small installments one after another.

I must admit my frailties in presenting *Śrīmad-Bhāgavatam,* but still I am hopeful of its good reception by the thinkers and leaders of society on the strength of the following statement of *Śrīmad-Bhāgavatam* (1.5.11):

tad-vāg-visargo janatāgha-viplavo
yasmin prati-ślokam abaddhavaty api

nāmāny anantasya yaśo 'ṅkitāni yac
chṛṇvanti gāyanti gṛṇanti sādhavaḥ

"On the other hand, that literature which is full with descriptions of the transcendental glories of the name, fame, form and pastimes of the unlimited Supreme Lord is a transcendental creation meant to bring about a revolution in the impious life of a misdirected civilization. Such transcendental literatures, even though irregularly composed, are heard, sung and accepted by purified men who are thoroughly honest."

Oṁ tat sat

A. C. Bhaktivedanta Swami

Introduction

"This *Bhāgavata Purāṇa* is as brilliant as the sun, and it has arisen just after the departure of Lord Kṛṣṇa to His own abode, accompanied by religion, knowledge, etc. Persons who have lost their vision due to the dense darkness of ignorance in the age of Kali shall get light from this *Purāṇa*." (*Śrīmad-Bhāgavatam* 1.3.43)

The timeless wisdom of India is expressed in the *Vedas*, ancient Sanskrit texts that touch upon all fields of human knowledge. Originally preserved through oral tradition, the *Vedas* were first put into writing five thousand years ago by Śrīla Vyāsadeva, the "literary incarnation of God." After compiling the *Vedas*, Vyāsadeva set forth their essence in the aphorisms known as *Vedānta-sūtras*. *Śrīmad-Bhāgavatam* is Vyāsadeva's commentary on his own *Vedānta-sūtras*. It was written in the maturity of his spiritual life under the direction of Nārada Muni, his spiritual master. Referred to as "the ripened fruit of the tree of Vedic literature," *Śrīmad-Bhāgavatam* is the most complete and authoritative exposition of Vedic knowledge.

After compiling the *Bhāgavatam*, Vyāsa impressed the synopsis of it upon his son, the sage Śukadeva Gosvāmī. Śukadeva Gosvāmī subsequently recited the entire *Bhāgavatam* to Mahārāja Parīkṣit in an assembly of learned saints on the bank of the Ganges at Hastināpura (now Delhi). Mahārāja Parīkṣit was the emperor of the world and was a great *rājarṣi* (saintly king). Having received a warning that he would die within a week, he renounced his entire kingdom and retired to the bank of the Ganges to fast until death and receive spiritual enlightenment. The *Bhāgavatam* begins with Emperor Parīkṣit's sober inquiry to Śukadeva Gosvāmī: "You are the spiritual master of great saints and devotees. I am therefore begging you to show the way of perfection for all persons, and especially for one who is about to die. Please let me know what a man should hear, chant, remember and worship, and also what he should not do. Please explain all this to me."

Śukadeva Gosvāmī's answer to this question, and numerous other questions posed by Mahārāja Parīkṣit, concerning everything from the nature of the self to the origin of the universe, held the assembled sages in rapt attention continuously for the seven days leading to the King's death. The sage Sūta Gosvāmī, who was present on the bank of the Ganges when Śukadeva Gosvāmī first recited *Śrīmad-Bhāgavatam*, later repeated the *Bhāgavatam* before a gathering of sages in the forest of Naimiṣāraṇya. Those sages, concerned about the spiritual welfare of the people in general, had gathered to perform a long, continuous chain of sacrifices to counteract the degrading influence of the incipient age of Kali. In response to the sages' request that he speak the essence of Vedic wisdom, Sūta Gosvāmī repeated from memory the entire eighteen thousand verses of *Śrīmad-Bhāgavatam*, as spoken by Śukadeva Gosvāmī to Mahārāja Parīkṣit.

The reader of *Śrīmad-Bhāgavatam* hears Sūta Gosvāmī relate the questions of Mahārāja Parīkṣit and the answers of Śukadeva Gosvāmī. Also, Sūta Gosvāmī sometimes responds directly to questions put by Śaunaka Ṛṣi, the spokesman for the sages gathered at Naimiṣāraṇya. One therefore simultaneously hears two dialogues: one between Mahārāja Parīkṣit and Śukadeva Gosvāmī on the bank of the Ganges, and another at Naimiṣāraṇya between Sūta Gosvāmī and the sages at Naimiṣāraṇya Forest, headed by Śaunaka Ṛṣi. Furthermore, while instructing King Parīkṣit, Śukadeva Gosvāmī often relates historical episodes and gives accounts of lengthy philosophical discussions between such great souls as the saint Maitreya and his disciple Vidura. With this understanding of the history of the *Bhāgavatam*, the reader will easily be able to follow its intermingling of dialogues and events from various sources. Since philosophical wisdom, not chronological order, is most important in the text, one need only be attentive to the subject matter of *Śrīmad-Bhāgavatam* to appreciate fully its profound message.

The translator of this edition compares the *Bhāgavatam* to sugar candy—wherever you taste it, you will find it equally sweet and relishable. Therefore, to taste the sweetness of the *Bhāgavatam*, one may begin by reading any of its volumes. After such an introductory taste, however, the serious reader is best advised to go back to Volume One of the First Canto and then proceed through the *Bhāgavatam*, volume after volume, in its natural order.

This edition of the *Bhāgavatam* is the first complete English translation of this important text with an elaborate commentary, and it is the first widely available to the English-speaking public. It is the product of the scholarly and devotional effort of His Divine Grace A. C. Bhaktivedanta Swami Prabhupāda, the world's most distinguished teacher of Indian religious and philosophical thought. His consummate Sanskrit scholarship and intimate familiarity with Vedic culture and thought as well as the modern way of life combine to reveal to the West a magnificent exposition of this important classic.

Readers will find this work of value for many reasons. For those interested in the classical roots of Indian civilization, it serves as a vast reservoir of detailed information on virtually every one of its aspects. For students of comparative philosophy and religion, the *Bhāgavatam* offers a penetrating view into the meaning of India's profound spiritual heritage. To sociologists and anthropologists, the *Bhāgavatam* reveals the practical workings of a peaceful and scientifically organized Vedic culture, whose institutions were integrated on the basis of a highly developed spiritual world view. Students of literature will discover the *Bhāgavatam* to be a masterpiece of majestic poetry. For students of psychology, the text provides important perspectives on the nature of consciousness, human behavior and the philosophical study of identity. Finally, to those seeking spiritual insight, the *Bhāgavatam* offers simple and practical guidance for attainment of the highest self-knowledge and realization of the Absolute Truth. The entire multivolume text, presented by the Bhaktivedanta Book Trust, promises to occupy a significant place in the intellectual, cultural and spiritual life of modern man for a long time to come.

—The Publishers

His Divine Grace
A. C. Bhaktivedanta Swami Prabhupāda
Founder-Ācārya of the International Society for Krishna Consciousness

PLATE ONE

To worship Lord Kṛṣṇa, Mahārāja Ambarīṣa, along with his Queen, observed the vow of Ekādaśī and Dvādaśī for one year. In the month of Kārtika, after observing that vow for one year, Mahārāja Ambarīṣa observed a fast for three nights, bathed in the Yamunā and worshiped the Supreme Personality of Godhead, Hari, in Madhuvana. Following the regulative principles of *mahābhiṣeka*, Mahārāja Ambarīṣa performed the bathing ceremony for the Deities of Śrī-Śrī Rādhā-Kṛṣṇa with all paraphernalia, and then he dressed the Deities with fine clothing, ornaments, fragrant flower garlands and other paraphernalia for worship. Finally, with attention and devotion, he performed *ārati* for the Deities as the assembled devotees sang songs glorifying the Lord and played musical instruments such as shenais, kettledrums, and sitars. *(pp. 112–114)*

PLATE TWO

Just as King Ambarīṣa was about to break his Ekādaśī fast, Durvāsā Muni, the great and powerful mystic, appeared on the scene unannounced. The King humbly requested the sage to eat, and Durvāsā gladly accepted. However, he asked the King to wait a few moments while he performed the necessary rituals of bathing and meditating in the Yamunā River. As the King waited and waited, the proper period for breaking the fast was rapidly expiring, yet he could not eat without offending Durvāsā. In this dilemma, the King consulted with the palace *brāhmaṇas* and decided to drink water—for drinking water is considered as both eating and not eating. When Durvāsā Muni returned, he could understand by his mystic power that the King had drunk water without his permission, and he angrily spoke as follows: "Alas, just see the behavior of this cruel man! He is not a devotee of Lord Viṣṇu. Being proud of his material opulence and his position, he considers himself God. Just see how he has transgressed the laws of religion. Mahārāja Ambarīṣa, you have invited me to eat as a guest, but instead of feeding me, you yourself have eaten first. Because of your misbehavior, I shall show you something to punish you." As Durvāsā Muni said this, his face became red with anger. Uprooting a bunch of hair from his head, he created a demon resembling the blazing fire of devastation to punish Mahārāja Ambarīṣa. *(pp. 116–123)*

PLATE THREE

Upon seeing that his attempt to curse King Ambarīṣa had failed and that the Lord's Sudarśana *cakra* was moving toward him, Durvāsā Muni became very frightened and began to run in all directions to save his life. As the blazing flames of a forest fire pursue a snake, the disc of the Supreme Personality of Godhead began following Durvāsā Muni. Durvāsā Muni saw that the disc was almost touching his back, and thus he ran very swiftly, desiring to enter a cave of Sumeru Mountain. Just to protect himself, Durvāsā Muni fled everywhere, in all directions—in the sky, on the surface of the earth, in caves, in the ocean, on different planets of the rulers of the three worlds, and even on the heavenly planets—but wherever he went he immediately saw following him the unbearable fire of the Sudarśana *cakra*. *(pp. 126–128)*

PLATE FOUR

After running throughout the material universes in fear of the Sudarśana disc, Durvāsā Muni finally went to Vaikuṇṭhadhāma, where the Supreme Personality of Godhead, Nārāyaṇa, resides with His consort, the goddess of fortune. Falling at the lotus feet of Nārāyaṇa, Durvāsā spoke as follows: "O infallible, unlimited Lord! I have greatly offended your dear devotee King Ambarīṣa. Please give me protection." Lord Nārāyaṇa said to the *brāhmaṇa:* "I cannot protect you, for I am completely under the control of My devotees. Indeed, I am not at all independent. Because my devotees are completely devoid of material desires, I sit only within the cores of their hearts. As chaste women bring their gentle husbands under control by service, the pure devotees, who are equal to everyone and completely attached to Me in the core of the heart, bring Me under their full control. O *brāhmaṇa*, let Me now advise you for your own protection. By offending Mahārāja Ambarīṣa, you have acted with self-envy, for one's so-called prowess, when employed against a devotee, certainly harms he who employs it. Therefore you should go to him immediately, without a moment's delay. If you can satisfy Mahārāja Ambarīṣa, then there will be peace for you." *(pp. 134–147)*

PLATE FIVE

Durvāsā Muni, who was very much harassed by the Sudarśana *cakra,* approached Mahārāja Ambarīṣa, fell down and clasped the King's lotus feet. Aggrieved at Durvāsā's fearful condition, King Ambarīṣa immediately began offering prayers to the great weapon of the Supreme Personality of Godhead: "O Sudarśana *cakra,* you are fire, you are the most powerful sun, and you are the moon, the master of all luminaries. You are religion, you are truth, you are the maintainer of the entire universe, and you are the supreme transcendental prowess in the hands of the Supreme Personality of Godhead. You are the original vision of the Lord, and therefore you are known as Sudarśana. Everything has been created by your activities, and therefore you are all-pervading. O protector of the universe, you are engaged by the Supreme Lord as His all-powerful weapon in killing the envious enemies. For the benefit of our entire dynasty, kindly favor this poor *brāhmaṇa.* This will certainly be a favor for all of us. If the Supreme Personality of Godhead, who is one without a second, who is the reservoir of all transcendental qualities, and who is the life and soul of all living entities, is pleased with us, we wish that this *brāhmaṇa,* Durvāsā Muni, be freed from the pain of being burned." *(pp. 150–159)*

PLATE SIX

After performing His wonderful pastimes in the Yamunā River, Lord Śrī Kṛṣṇa got up on the shore, taking with Him all His beloved *gopīs*. After putting on dry clothing, they went to a small jeweled house, where the *gopī* Vṛndā arranged to dress them in forest clothing by decorating them with fragrant flowers, green leaves and all kinds of other ornaments. In Vṛndāvana, the trees and creepers are wonderful because throughout the entire year they produce all kinds of fruits and flowers. The *gopīs* and maidservants in the bowers of Vṛndāvana picked these fruits and flowers and brought them before Rādhā and Kṛṣṇa. The *gopīs* peeled all the fruits and placed them together on large plates on a platform in the jeweled cottage. They arranged the fruit in orderly rows for eating, and in front of it they made a place to sit. Among the fruits were many varieties of mango, bananas, berries, jackfruits, dates, tangerines, oranges, blackberries, grapes, and all kinds of dry fruit. At home Śrīmatī Rādhārāṇī had made various types of sweetmeats from milk and sugar, and she had brought them all for Kṛṣṇa. When Kṛṣṇa saw the very nice arrangement of food, He happily sat down and had a forest picnic.

PLATE SEVEN

Sagara Mahārāja performed *aśvamedha* sacrifices and thus satisfied the Supreme Lord, but Indra, the King of heaven, stole the horse meant to be offered at the sacrifice. Then King Sagara ordered the sixty-thousand sons of his wife Sumati to search for the lost horse. They finally found the horse near the *āśrama* of Kapila Muni, the great saint and incarnation of Lord Viṣṇu. "Here is the man who has stolen the horse," they said. "He is staying there with closed eyes. Certainly he is very sinful. Kill him! Kill him!" Shouting like this, the sons of Sagara raised their weapons. Then, because they had lost their intelligence and disrespected a great personality, fire emanated from their own bodies, and the sons of Sagara were immediately burned to ashes. Later, King Sagara's grandson, Aṁśumān, also searched for the lost horse and came upon Lord Kapila sitting near the remains of Aṁśumān's uncles. When Aṁśumān saw Kapila sitting by the lost sacrificial horse, he offered Him respectful obeisances, folded his hands and prayed with great attention: "O Supersoul of all living entities, O Personality of Godhead, simply by seeing You I have now been freed from all lusty desires, which are the root cause of insurmountable illusion and bondage in the material world." Thereupon, out of His causeless mercy, the Personality of Godhead said: "My dear Aṁśumān, here is the animal sought by your grandfather for sacrifice. Please take it. As for your forefathers, who have been burned to ashes, they can be delivered only by Ganges water, and not by any other means." *(pp. 242–259)*

CHAPTER ONE

King Sudyumna Becomes a Woman

This chapter describes how Sudyumna became a woman and how the dynasty of Vaivasvata Manu was amalgamated with the Soma-vaṁśa, the dynasty coming from the moon.

By the desire of Mahārāja Parīkṣit, Śukadeva Gosvāmī told about the dynasty of Vaivasvata Manu, who was formerly King Satyavrata, the ruler of Draviḍa. While describing this dynasty, he also described how the Supreme Personality of Godhead, while lying down in the waters of devastation, gave birth to Lord Brahmā from a lotus generated from His navel. From the mind of Lord Brahmā, Marīci was generated, and his son was Kaśyapa. From Kaśyapa, through Aditi, Vivasvān was generated, and from Vivasvān came Śrāddhadeva Manu, who was born from the womb of Saṁjñā. Śrāddhadeva's wife, Śraddhā, gave birth to ten sons, such as Ikṣvāku and Nṛga.

Śrāddhadeva, or Vaivasvata Manu, the father of Mahārāja Ikṣvāku, was sonless before Ikṣvāku's birth, but by the grace of the great sage Vasiṣṭha he performed a *yajña* to satisfy Mitra and Varuṇa. Then, although Vaivasvata Manu wanted a son, by the desire of his wife he got a daughter named Ilā. Manu, however, was not satisfied with the daughter. Consequently, for Manu's satisfaction, the great sage Vasiṣṭha prayed for Ilā to be transformed into a boy, and his prayer was fulfilled by the Supreme Personality of Godhead. Thus Ilā became a beautiful young man named Sudyumna.

Once upon a time, Sudyumna went on tour with his ministers. At the foot of the mountain Sumeru there is a forest named Sukumāra, and as soon as they entered that forest, they were all transformed into women. When Mahārāja Parīkṣit inquired from Śukadeva Gosvāmī about the reason for this transformation, Śukadeva Gosvāmī described how Sudyumna, being transformed into a woman, accepted Budha, the son of the moon, as her husband and had a son named Purūravā. By the grace of Lord Śiva, Sudyumna received the benediction that he would live one month as a woman and one month as a man. Thus he regained his kingdom and had three sons, named Utkala, Gaya and Vimala, who were all very religious. Thereafter, he entrusted his kingdom to Purūravā and took the order of *vānaprastha* life.

TEXT 1

श्रीराजोवाच
मन्वन्तराणि सर्वाणि त्वयोक्तानि श्रुतानि मे ।
वीर्याण्यनन्तवीर्यस्य हरेस्तत्र कृतानि च ॥ १ ॥

śrī-rājovāca
manvantarāṇi sarvāṇi
tvayoktāni śrutāni me
vīryāṇy ananta-vīryasya
hares tatra kṛtāni ca

śrī-rājā uvāca—King Parīkṣit said; *manvantarāṇi*—all about the periods of the various Manus; *sarvāṇi*—all of them; *tvayā*—by you; *uktāni*—have been described; *śrutāni*—have been listened to; *me*—by me; *vīryāṇi*—wonderful activities; *ananta-vīryasya*—of the Supreme Personality of Godhead, who has unlimited potency; *hareḥ*—of the Supreme Lord, Hari; *tatra*—in those *manvantara* periods; *kṛtāni*—which have been performed; *ca*—also.

TRANSLATION

King Parīkṣit said: My lord, Śukadeva Gosvāmī, you have elaborately described all the periods of the various Manus and, within those periods, the wonderful activities of the Supreme Personality of Godhead, who has unlimited potency. I am fortunate to have heard all of this from you.

TEXTS 2–3

योऽसौ सत्यव्रतो नाम राजर्षिर्द्रविडेश्वरः ।
ज्ञानं योऽतीतकल्पान्ते लेभे पुरुषसेवया ॥ २ ॥
स वै विवस्वतः पुत्रो मनुरासीदिति श्रुतम् ।
त्वत्तस्तस्य सुताःप्रोक्ता इक्ष्वाकुप्रमुखा नृपाः॥ ३ ॥

yo 'sau satyavrato nāma
rājarṣir draviḍeśvaraḥ
jñānaṁ yo 'tīta-kalpānte
lebhe puruṣa-sevayā

sa vai vivasvataḥ putro
manur āsīd iti śrutam
tvattas tasya sutāḥ proktā
ikṣvāku-pramukhā nṛpāḥ

yaḥ asau—he who was known; *satyavrataḥ*—Satyavrata; *nāma*—by the name; *rāja-ṛṣiḥ*—the saintly king; *draviḍa-īśvaraḥ*—the ruler of the Draviḍa countries; *jñānam*—knowledge; *yaḥ*—one who; *atīta-kalpa-ante*—at the end of the period of the last Manu, or at the end of the last millennium; *lebhe*—received; *puruṣa-sevayā*—by rendering service to the Supreme Personality of Godhead; *saḥ*—he; *vai*—indeed; *vivasvataḥ*—of Vivasvān; *putraḥ*—son; *manuḥ āsīt*—became the Vaivasvata Manu; *iti*—thus; *śrutam*—I have already heard; *tvattaḥ*—from you; *tasya*—his; *sutāḥ*—sons; *proktāḥ*—have been explained; *ikṣvāku-pramukhāḥ*—headed by Ikṣvāku; *nṛpāḥ*—many kings.

TRANSLATION

Satyavrata, the saintly king of Draviḍadeśa who received spiritual knowledge at the end of the last millennium by the grace of the Supreme, later became Vaivasvata Manu, the son of Vivasvān, in the next manvantara [period of Manu]. I have received this knowledge from you. I also understand that such kings as Ikṣvāku were his sons, as you have already explained.

TEXT 4

तेषां वंशं पृथग् ब्रह्मन् वंशानुचरितानि च ।
कीर्तयस्व महाभाग नित्यं शुश्रूषतां हि नः ॥ ४ ॥

teṣāṁ vaṁśaṁ pṛthag brahman
vaṁśānucaritāni ca

kīrtayasva mahā-bhāga
nityaṁ śuśrūṣatāṁ hi naḥ

teṣām—of all those kings; *vaṁśam*—the dynasties; *pṛthak*—separately; *brahman*—O great *brāhmaṇa* (Śukadeva Gosvāmī); *vaṁśa-anucaritāni ca*—and their dynasties and characteristics; *kīrtayasva*—kindly describe; *mahā-bhāga*—O greatly fortunate one; *nityam*—eternally; *śuśrūṣatām*—who are engaged in your service; *hi*—indeed; *naḥ*—of ourselves.

TRANSLATION

O greatly fortunate Śukadeva Gosvāmī, O great brāhmaṇa, kindly describe to us separately the dynasties and characteristics of all those kings, for we are always eager to hear such topics from you.

TEXT 5

ये भूता ये भविष्याश्च भवन्त्यद्यतनाश्च ये ।
तेषां नः पुण्यकीर्तीनां सर्वेषां वद विक्रमान् ॥ ५ ॥

ye bhūtā ye bhaviṣyāś ca
bhavanty adyatanāś ca ye
teṣāṁ naḥ puṇya-kīrtīnāṁ
sarveṣāṁ vada vikramān

ye—all of whom; *bhūtāḥ*—have already appeared; *ye*—all of whom; *bhaviṣyāḥ*—will appear in the future; *ca*—also; *bhavanti*—are existing; *adyatanāḥ*—at present; *ca*—also; *ye*—all of whom; *teṣām*—of all of them; *naḥ*—unto us; *puṇya-kīrtīnām*—who were all pious and celebrated; *sarveṣām*—of all of them; *vada*—kindly explain; *vikramān*—about the abilities.

TRANSLATION

Kindly tell us about the abilities of all the celebrated kings born in the dynasty of Vaivasvata Manu, including those who have already passed, those who may appear in the future, and those who exist at present.

TEXT 6

श्रीसूत उवाच
एवं परीक्षिता राज्ञा सदसि ब्रह्मवादिनाम् ।
पृष्टः प्रोवाच भगवाञ्छुकः परमधर्मवित् ॥ ६ ॥

śrī-sūta uvāca
evaṁ parīkṣitā rājñā
sadasi brahma-vādinām
pṛṣṭaḥ provāca bhagavāñ
chukaḥ parama-dharma-vit

śrī-sūtaḥ uvāca—Śrī Sūta Gosvāmī said; *evam*—in this way; *parīkṣitā*—by Mahārāja Parīkṣit; *rājñā*—by the King; *sadasi*—in the assembly; *brahma-vādinām*—of all the great saintly experts in Vedic knowledge; *pṛṣṭaḥ*—having been asked; *provāca*—answered; *bhagavān*—the most powerful; *śukaḥ*—Śuka Gosvāmī; *parama-dharma-vit*—the most learned scholar in religious principles.

TRANSLATION

Sūta Gosvāmī said: When Śukadeva Gosvāmī, the greatest knower of religious principles, was thus requested by Mahārāja Parīkṣit in the assembly of all the scholars learned in Vedic knowledge, he then proceeded to speak.

TEXT 7

श्रीशुक उवाच
श्रूयतां मानवो वंशः प्राचुर्येण परंतप ।
न शक्यते विस्तरतो वक्तुं वर्षशतैरपि ॥ ७ ॥

śrī-śuka uvāca
śrūyatāṁ mānavo vaṁśaḥ
prācuryeṇa parantapa
na śakyate vistarato
vaktuṁ varṣa-śatair api

śrī-śukaḥ uvāca—Śrī Śukadeva Gosvāmī said; *śrūyatām*—just hear from me; *mānavaḥ vaṁśaḥ*—the dynasty of Manu; *prācuryeṇa*—as expansive as possible; *parantapa*—O King, who can subdue your enemies; *na*—not; *śakyate*—one is able; *vistarataḥ*—very broadly; *vaktum*—to speak; *varṣa-śataiḥ api*—even if he does so for hundreds of years.

TRANSLATION

Śukadeva Gosvāmī continued: O King, subduer of your enemies, now hear from me in great detail about the dynasty of Manu. I shall explain as much as possible, although one could not say everything about it, even in hundreds of years.

TEXT 8

परावरेषां भूतानामात्मा यः पुरुषः परः ।
स एवासीदिदं विश्वं कल्पान्तेऽन्यन्न किञ्चन ॥ ८ ॥

parāvareṣāṁ bhūtānām
ātmā yaḥ puruṣaḥ paraḥ
sa evāsīd idaṁ viśvaṁ
kalpānte 'nyan na kiñcana

para-avareṣām—of all living entities, in higher or lower statuses of life; *bhūtānām*—of those who have taken material bodies (the conditioned souls); *ātmā*—the Supersoul; *yaḥ*—one who is; *puruṣaḥ*—the Supreme Person; *paraḥ*—transcendental; *saḥ*—He; *eva*—indeed; *āsīt*—was existing; *idam*—this; *viśvam*—universe; *kalpa-ante*—at the end of the millennium; *anyat*—anything else; *na*—not; *kiñcana*—anything whatsoever.

TRANSLATION

The transcendental Supreme Person, the Supersoul of all living entities, who are in different statuses of life, high and low, existed at the end of the millennium, when neither this manifested cosmos nor anything else but Him existed.

PURPORT

Taking the proper position from which to describe the dynasty of Manu, Śukadeva Gosvāmī begins by saying that when the entire world is inundated, only the Supreme Personality of Godhead exists, and nothing else. Śukadeva Gosvāmī will now describe how the Lord creates other things, one after another.

TEXT 9

तस्य नाभेः समभवत् पद्मकोशो हिरण्मयः ।
तस्मिञ्जज्ञे महाराज स्वयंभूश्चतुराननः ॥ ९ ॥

tasya nābheḥ samabhavat
padma-koṣo hiraṇmayaḥ
tasmiñ jajñe mahārāja
svayambhūś catur-ānanaḥ

tasya—of Him (the Supreme Personality of Godhead); *nābheḥ*—from the navel; *samabhavat*—generated; *padma-koṣaḥ*—a lotus; *hiraṇ-mayaḥ*—known as Hiraṇmaya, or golden; *tasmin*—on that golden lotus; *jajñe*—appeared; *mahārāja*—O King; *svayambhūḥ*—one who is self-manifested, who takes birth without a mother; *catuḥ-ānanaḥ*—with four heads.

TRANSLATION

O King Parīkṣit, from the navel of the Supreme Personality of Godhead was generated a golden lotus, on which the four-faced Lord Brahmā took his birth.

TEXT 10

मरीचिर्मनसस्तस्य जज्ञे तस्यापि कश्यपः ।
दाक्षायण्यां ततोऽदित्यां विवस्वानभवत् सुतः ॥१०॥

marīcir manasas tasya
jajñe tasyāpi kaśyapaḥ
dākṣāyaṇyāṁ tato 'dityāṁ
vivasvān abhavat sutaḥ

marīciḥ—the great saintly person known as Marīci; *manasaḥ tasya*—from the mind of Lord Brahmā; *jajñe*—took birth; *tasya api*—from Marīci; *kaśyapaḥ*—Kaśyapa (took birth); *dākṣāyaṇyām*—in the womb of the daughter of Mahārāja Dakṣa; *tataḥ*—thereafter; *adityām*—in the womb of Aditi; *vivasvān*—Vivasvān; *abhavat*—took birth; *sutaḥ*—a son.

TRANSLATION

From the mind of Lord Brahmā, Marīci took birth, and from the semen of Marīci, Kaśyapa appeared from the womb of the daughter of Dakṣa Mahārāja. From Kaśyapa, by the womb of Aditi, Vivasvān took birth.

TEXTS 11–12

ततो मनुः श्राद्धदेवः संज्ञायामास भारत ।
श्रद्धायां जनयामास दश पुत्रान् स आत्मवान् ॥११॥
इक्ष्वाकुनृगशर्यातिदिष्टधृष्टकरूषकान् ।
नरिष्यन्तं पृषध्रं च नभगं च कविं विभुः ॥१२॥

tato manuḥ śrāddhadevaḥ
saṁjñāyām āsa bhārata
śraddhāyāṁ janayām āsa
daśa putrān sa ātmavān

ikṣvāku-nṛga-śaryāti-
diṣṭa-dhṛṣṭa-karūṣakān
nariṣyantaṁ pṛṣadhraṁ ca
nabhagaṁ ca kaviṁ vibhuḥ

tataḥ—from Vivasvān; *manuḥ śrāddhadevaḥ*—the Manu named Śrāddhadeva; *saṁjñāyām*—in the womb of Saṁjñā (the wife of Vivasvān); *āsa*—was born; *bhārata*—O best of the Bhārata dynasty; *śraddhāyām*—in the womb of Śraddhā (the wife of Śrāddhadeva); *janayām āsa*—begot; *daśa*—ten; *putrān*—sons; *saḥ*—that Śrāddhadeva; *ātmavān*—having conquered his senses; *ikṣvāku-nṛga-śaryāti-*

diṣṭa-dhṛṣṭa-karūṣakān—named Ikṣvāku, Nṛga, Śaryāti, Diṣṭa, Dhṛṣṭa and Karūṣaka; *nariṣyantam*—Nariṣyanta; *pṛṣadhram ca*—and Pṛṣadhra; *nabhagam ca*—and Nabhaga; *kavim*—Kavi; *vibhuḥ*—the great.

TRANSLATION

O King, best of the Bhārata dynasty, from Vivasvān, by the womb of Saṁjñā, Śrāddhadeva Manu was born. Śrāddhadeva Manu, having conquered his senses, begot ten sons in the womb of his wife, Śraddhā. The names of these sons were Ikṣvāku, Nṛga, Śaryāti, Diṣṭa, Dhṛṣṭa, Karūṣaka, Nariṣyanta, Pṛṣadhra, Nabhaga and Kavi.

TEXT 13

अप्रजस्य मनोः पूर्वं वसिष्ठो भगवान् किल ।
मित्रावरुणयोरिष्टिं प्रजार्थमकरोद् विभुः ॥१३॥

aprajasya manoḥ pūrvaṁ
vasiṣṭho bhagavān kila
mitrā-varuṇayor iṣṭiṁ
prajārtham akarod vibhuḥ

aprajasya—of he who had no son; *manoḥ*—of Manu; *pūrvam*—formerly; *vasiṣṭhaḥ*—the great saint Vasiṣṭha; *bhagavān*—powerful; *kila*—indeed; *mitrā-varuṇayoḥ*—of the demigods named Mitra and Varuṇa; *iṣṭim*—a sacrifice; *prajā-artham*—for the sake of getting sons; *akarot*—executed; *vibhuḥ*—the great person.

TRANSLATION

Manu at first had no sons. Therefore, in order to get a son for him, the great saint Vasiṣṭha, who was very powerful in spiritual knowledge, performed a sacrifice to satisfy the demigods Mitra and Varuṇa.

TEXT 14

तत्र श्रद्धा मनोः पत्नी होतारं समयाचत ।
दुहित्रर्थमुपागम्य प्रणिपत्य पयोव्रता ॥१४॥

tatra śraddhā manoḥ patnī
hotāraṁ samayācata
duhitrartham upāgamya
praṇipatya payovratā

tatra—in that sacrifice; *śraddhā*—Śraddhā; *manoḥ*—of Manu; *patnī*—the wife; *hotāram*—to the priest performing the *yajña; samayācata*—begged properly; *duhitṛ-artham*—for a daughter; *upāgamya*—coming near; *praṇipatya*—offering obeisances; *payaḥ-vratā*—who was observing the vow of drinking only milk.

TRANSLATION

During that sacrifice, Śraddhā, Manu's wife, who was observing the vow of subsisting only by drinking milk, approached the priest offering the sacrifice, offered obeisances to him and begged for a daughter.

TEXT 15

प्रेषितोऽध्वर्युणा होता व्यचरत् तत् समाहितः ।
गृहीते हविषि वाचा वषट्कारं गृणन्द्विजः ॥१५॥

preṣito 'dhvaryuṇā hotā
vyacarat tat samāhitaḥ
gṛhīte haviṣi vācā
vaṣaṭ-kāraṁ gṛṇan dvijaḥ

preṣitaḥ—being told to execute the sacrifice; *adhvaryuṇā*—by the *ṛtvik* priest; *hotā*—the priest in charge of offering oblations; *vyacarat*—executed; *tat*—that (sacrifice); *samāhitaḥ*—with great attention; *gṛhīte haviṣi*—upon taking the clarified butter for the first oblation; *vācā*—by chanting the *mantra; vaṣaṭ-kāram*—the *mantra* beginning with the word *vaṣaṭ; gṛṇan*—reciting; *dvijaḥ*—the *brāhmaṇa.*

TRANSLATION

Told by the chief priest "Now offer oblations," the person in charge of oblations took clarified butter to offer. He then remem-

bered the request of Manu's wife and performed the sacrifice while chanting the word "vaṣaṭ."

TEXT 16

होतुस्तद्‌व्यभिचारेण कन्येला नाम साभवत् ।
तां विलोक्य मनुः प्राह नातितुष्टमना गुरुम् ॥१६॥

hotus tad-vyabhicāreṇa
kanyelā nāma sābhavat
tāṁ vilokya manuḥ prāha
nātituṣṭamanā gurum

hotuḥ—of the priest; *tat*—of the *yajña; vyabhicāreṇa*—by that transgression; *kanyā*—a daughter; *ilā*—Ilā; *nāma*—by the name; *sā*—that daughter; *abhavat*—was born; *tām*—unto her; *vilokya*—seeing; *manuḥ*—Manu; *prāha*—said; *na*—not; *atituṣṭamanāḥ*—very much satisfied; *gurum*—unto his *guru.*

TRANSLATION

Manu had begun that sacrifice for the sake of getting a son, but because the priest was diverted by the request of Manu's wife, a daughter named Ilā was born. Upon seeing the daughter, Manu was not very satisfied. Thus he spoke to his guru, Vasiṣṭha, as follows.

PURPORT

Because Manu had no issue, he was pleased at the birth of the child, even though a daughter, and gave her the name Ilā. Later, however, he was not very satisfied to see the daughter instead of a son. Because he had no issue, he was certainly very glad at the birth of Ilā, but his pleasure was temporary.

TEXT 17

भगवन् किमिदं जातं कर्म वो ब्रह्मवादिनाम् ।
विपर्ययमहो कष्टं मैवं स्याद् ब्रह्मविक्रिया ॥१७॥

bhagavan kim idaṁ jātaṁ
karma vo brahma-vādinām
viparyayam aho kaṣṭaṁ
maivaṁ syād brahma-vikriyā

bhagavan—O my lord; *kim idam*—what is this; *jātam*—born; *karma*—fruitive activities; *vaḥ*—of all of you; *brahma-vādinām*—of you, who are expert in chanting the Vedic *mantras; viparyayam*—deviation; *aho*—alas; *kaṣṭam*—painful; *mā evam syāt*—thus it should not have been; *brahma-vikriyā*—this opposite action of the Vedic *mantras.*

TRANSLATION

My lord, all of you are expert in chanting the Vedic mantras. How then has the result been opposite to the one desired? This is a matter for lamentation. There should not have been such a reversal of the results of the Vedic mantras.

PURPORT

In this age, the performance of *yajña* has been forbidden because no one can properly chant the Vedic *mantras.* If Vedic *mantras* are chanted properly, the desire for which a sacrifice is performed must be successful. Therefore the Hare Kṛṣṇa chant is called the *mahā-mantra,* the great, exalted *mantra* above all other Vedic *mantras,* because simply chanting the Hare Kṛṣṇa *mahā-mantra* brings so many beneficial effects. As explained by Śrī Caitanya Mahāprabhu (*Śikṣāṣṭaka* 1):

ceto-darpaṇa-mārjanaṁ bhava-mahā-dāvāgni-nirvāpaṇaṁ
śreyaḥ-kairava-candrikā-vitaraṇaṁ vidyā-vadhū-jīvanam
ānandāmbudhi-vardhanaṁ prati-padaṁ pūrṇāmṛtāsvādanaṁ
sarvātma-snapanaṁ paraṁ vijayate śrī-kṛṣṇa-saṅkīrtanam

"Glory to the Śrī Kṛṣṇa *saṅkīrtana,* which cleanses the heart of all the dust accumulated for years and extinguishes the fire of conditional life, of repeated birth and death. This *saṅkīrtana* movement is the prime benediction for humanity at large because it spreads the rays of the benediction moon. It is the life of all transcendental knowledge. It increases the ocean of transcendental bliss, and it enables us to fully taste the nectar for which we are always anxious."

Therefore, the best performance of *yajña* given to us is the *saṅkīrtana-yajña. Yajñaiḥ saṅkīrtana-prāyair yajanti hi sumedhasaḥ* (*Bhāg.* 11.5.32). Those who are intelligent take advantage of the greatest *yajña* in this age by chanting the Hare Kṛṣṇa *mahā-mantra* in congregation. When the Hare Kṛṣṇa *mantra* is chanted by many men together, the chanting is called *saṅkīrtana,* and as a result of such a *yajña* there will be clouds in the sky (*yajñād bhavati parjanyaḥ*). In these days of drought, people can gain relief from scarcity of rain and food by the simple method of the Hare Kṛṣṇa *yajña.* Indeed, this can relieve all of human society. At present there are droughts throughout Europe and America, and people are suffering, but if people take this Kṛṣṇa consciousness movement seriously, if they stop their sinful activities and chant the Hare Kṛṣṇa *mahā-mantra,* all their problems will be solved without difficulty. In other processes of *yajña* there are difficulties because there are no learned scholars who can chant the *mantras* perfectly well, nor is it possible to secure the ingredients to perform the *yajña.* Because human society is poverty-stricken and men are devoid of Vedic knowledge and the power to chant the Vedic *mantras,* the Hare Kṛṣṇa *mahā-mantra* is the only shelter. People should be intelligent enough to chant it. *Yajñaiḥ saṅkīrtana-prāyair yajanti hi sumedhasaḥ.* Those whose brains are dull cannot understand this chanting, nor can they take to it.

TEXT 18

यूयं ब्रह्मविदो युक्तास्तपसा दग्धकिल्बिषाः ।
कुतः संकल्पवैषम्यमनृतं विबुधेष्विव ॥१८॥

yūyaṁ brahma-vido yuktās
tapasā dagdha-kilbiṣāḥ
kutaḥ saṅkālpa-vaiṣamyam
anṛtaṁ vibudheṣv iva

yūyam—of all you; *brahma-vidaḥ*—completely in awareness of the Absolute Truth; *yuktāḥ*—self-controlled and well balanced; *tapasā*—by dint of austerity and penances; *dagdha-kilbiṣāḥ*—all kinds of material contamination having been burnt out; *kutaḥ*—then how; *saṅkalpa-vaiṣamyam*—discrepancy in the matter of determination; *anṛtam*—false promise, false statement; *vibudheṣu*—in the society of the demigods; *iva*—or.

TRANSLATION

You are all self-controlled, well balanced in mind, and aware of the Absolute Truth. And because of austerities and penances you are completely cleansed of all material contamination. Your words, like those of the demigods, are never baffled. Then how is it possible that your determination has failed?

PURPORT

We have learned from many Vedic literatures that a benediction or curse given by the demigods never proves false. By performing austerities and penances, by controlling the senses and mind, and by achieving full knowledge of the Absolute Truth, one is fully cleansed of material contamination. Then one's words and blessings, like those of the demigods, are never a failure.

TEXT 19

निशम्य तद् वचस्तस्य भगवान् प्रपितामहः ।
होतुर्व्यतिक्रमं ज्ञात्वा बभाषे रविनन्दनम् ॥१९॥

niśamya tad vacas tasya
bhagavān prapitāmahaḥ
hotur vyatikramaṁ jñātvā
babhāṣe ravi-nandanam

niśamya—after hearing; *tat vacaḥ*—those words; *tasya*—of him (Manu); *bhagavān*—the most powerful; *prapitāmahaḥ*—the great-grandfather Vasiṣṭha; *hotuḥ vyatikramam*—discrepancy on the part of the *hotā* priest; *jñātvā*—understanding; *babhāṣe*—spoke; *ravi-nandanam*—unto Vaivasvata Manu, son of the sun-god.

TRANSLATION

The most powerful great-grandfather Vasiṣṭha, after hearing these words of Manu, understood the discrepancy on the part of the priest. Thus he spoke as follows to the son of the sun-god.

TEXT 20

एतत् संकल्पवैषम्यं होतुस्ते व्यभिचारतः ।
तथापि साधयिष्ये ते सुप्रजास्त्वं स्वतेजसा ॥२०॥

etat saṅkalpa-vaiṣamyaṁ
hotus te vyabhicārataḥ
tathāpi sādhayiṣye te
suprajāstvaṁ sva-tejasā

etat—this; *saṅkalpa-vaiṣamyam*—discrepancy in the objective; *hotuḥ*—of the priest; *te*—your; *vyabhicārataḥ*—from deviating from the prescribed purpose; *tathā api*—still; *sādhayiṣye*—I shall execute; *te*—for you; *su-prajāstvam*—a very nice son; *sva-tejasā*—by my own prowess.

TRANSLATION

This discrepancy in the objective is due to your priest's deviation from the original purpose. However, by my own prowess I shall give you a good son.

TEXT 21

एवं व्यवसितो राजन् भगवान् स महायशाः ।
अस्तौषीदादिपुरुषमिलायाः पुंस्त्वकाम्यया ॥२१॥

evaṁ vyavasito rājan
bhagavān sa mahā-yaśāḥ
astauṣīd ādi-puruṣam
ilāyāḥ puṁstva-kāmyayā

evam—thus; *vyavasitaḥ*—deciding; *rājan*—O King Parīkṣit; *bhagavān*—the most powerful; *saḥ*—Vasiṣṭha; *mahā-yaśāḥ*—very famous; *astauṣīt*—offered prayers; *ādi-puruṣam*—unto the Supreme

Person, Lord Viṣṇu; *ilāyāḥ*—of Ilā; *puṁstva-kāmyayā*—for the transformation into a male.

TRANSLATION

Śukadeva Gosvāmī said: O King Parīkṣit, after the most famous and powerful Vasiṣṭha made this decision, he offered prayers to the Supreme Person, Viṣṇu, to transform Ilā into a male.

TEXT 22

तस्मै कामवरं तुष्टो भगवान् हरिरीश्वरः ।
ददाविलाभवत् तेन सुद्युम्नः पुरुषर्षभः ॥२२॥

tasmai kāma-varaṁ tuṣṭo
bhagavān harir īśvaraḥ
dadāv ilābhavat tena
sudyumnaḥ puruṣarṣabhaḥ

tasmai—unto him (Vasiṣṭha); *kāma-varam*—the desired benediction; *tuṣṭaḥ*—being pleased; *bhagavān*—the Supreme Personality; *hariḥ īśvaraḥ*—the supreme controller, the Lord; *dadau*—gave; *ilā*—the girl, Ilā; *abhavat*—became; *tena*—because of this benediction; *sudyumnaḥ*—by the name Sudyumna; *puruṣa-ṛṣabhaḥ*—a nice male.

TRANSLATION

The Supreme Personality of Godhead, the supreme controller, being pleased with Vasiṣṭha, gave him the benediction he desired. Thus Ilā was transformed into a very fine male named Sudyumna.

TEXTS 23–24

स एकदा महाराज विचरन् मृगयां वने ।
वृतः कतिपयामात्यैरश्वमारुह्य सैन्धवम् ॥२३॥
प्रगृह्य रुचिरं चापं शरांश्च परमाद्भुतान् ।
दंशितोऽनुमृगं वीरो जगाम दिशमुत्तराम् ॥२४॥

sa ekadā mahārāja
vicaran mṛgayāṁ vane
vṛtaḥ katipayāmātyair
aśvam āruhya saindhavam

pragṛhya ruciraṁ cāpaṁ
śarāṁś ca paramādbhutān
daṁśito 'numṛgaṁ vīro
jagāma diśam uttarām

saḥ—Sudyumna; *ekadā*—once upon a time; *mahārāja*—O King Parīkṣit; *vicaran*—touring; *mṛgayām*—for hunting; *vane*—in the forest; *vṛtaḥ*—accompanied; *katipaya*—a few; *amātyaiḥ*—by ministers or associates; *aśvam*—upon a horse; *āruhya*—riding; *saindhavam*—born in the Sindhupradeśa; *pragṛhya*—holding in hand; *ruciram*—beautiful; *cāpam*—bow; *śarān ca*—and arrows; *parama-adbhutān*—very wonderful, uncommon; *daṁśitaḥ*—wearing armor; *anumṛgam*—behind the animals; *vīraḥ*—the hero; *jagāma*—went toward; *diśam uttarām*—the north.

TRANSLATION

O King Parīkṣit, that hero Sudyumna, accompanied by a few ministers and associates and riding on a horse brought from Sindhupradeśa, once went into the forest to hunt. He wore armor and was decorated with bows and arrows, and he was very beautiful. While following the animals and killing them, he reached the northern part of the forest.

TEXT 25

सुकुमारवनं मेरोरधस्तात् प्रविवेश ह ।
यत्रास्ते भगवाञ्छर्वो रममाणः सहोमया ॥२५॥

sukumāra-vanaṁ meror
adhastāt praviveśa ha
yatrāste bhagavāñ charvo
ramamāṇaḥ sahomayā

sukumāra-vanam—the forest known as Sukumāra; *meroḥ adhastāt*—at the foot of Mount Meru; *praviveśa ha*—he entered; *yatra*—wherein; *āste*—was; *bhagavān*—the most powerful (demigod); *śarvaḥ*—Lord Śiva; *ramamāṇaḥ*—engaged in enjoyment; *saha umayā*—with Umā, his wife.

TRANSLATION

There in the north, at the bottom of Mount Meru, is a forest known as Sukumāra where Lord Śiva always enjoys with Umā. Sudyumna entered that forest.

TEXT 26

तस्मिन् प्रविष्ट एवासौ सुद्युम्नः परवीरहा ।
अपश्यत् स्त्रियमात्मानमश्वं च वडवां नृप ॥२६॥

tasmin praviṣṭa evāsau
sudyumnaḥ para-vīra-hā
apaśyat striyam ātmānam
aśvaṁ ca vaḍavāṁ nṛpa

tasmin—in that forest; *praviṣṭaḥ*—having entered; *eva*—indeed; *asau*—he; *sudyumnaḥ*—Prince Sudyumna; *para-vīra-hā*—who could very well subdue his enemies; *apaśyat*—observed; *striyam*—female; *ātmānam*—himself; *aśvam ca*—and his horse; *vaḍavām*—a mare; *nṛpa*—O King Parīkṣit.

TRANSLATION

O King Parīkṣit, as soon as Sudyumna, who was expert in subduing enemies, entered the forest, he saw himself transformed into a female and his horse transformed into a mare.

TEXT 27

तथा तदनुगाः सर्वे आत्मलिङ्गविपर्ययम् ।
दृष्ट्वा विमनसोऽभूवन् वीक्षमाणाः परस्परम् ॥२७॥

tathā tad-anugāḥ sarve
ātma-liṅga-viparyayam
dṛṣṭvā vimanaso 'bhūvan
vīkṣamāṇāḥ parasparam

tathā—similarly; *tat-anugāḥ*—the companions of Sudyumna; *sarve*—all of them; *ātma-liṅga-viparyayam*—the transformation of their sex into the opposite; *dṛṣṭvā*—seeing; *vimanasaḥ*—morose; *abhūvan*—they became; *vīkṣamāṇāḥ*—looking over; *parasparam*—one another.

TRANSLATION

When his followers also saw their identities transformed and their sex reversed, they were all very morose and just looked at one another.

TEXT 28

श्रीराजोवाच

कथमेवं गुणो देशः केन वा भगवन् कृतः ।
प्रश्नमेनं समाचक्ष्व परं कौतूहलं हि नः ॥२८॥

śrī-rājovāca
katham evaṁ guṇo deśaḥ
kena vā bhagavan kṛtaḥ
praśnam enaṁ samācakṣva
paraṁ kautūhalaṁ hi naḥ

śrī-rājā uvāca—Mahārāja Parīkṣit said; *katham*—how; *evam*—this; *guṇaḥ*—quality; *deśaḥ*—the country; *kena*—why; *vā*—either; *bhagavan*—O most powerful; *kṛtaḥ*—it was so done; *praśnam*—question; *enam*—this; *samācakṣva*—just deliberate; *param*—very much; *kautūhalam*—eagerness; *hi*—indeed; *naḥ*—our.

TRANSLATION

Mahārāja Parīkṣit said: O most powerful brāhmaṇa, why was this place so empowered, and who made it so powerful? Kindly answer this question, for I am very eager to hear about this.

TEXT 29

श्रीशुक उवाच

एकदा गिरिशं द्रष्टुमृषयस्तत्र सुव्रताः ।
दिशो वितिमिराभासाः कुर्वन्तः समुपागमन् ॥२९॥

śrī-śuka uvāca
ekadā giriśaṁ draṣṭum
ṛṣayas tatra suvratāḥ
diśo vitimirābhāsāḥ
kurvantaḥ samupāgaman

śrī-śukaḥ uvāca—Śrī Śukadeva Gosvāmī said; *ekadā*—once upon a time; *giriśam*—Lord Śiva; *draṣṭum*—to see; *ṛṣayaḥ*—very saintly persons; *tatra*—in that forest; *su-vratāḥ*—highly elevated in spiritual power; *diśaḥ*—all directions; *vitimira-ābhāsāḥ*—having been cleared of all darkness whatsoever; *kurvantaḥ*—doing so; *samupāgaman*—arrived.

TRANSLATION

Śukadeva Gosvāmī answered: Great saintly persons who strictly observed the spiritual rules and regulations and whose own effulgence dissipated all the darkness of all directions once came to see Lord Śiva in that forest.

TEXT 30

तान् विलोक्याम्बिका देवी विवासा व्रीडिता भृशम् ।
भर्तुरङ्कात् समुत्थाय नीवीमाश्वथ पर्यधात् ॥३०॥

tān vilokyāmbikā devī
vivāsā vrīḍitā bhṛśam
bhartur aṅkāt samutthāya
nīvīm āśv atha paryadhāt

tān—all the saintly persons; *vilokya*—seeing them; *ambikā*—mother Durgā; *devī*—the goddess; *vivāsā*—because she was naked; *vrīḍitā*—ashamed; *bhṛśam*—highly; *bhartuḥ*—of her husband; *aṅkāt*—from the lap; *samutthāya*—getting up; *nīvīm*—breast; *āśu atha*—very quickly; *paryadhāt*—covered with cloth.

TRANSLATION

When the goddess Ambikā saw the great saintly persons, she was very much ashamed because at that time she was naked. She immediately got up from the lap of her husband and tried to cover her breast.

TEXT 31

ऋषयोऽपि तयोर्वीक्ष्य प्रसङ्गं रममाणयोः ।
निवृत्ताः प्रययुस्तस्मान्नरनारायणाश्रमम् ॥३१॥

ṛṣayo 'pi tayor vīkṣya
prasaṅgaṁ ramamāṇayoḥ
nivṛttāḥ prayayus tasmān
nara-nārāyaṇāśramam

ṛṣayaḥ—all the great saintly persons; *api*—also; *tayoḥ*—of both of them; *vīkṣya*—seeing; *prasaṅgam*—engagement in sexual matters; *ramamāṇayoḥ*—who were enjoying in that way; *nivṛttāḥ*—desisted from going further; *prayayuḥ*—immediately departed; *tasmāt*—from that place; *nara-nārāyaṇa-āśramam*—to the *āśrama* of Nara-Nārāyaṇa.

TRANSLATION

Seeing Lord Śiva and Pārvatī engaged in sexual affairs, all the great saintly persons immediately desisted from going further and departed for the āśrama of Nara-Nārāyaṇa.

TEXT 32

तदिदं भगवानाह प्रियायाः प्रियकाम्यया ।
स्थानं यः प्रविशेदेतत् स वै योषिद् भवेदिति ॥३२॥

tad idaṁ bhagavān āha
priyāyāḥ priya-kāmyayā
sthānaṁ yaḥ praviśed etat
sa vai yoṣid bhaved iti

tat—because; *idam*—this; *bhagavān*—Lord Śiva; *āha*—said; *priyāyāḥ*—of his dear wife; *priya-kāmyayā*—for the pleasure; *sthānam*—place; *yaḥ*—anyone who; *praviśet*—will enter; *etat*—here; *saḥ*—that person; *vai*—indeed; *yoṣit*—female; *bhavet*—shall become; *iti*—thus.

TRANSLATION

Thereupon, just to please his wife, Lord Śiva said, "Any male entering this place shall immediately become a female!"

TEXT 33

तत ऊर्ध्वं वनं तद् वै पुरुषा वर्जयन्ति हि ।
सा चानुचरसंयुक्ता विचचार वनाद् वनम् ॥३३॥

tata ūrdhvaṁ vanaṁ tad vai
puruṣā varjayanti hi
sā cānucara-saṁyuktā
vicacāra vanād vanam

tataḥ ūrdhvam—from that time onward; *vanam*—forest; *tat*—that; *vai*—in particular; *puruṣāḥ*—males; *varjayanti*—do not enter; *hi*—indeed; *sā*—Sudyumna in the form of a woman; *ca*—also; *anucara-saṁyuktā*—accompanied by his companions; *vicacāra*—walked; *vanāt vanam*—within the forest from one place to another.

TRANSLATION

Since that time, no male had entered that forest. But now King Sudyumna, having been transformed into a female, began to walk with his associates from one forest to another.

PURPORT

In *Bhagavad-gītā* (2.22) it is said:

vāsāṁsi jīrṇāni yathā vihāya
navāni gṛhṇāti naro 'parāṇi
tathā sarīrāṇi vihāya jīrṇāny
anyāni saṁyāti navāni dehī

"As a person puts on new garments, giving up old ones, the soul accepts new material bodies, giving up the old and useless ones."

The body is just like a dress, and here this is proved. Sudyumna and his associates were all male, which means that their souls were covered by male dress, but now they became female, which means that their dress was changed. The soul, however, remains the same. It is said that by modern medical treatment a male can be transformed into a female, and a female into a male. The body, however, has no connection with the soul. The body can be changed, either in this life or the next. Therefore, one who has knowledge of the soul and how the soul transmigrates from one body to another does not pay attention to the body, which is nothing but a covering dress. *Paṇḍitāḥ sama-darśinaḥ.* Such a person sees the soul, which is part and parcel of the Supreme Lord. Therefore he is a *sama-darśī*, a learned person.

TEXT 34

अथ तामाश्रमाभ्याशे चरन्तीं प्रमदोत्तमाम् ।
स्त्रीभिः परिवृतां वीक्ष्य चकमे भगवान् बुधः ॥३४॥

atha tām āśramābhyāśe
carantīṁ pramadottamām
strībhiḥ parivṛtāṁ vīkṣya
cakame bhagavān budhaḥ

atha—in this way; *tām*—her; *āśrama-abhyāśe*—in the neighborhood of his *āśrama; carantīm*—loitering; *pramadā-uttamām*—the best of beautiful women who excite sex; *strībhiḥ*—by other women; *parivṛtām*—surrounded; *vīkṣya*—seeing her; *cakame*—desired sex; *bhagavān*—the most powerful; *budhaḥ*—Budha, the son of the moon and predominating deity of the planet known as Budha, or Mercury.

TRANSLATION

Sudyumna had been transformed into the best of beautiful women who excite sexual desire and was surrounded by other women. Upon seeing this beautiful woman loitering near his āśrama, Budha, the son of the moon, immediately desired to enjoy her.

TEXT 35

सापि तं चकमे सुभ्रूः सोमराजसुतं पतिम् ।
स तस्यां जनयामास पुरूरवसमात्मजम् ॥३५॥

sāpi taṁ cakame subhrūḥ
somarāja-sutaṁ patim
sa tasyāṁ janayām āsa
purūravasam ātmajam

sā—Sudyumna, transformed into a woman; *api*—also; *tam*—unto him (Budha); *cakame*—desired sex; *su-bhrūḥ*—very beautiful; *somarāja-sutam*—unto the son of the king of the moon; *patim*—as her husband; *saḥ*—he (Budha); *tasyām*—in her womb; *janayām āsa*—begot; *purūravasam*—named Purūravā; *ātma-jam*—a son.

TRANSLATION

The beautiful woman also desired to accept Budha, the son of the king of the moon, as her husband. Thus Budha begot in her womb a son named Purūravā.

TEXT 36

एवं स्त्रीत्वमनुप्राप्तः सुद्युम्नो मानवो नृपः ।
सस्मार स कुलाचार्यं वसिष्ठमिति शुश्रुम ॥३६॥

evaṁ strītvam anuprāptaḥ
sudyumno mānavo nṛpaḥ
sasmāra sa kulācāryaṁ
vasiṣṭham iti śuśruma

evam—in this way; *strītvam*—femininity; *anuprāptaḥ*—having achieved in that way; *sudyumnaḥ*—the male named Sudyumna; *mānavaḥ*—the son of Manu; *nṛpaḥ*—the king; *sasmāra*—remembered; *saḥ*—he; *kula-ācāryam*—the familial spiritual master; *vasiṣṭham*—the most powerful Vasiṣṭha; *iti śuśruma*—I have heard it (from reliable sources).

TRANSLATION

I heard from reliable sources that King Sudyumna, the son of Manu, having thus achieved femininity, remembered his familial spiritual master, Vasiṣṭha.

TEXT 37

स तस्य तां दशां दृष्ट्वा कृपया भृशपीडितः ।
सुद्युम्नस्याशयन् पुंस्त्वमुपाधावत शङ्करम् ॥३७॥

sa tasya tāṁ daśāṁ dṛṣṭvā
kṛpayā bhṛśa-pīḍitaḥ
sudyumnasyāśayan puṁstvam
upādhāvata śaṅkaram

saḥ—he, Vasiṣṭha; *tasya*—of Sudyumna; *tām*—that; *daśām*—condition; *dṛṣṭvā*—seeing; *kṛpayā*—out of mercy; *bhṛśa-pīḍitaḥ*—being very much aggrieved; *sudyumnasya*—of Sudyumna; *āśayan*—desiring; *puṁstvam*—the maleness; *upādhāvata*—began to worship; *śaṅkaram*—Lord Śiva.

TRANSLATION

Upon seeing Sudyumna's deplorable condition, Vasiṣṭha was very much aggrieved. Desiring for Sudyumna to regain his maleness, Vasiṣṭha again began to worship Lord Śaṅkara [Śiva].

TEXTS 38–39

तुष्टस्तस्मै स भगवानृषये प्रियमावहन् ।
स्वां च वाचमृतां कुर्वन्निदमाह विशांपते ॥३८॥
मासं पुमान् स भविता मासं स्त्री तव गोत्रजः ।
इत्थं व्यवस्थया कामं सुद्युम्नोऽवतु मेदिनीम् ॥३९॥

tuṣṭas tasmai sa bhagavān
ṛṣaye priyam āvahan
svāṁ ca vācam ṛtāṁ kurvann
idam āha viśāmpate

māsaṁ pumān sa bhavitā
māsaṁ strī tava gotrajaḥ
itthaṁ vyavasthayā kāmaṁ
sudyumno 'vatu medinīm

tuṣṭaḥ—being pleased; *tasmai*—unto Vasiṣṭha; *saḥ*—he (Lord Śiva); *bhagavān*—the most powerful; *ṛṣaye*—unto the great sage; *priyam āvahan*—just to please him; *svām ca*—his own; *vācam*—word; *ṛtām*—true; *kurvan*—and keeping; *idam*—this; *āha*—said; *viśāmpate*—O King Parīkṣit; *māsam*—one month; *pumān*—male; *saḥ*—Sudyumna; *bhavitā*—will become; *māsam*—another month; *strī*—female; *tava*—your; *gotra-jaḥ*—disciple born in your disciplic succession; *ittham*—in this way; *vyavasthayā*—by settlement; *kāmam*—according to desire; *sudyumnaḥ*—King Sudyumna; *avatu*—may rule; *medinīm*—the world.

TRANSLATION

O King Parīkṣit, Lord Śiva was pleased with Vasiṣṭha. Therefore, to satisfy him and to keep his own word to Pārvatī, Lord Śiva said to that saintly person, "Your disciple Sudyumna may remain a male for one month and a female for the next. In this way he may rule the world as he likes."

PURPORT

The word *gotrajaḥ* is significant in this connection. *Brāhmaṇas* generally act as spiritual masters of two dynasties. One is their disciplic succession, and the other is the dynasty born of their semen. Both descendants belong to the same *gotra*, or dynasty. In the Vedic system we sometimes find that both *brāhmaṇas* and *kṣatriyas* and even *vaiśyas* come in the disciplic succession of the same *ṛṣis*. Because the *gotra* and dynasty are one, there is no difference between the disciples and the family born of the semen. The same system still prevails in Indian society, especially in regard to marriage, for which the *gotra* is calculated. Here the word *gotrajaḥ* refers to those born in the same dynasty, whether they be disciples or members of the family.

TEXT 40

आचार्यानुग्रहात् कामं लब्ध्वा पुंस्त्वं व्यवस्थया ।
पालयामास जगतीं नाभ्यनन्दन् स्म तं प्रजाः ॥४०॥

ācāryānugrahāt kāmaṁ
labdhvā puṁstvaṁ vyavasthayā
pālayām āsa jagatīṁ
nābhyanandan sma taṁ prajāḥ

ācārya-anugrahāt—by the mercy of the spiritual master; *kāmam*—desired; *labdhvā*—having achieved; *puṁstvam*—maleness; *vyavasthayā*—by this settlement of Lord Śiva; *pālayām āsa*—he ruled; *jagatīm*—the whole world; *na abhyanandan sma*—were not satisfied with; *tam*—to the king; *prajāḥ*—the citizens.

TRANSLATION

Thus being favored by the spiritual master, according to the words of Lord Śiva, Sudyumna regained his desired maleness every alternate month and in this way ruled the kingdom, although the citizens were not satisfied with this.

PURPORT

The citizens could understand that the king was transformed into a female every alternate month and therefore could not discharge his royal duty. Consequently they were not very satisfied.

TEXT 41

तस्योत्कलो गयो राजन् विमलश्च त्रयः सुताः ।
दक्षिणापथराजानो बभूवुर्धर्मवत्सलाः ॥४१॥

tasyotkalo gayo rājan
vimalaś ca trayaḥ sutāḥ
dakṣiṇā-patha-rājāno
babhūvur dharma-vatsalāḥ

tasya—of Sudyumna; *utkalaḥ*—by the name Utkala; *gayaḥ*—by the name Gaya; *rājan*—O King Parīkṣit; *vimalaḥ ca*—and Vimala; *trayaḥ*—three; *sutāḥ*—sons; *dakṣiṇā-patha*—of the southern part of the world; *rājānaḥ*—kings; *babhūvuḥ*—they became; *dharma-vatsalāḥ*—very religious.

TRANSLATION

O King, Sudyumna had three very pious sons, named Utkala, Gaya and Vimala, who became the kings of the Dakṣiṇā-patha.

TEXT 42

ततः परिणते काले प्रतिष्ठानपतिः प्रभुः ।
पुरूरवस उत्सृज्य गां पुत्राय गतो वनम् ॥४२॥

tataḥ pariṇate kāle
pratiṣṭhāna-patiḥ prabhuḥ
purūravasa utsṛjya
gāṁ putrāya gato vanam

tataḥ—thereafter; *pariṇate kāle*—when the time was ripe; *pratiṣṭhāna-patiḥ*—the master of the kingdom; *prabhuḥ*—very powerful; *purūravase*—unto Purūravā; *utsṛjya*—delivering; *gām*—the world; *putrāya*—unto his son; *gataḥ*—departed; *vanam*—to the forest.

TRANSLATION

Thereafter, when the time was ripe, when Sudyumna, the king of the world, was sufficiently old, he delivered the entire kingdom to his son Purūravā and entered the forest.

PURPORT

According to the Vedic system, one within the institution of *varṇa* and *āśrama* must leave his family life after he reaches fifty years of age (*pañcāśad ūrdhvaṁ vanaṁ vrajet*). Thus Sudyumna followed the prescribed regulations of *varṇāśrama* by leaving the kingdom and going to the forest to complete his spiritual life.

Thus end the Bhaktivedanta purports of the Ninth Canto, First Chapter, of the Śrīmad-Bhāgavatam, *entitled "King Sudyumna Becomes a Woman."*

CHAPTER TWO

The Dynasties of the Sons of Manu

This Second Chapter describes the dynasties of the sons of Manu, headed by Karūṣa.

After Sudyumna accepted the order of *vānaprastha* and departed for the forest, Vaivasvata Manu, being desirous of sons, worshiped the Supreme Personality of Godhead and consequently begot ten sons like Mahārāja Ikṣvāku, all of whom were like their father. One of these sons, Pṛṣadhra, was engaged in the duty of protecting cows at night with a sword in his hand. Following the order of his spiritual master, he would stand in this way for the entire night. Once, in the darkness of night, a tiger seized a cow from the cowshed, and when Pṛṣadhra came to know this, he took a sword in his hand and followed the tiger. Unfortunately, when he finally approached the tiger, he could not distinguish between the cow and the tiger in the dark, and thus he killed the cow. Because of this, his spiritual master cursed him to take birth in a *śūdra* family, but Pṛṣadhra practiced mystic *yoga*, and in *bhakti-yoga* he worshiped the Supreme Personality of Godhead. Then he voluntarily entered a blazing forest fire, thus relinquishing his material body and going back home, back to Godhead.

Kavi, the youngest son of Manu, was a great devotee of the Supreme Personality of Godhead from his very childhood. From Manu's son known as Karūṣa, a sect of *kṣatriyas* known as Kārūṣas was generated. Manu also had a son known as Dhṛṣṭa, from whom another sect of *kṣatriyas* was generated, but although they were born of one who had the qualities of a *kṣatriya*, they became *brāhmaṇas*. From Nṛga, another son of Manu, came the sons and grandsons known as Sumati, Bhūtajyoti and Vasu. From Vasu, in succession, came Pratīka, and from him came Oghavān. Descending in order from the seminal dynasty of Nariṣyanta, another son of Manu, were Citrasena, Ṛkṣa, Mīḍhvān, Pūrṇa, Indrasena, Vītihotra, Satyaśravā, Uruśravā, Devadatta and Agniveśya. From the *kṣatriya* known as Agniveśya came the celebrated *brāhmaṇa* dynasty known as Āgniveśyāyana. From the seminal dynasty of Diṣṭa, another son of Manu, came Nābhāga, and from him in succession came

Bhalandana, Vatsaprīti, Prāṁśu, Pramati, Khanitra, Cākṣuṣa, Viviṁśati, Rambha, Khanīnetra, Karandhama, Avīkṣit, Marutta, Dama, Rājyavardhana, Sudhṛti, Nara, Kevala, Dhundhumān, Vegavān, Budha and Tṛṇabindu. In this way, many sons and grandsons were born in this dynasty. From Tṛṇabindu came a daughter named Ilavilā, from whom Kuvera took birth. Tṛṇabindu also had three sons, named Viśāla, Śūnyabandhu and Dhūmraketu. The son of Viśāla was Hemacandra, his son was Dhūmrākṣa, and his son was Saṁyama. The sons of Saṁyama were Devaja and Kṛśāśva. Kṛśāśva's son, Somadatta, performed an Aśvamedha sacrifice, and by worshiping the Supreme Personality of Godhead, Viṣṇu, he achieved the supreme perfection of going back home, back to Godhead.

TEXT 1

श्रीशुक उवाच

एवं गतेऽथ सुद्युम्ने मनुर्वैवस्वतः सुते ।
पुत्रकामस्तपस्तेपे यमुनायां शतं समाः ॥ १ ॥

śrī-śuka uvāca
evaṁ gate 'tha sudyumne
manur vaivasvataḥ sute
putra-kāmas tapas tepe
yamunāyāṁ śataṁ samāḥ

śrī-śukaḥ uvāca—Śrī Śukadeva Gosvāmī said; *evam*—thus; *gate*—had accepted the order of *vānaprastha; atha*—thereafter; *sudyumne*—when Sudyumna; *manuḥ vaivasvataḥ*—Vaivasvata Manu, known as Śrāddhadeva; *sute*—his son; *putra-kāmaḥ*—desiring to get sons; *tapaḥ tepe*—executed severe austerities; *yamunāyām*—on the bank of the Yamunā; *śatam samāḥ*—for one hundred years.

TRANSLATION

Śukadeva Gosvāmī said: Thereafter, when his son Sudyumna had thus gone to the forest to accept the order of vānaprastha, Vaivasvata Manu [Śrāddhadeva], being desirous of getting more

sons, performed severe austerities on the bank of the Yamunā for one hundred years.

TEXT 2

ततोऽयजन्मनुर्देवमपत्यार्थं हरिं प्रभुम् ।
इक्ष्वाकुपूर्वजान् पुत्रान्लेभे स्वसदृशान् दश ॥ २ ॥

tato 'yajan manur devam
apatyārthaṁ hariṁ prabhum
ikṣvāku-pūrvajān putrān
lebhe sva-sadṛśān daśa

tataḥ—thereafter; *ayajat*—worshiped; *manuḥ*—Vaivasvata Manu; *devam*—unto the Supreme Personality of Godhead; *apatya-artham*—with a desire to get sons; *harim*—unto Hari, the Supreme Personality of Godhead; *prabhum*—the Lord; *ikṣvāku-pūrva-jān*—of whom the eldest was named Ikṣvāku; *putrān*—sons; *lebhe*—got; *sva-sadṛśān*—exactly like himself; *daśa*—ten.

TRANSLATION

Then, because of this desire for sons, the Manu known as Śrāddhadeva worshiped the Supreme Lord, the Personality of Godhead, the Lord of the demigods. Thus he got ten sons exactly like himself. Among them all, Ikṣvāku was the eldest.

TEXT 3

पृषध्रस्तु मनोः पुत्रो गोपालो गुरुणा कृतः ।
पालयामास गा यत्तो रात्र्यां वीरासनव्रतः ॥ ३ ॥

pṛṣadhras tu manoḥ putro
go-pālo guruṇā kṛtaḥ
pālayām āsa gā yatto
rātryāṁ vīrāsana-vrataḥ

pṛṣadhraḥ tu—among them, Pṛṣadhra; *manoḥ*—of Manu; *putraḥ*—the son; *go-pālaḥ*—herding cows; *guruṇā*—by the order of his spiritual master; *kṛtaḥ*—having been engaged; *pālayām āsa*—he protected; *gāḥ*—cows; *yattaḥ*—so engaged; *rātryām*—at night; *vīrāsana-vrataḥ*—taking the vow of *vīrāsana*, standing with a sword.

TRANSLATION

Among these sons, Pṛṣadhra, following the order of his spiritual master, was engaged as a protector of cows. He would stand all night with a sword to give the cows protection.

PURPORT

One who becomes *vīrāsana* takes the vow to stand all night with a sword to give protection to the cows. Because Pṛṣadhra was engaged in this way, it is to be understood that he had no dynasty. We can further understand from this vow accepted by Pṛṣadhra how essential it is to protect the cows. Some son of a *kṣatriya* would take this vow to protect the cows from ferocious animals, even at night. What then is to be said of sending cows to slaughterhouses? This is the most sinful activity in human society.

TEXT 4

एकदा प्राविशद् गोष्ठं शार्दूलो निशि वर्षति ।
शयाना गाव उत्थाय भीतास्ता बभ्रमुर्व्रजे ॥ ४ ॥

ekadā prāviśad goṣṭhaṁ
śārdūlo niśi varṣati
śayānā gāva utthāya
bhītās tā babhramur vraje

ekadā—once upon a time; *prāviśat*—entered; *goṣṭham*—the land of the cowshed; *śārdūlaḥ*—a tiger; *niśi*—at night; *varṣati*—while it was raining; *śayānāḥ*—lying down; *gāvaḥ*—cows; *utthāya*—getting up; *bhītāḥ*—fearing; *tāḥ*—all of them; *babhramuḥ*—scattered here and there; *vraje*—in the land surrounding the cowshed.

TRANSLATION

Once at night, while it was raining, a tiger entered the land of the cowshed. Upon seeing the tiger, all the cows, who were lying down, got up in fear and scattered here and there on the land.

TEXTS 5–6

एकां जग्राह बलवान् सा चुक्रोश भयातुरा ।
तस्यास्तु क्रन्दितं श्रुत्वा पृषध्रोऽनुससार ह ॥ ५ ॥
खड्गमादाय तरसा प्रलीनोडुगणे निशि ।
अजानन्नच्छिनोद् बभ्रोः शिरः शार्दूलशङ्कया ॥ ६ ॥

ekāṁ jagrāha balavān
sā cukrośa bhayāturā
tasyās tu kranditaṁ śrutvā
pṛṣadhro 'nusasāra ha

khaḍgam ādāya tarasā
pralīnoḍu-gaṇe niśi
ajānann acchinod babhroḥ
śiraḥ śārdūla-śaṅkayā

ekām—one of the cows; *jagrāha*—seized; *balavān*—the strong tiger; *sā*—that cow; *cukrośa*—began to cry; *bhaya-āturā*—in distress and fear; *tasyāḥ*—of her; *tu*—but; *kranditam*—the screaming; *śrutvā*—hearing; *pṛṣadhraḥ*—Pṛṣadhra; *anusasāra ha*—followed; *khaḍgam*—sword; *ādāya*—taking; *tarasā*—very hastily; *pralīna-uḍu-gaṇe*—when the stars were covered by clouds; *niśi*—at night; *ajānan*—without knowledge; *acchinot*—cut off; *babhroḥ*—of the cow; *śiraḥ*—the head; *śārdūla-śaṅkayā*—mistaking it for the head of the tiger.

TRANSLATION

When the very strong tiger seized the cow, the cow screamed in distress and fear, and Pṛṣadhra, hearing the screaming, immediately followed the sound. He took up his sword, but because

the stars were covered by clouds, he mistook the cow for the tiger and mistakenly cut off the cows' head with great force.

TEXT 7

व्याघ्रोऽपि वृक्णश्रवणो निस्त्रिंशाग्राहतस्ततः ।
निश्चक्राम भृशं भीतो रक्तं पथि समुत्सृजन् ॥ ७ ॥

vyāghro 'pi vṛkṇa-śravaṇo
nistriṁśāgrāhatas tataḥ
niścakrāma bhṛśaṁ bhīto
raktaṁ pathi samutsṛjan

vyāghraḥ—the tiger; *api*—also; *vṛkṇa-śravaṇaḥ*—its ear being cut off; *nistriṁśa-agra-āhataḥ*—because of being cut by the tip of the sword; *tataḥ*—thereafter; *niścakrāma*—fled (from that place); *bhṛśam*—very much; *bhītaḥ*—being afraid; *raktam*—blood; *pathi*—on the road; *samutsṛjan*—discharging.

TRANSLATION

Because the tiger's ear had been cut by the edge of the sword, the tiger was very afraid, and it fled from that place, while bleeding on the street.

TEXT 8

मन्यमानो हतं व्याघ्रं पृषध्रः परवीरहा ।
अद्राक्षीत् स्वहतां बभ्रुं व्युष्टायां निशि दुःखितः ॥८॥

manyamāno hataṁ vyāghraṁ
pṛṣadhraḥ para-vīra-hā
adrākṣīt sva-hatāṁ babhruṁ
vyuṣṭāyāṁ niśi duḥkhitaḥ

manyamānaḥ—thinking that; *hatam*—has been killed; *vyāghram*—the tiger; *pṛṣadhraḥ*—Manu's son Pṛṣadhra; *para-vīra-hā*—although quite able to punish the enemy; *adrākṣīt*—saw; *sva-hatām*—had been killed by him; *babhrum*—the cow; *vyuṣṭāyām niśi*—when the night had passed (in the morning); *duḥkhitaḥ*—became very much unhappy.

TRANSLATION

In the morning, when Pṛṣadhra, who was quite able to subdue his enemy, saw that he had killed the cow although at night he thought he had killed the tiger, he was very unhappy.

TEXT 9

तं शशाप कुलाचार्यः कृतागसमकामतः ।
न क्षत्रबन्धुः शूद्रस्त्वं कर्मणा भवितामुना ॥ ९ ॥

taṁ śaśāpa kulācāryaḥ
kṛtāgasam akāmataḥ
na kṣatra-bandhuḥ śūdras tvaṁ
karmaṇā bhavitāmunā

tam—him (Pṛṣadhra); *śaśāpa*—cursed; *kula-ācāryaḥ*—the family priest, Vasiṣṭha; *kṛta-āgasam*—because of committing the great sin of killing a cow; *akāmataḥ*—although he did not want to do it; *na*—not; *kṣatra-bandhuḥ*—the family member of a *kṣatriya; śūdraḥ tvam*—you have behaved like a *śūdra; karmaṇā*—therefore by your fruitive reaction; *bhavitā*—you shall become a *śūdra; amunā*—because of killing the cow.

TRANSLATION

Although Pṛṣadhra had committed the sin unknowingly, his family priest, Vasiṣṭha, cursed him, saying, "In your next life you shall not be able to become a kṣatriya. Instead, you shall take birth as a śūdra because of killing the cow."

PURPORT

It appears that Vasiṣṭha was not free from *tamo-guṇa*, the mode of ignorance. As the family priest or spiritual master of Pṛṣadhra, Vasiṣṭha should have taken Pṛṣadhra's offense very lightly, but instead Vasiṣṭha cursed him to become a *śūdra*. It is the duty of a family priest not to curse a disciple but to give him relief through the performance of some sort of atonement. Vasiṣṭha, however, did just the opposite. Therefore Śrīla Viśvanātha Cakravartī Ṭhākura says that he was *durmati;* in other words, his intelligence was not very good.

TEXT 10

एवं शप्तस्तु गुरुणा प्रत्यगृह्णात् कृताञ्जलिः ।
अधारयद् व्रतं वीर ऊर्ध्वरेता मुनिप्रियम् ॥१०॥

evaṁ śaptas tu guruṇā
pratyagṛhṇāt kṛtāñjaliḥ
adhārayad vrataṁ vīra
ūrdhva-retā muni-priyam

evam—in this way; *śaptaḥ*—having been cursed; *tu*—but; *guruṇā*—by his spiritual master; *pratyagṛhṇāt*—he (Pṛṣadhra) accepted; *kṛta-añjaliḥ*—with folded hands; *adhārayat*—took up, assumed; *vratam*—the vow of *brahmacarya; vīraḥ*—that hero; *ūrdhva-retāḥ*—having controlled his senses; *muni-priyam*—which is approved by the great sages.

TRANSLATION

When the hero Pṛṣadhra was thus cursed by his spiritual master, he accepted the curse with folded hands. Then, having controlled his senses, he took the vow of brahmacarya, which is approved by all great sages.

TEXTS 11–13

वासुदेवे भगवति सर्वात्मनि परेऽमले ।
एकान्तित्वं गतो भक्त्या सर्वभूतसुहृत् समः ॥११॥
विमुक्तसङ्गः शान्तात्मा संयताक्षोऽपरिग्रहः ।
यदृच्छयोपपन्नेन कल्पयन् वृत्तिमात्मनः ॥१२॥
आत्मन्यात्मानमाधाय ज्ञानतृप्तः समाहितः ।
विचचार महीमेतां जडान्धबधिराकृतिः ॥१३॥

vāsudeve bhagavati
sarvātmani pare 'male
ekāntitvaṁ gato bhaktyā
sarva-bhūta-suhṛt samaḥ

vimukta-saṅgaḥ śāntātmā
saṁyatākṣo 'parigrahaḥ
yad-ṛcchayopapannena
kalpayan vṛttim ātmanaḥ

ātmany ātmānam ādhāya
jñāna-tṛptaḥ samāhitaḥ
vicacāra mahīm etāṁ
jaḍāndha-badhirākṛtiḥ

vāsudeve—unto the Supreme Personality of Godhead; *bhagavati*—unto the Lord; *sarva-ātmani*—unto the Supersoul; *pare*—unto the Transcendence; *amale*—unto the Supreme Person, who is without material contamination; *ekāntitvam*—rendering devotional service without diversion; *gataḥ*—being situated in that position; *bhaktyā*—because of pure devotion; *sarva-bhūta-suhṛt samaḥ*—because of being a devotee, friendly and equal to everyone; *vimukta-saṅgaḥ*—without material contamination; *śānta-ātmā*—a peaceful attitude; *saṁyata*—self-controlled; *akṣaḥ*—the vision of whom; *aparigrahaḥ*—without accepting any charity from anyone else; *yat-ṛcchayā*—by the grace of the Lord; *upapannena*—by whatever was available for bodily necessities; *kalpayan*—in this way arranging; *vṛttim*—the necessities of the body; *ātmanaḥ*—for the benefit of the soul; *ātmani*—within the mind; *ātmānam*—the Supreme Soul, the Personality of Godhead; *ādhāya*—keeping always; *jñāna-tṛptaḥ*—fully satisfied in transcendental knowledge; *samāhitaḥ*—always in trance; *vicacāra*—traveled all over; *mahīm*—the earth; *etām*—this; *jaḍa*—dumb; *andha*—blind; *badhira*—deaf; *ākṛtiḥ*—appearing as if.

TRANSLATION

Thereafter, Pṛṣadhra gained relief from all responsibilities, became peaceful in mind, and established control over all his senses.

Being unaffected by material conditions, being pleased with whatever was available by the grace of the Lord to maintain body and soul together, and being equal toward everyone, he gave full attention to the Supreme Personality of Godhead, Vāsudeva, who is the transcendental Supersoul, free from material contamination. Thus Pṛṣadhra, fully satisfied in pure knowledge, always keeping his mind on the Supreme Personality of Godhead, achieved pure devotional service to the Lord and began traveling all over the world, without affection for material activities, as if he were deaf, dumb and blind.

TEXT 14

एवं वृत्तो वनं गत्वा दृष्ट्वा दावाग्निमुत्थितम् ।
तेनोपयुक्तकरणो ब्रह्म प्राप परं मुनिः ॥१४॥

evaṁ vṛtto vanaṁ gatvā
dṛṣṭvā dāvāgnim utthitam
tenopayukta-karaṇo
brahma prāpa paraṁ muniḥ

evam vṛttaḥ—being situated in such an order of life; *vanam*—to the forest; *gatvā*—after going; *dṛṣṭvā*—when he saw; *dāva-agnim*—a forest fire; *utthitam*—existing there; *tena*—by that (fire); *upayukta-karaṇaḥ*—engaging all the senses of the body by burning; *brahma*—transcendence; *prāpa*—he achieved; *param*—the ultimate goal; *muniḥ*—as a great saintly person.

TRANSLATION

With this attitude, Pṛṣadhra became a great saint, and when he entered the forest and saw a blazing forest fire, he took this opportunity to burn his body in the fire. Thus he achieved the transcendental, spiritual world.

PURPORT

The Lord says in *Bhagavad-gītā* (4.9):

janma karma ca me divyam
evaṁ yo vetti tattvataḥ
tyaktvā dehaṁ punar janma
naiti mām eti so 'rjuna

"One who knows the transcendental nature of My appearance and activities does not, upon leaving the body, take his birth again in this material world, but attains My eternal abode, O Arjuna." Pṛṣadhra, because of his *karma*, was cursed to take his next birth as a *śūdra*, but because he took to saintly life, specifically concentrating his mind always upon the Supreme Personality of Godhead, he became a pure devotee. Immediately after giving up his body in the fire, he reached the spiritual world, as mentioned in *Bhagavad-gītā* (*mām eti*), as a result of his devotional situation. Devotional service performed by thinking of the Supreme Personality of Godhead is so powerful that although Pṛṣadhra was cursed he avoided the terrible consequence of becoming a *śūdra* and instead returned home, back to Godhead. As stated in *Brahma-saṁhitā* (5.54):

yas tv indra-gopam athavendram aho sva-karma-
bandhānurūpa-phala-bhājanam ātanoti
karmāṇi nirdahati kintu ca bhakti-bhājāṁ
govindam ādi-puruṣaṁ tam ahaṁ bhajāmi

Those who engage in devotional service are unaffected by the results of their material activities. Otherwise, everyone, from the smallest microbe up to the King of heaven, Indra, is subject to the laws of *karma*. A pure devotee, being always engaged in the service of the Lord, is exempt from these laws.

TEXT 15

कविः कनीयान् विषयेषु निःस्पृहो
विसृज्य राज्यं सह बन्धुभिर्वनम् ।
निवेश्य चित्ते पुरुषं स्वरोचिषं
विवेश कैशोरवयाः परं गतः ॥१५॥

kaviḥ kanīyān viṣayeṣu niḥspṛho
visṛjya rājyaṁ saha bandhubhir vanam
niveśya citte puruṣaṁ sva-rociṣaṁ
viveśa kaiśora-vayāḥ paraṁ gataḥ

kaviḥ—another son, known as Kavi; *kanīyān*—who was the youngest; *viṣayeṣu*—in material enjoyments; *niḥspṛhaḥ*—being without attachment; *visṛjya*—after giving up; *rājyam*—his father's property, the kingdom; *saha bandhubhiḥ*—accompanied by friends; *vanam*—the forest; *niveśya*—keeping always; *citte*—within the core of the heart; *puruṣam*—the Supreme Person; *sva-rociṣam*—self-effulgent; *viveśa*—entered; *kaiśora-vayāḥ*—a young man not fully in youth; *param*—the transcendental world; *gataḥ*—entered.

TRANSLATION

Being reluctant to accept material enjoyment, Manu's youngest son, whose name was Kavi, gave up the kingdom before attaining full youth. Accompanied by his friends, he went to the forest, always thinking of the self-effulgent Supreme Personality of Godhead within the core of his heart. Thus he attained perfection.

TEXT 16

करूषान्मानवादासन् कारूषाः क्षत्रजातयः ।
उत्तरापथगोप्तारो ब्रह्मण्या धर्मवत्सलाः ॥१६॥

karūṣān mānavād āsan
kārūṣāḥ kṣatra-jātayaḥ
uttarā-patha-goptāro
brahmaṇyā dharma-vatsalāḥ

karūṣāt—from Karūṣa; *mānavāt*—from the son of Manu; *āsan*—there was; *kārūṣāḥ*—called the Kārūṣas; *kṣatra-jātayaḥ*—a group of *kṣatriyas; uttarā*—northern; *patha*—of the direction; *goptāraḥ*—kings; *brahmaṇyāḥ*—celebrated protectors of the brahminical culture; *dharma-vatsalāḥ*—extremely religious.

TRANSLATION

From Karūṣa, another son of Manu, came the Kārūṣa dynasty, a family of kṣatriyas. The Kārūṣa kṣatriyas were the kings of the northern direction. They were celebrated protectors of brahminical culture and were all firmly religious.

TEXT 17

धृष्टाद् धार्ष्टमभूत् क्षत्रं ब्रह्मभूयं गतं क्षितौ ।
नृगस्य वंशः सुमतिर्भूतज्योतिस्ततो वसुः ॥१७॥

dhṛṣṭād dhārṣṭam abhūt kṣatraṁ
brahma-bhūyaṁ gataṁ kṣitau
nṛgasya vaṁśaḥ sumatir
bhūtajyotis tato vasuḥ

dhṛṣṭāt—from Dhṛṣṭa, another son of Manu; *dhārṣṭam*—a caste of the name Dhārṣṭa; *abhūt*—was produced; *kṣatram*—belonging to the *kṣatriya* group; *brahma-bhūyam*—the position of *brāhmaṇas; gatam*—had achieved; *kṣitau*—on the surface of the world; *nṛgasya*—of Nṛga, another son of Manu; *vaṁśaḥ*—the dynasty; *sumatiḥ*—of the name Sumati; *bhūtajyotiḥ*—of the name Bhūtajyoti; *tataḥ*—thereafter; *vasuḥ*—by the name Vasu.

TRANSLATION

From the son of Manu named Dhṛṣṭa came a kṣatriya caste called Dhārṣṭa, whose members achieved the position of brāhmaṇas in this world. Then, from the son of Manu named Nṛga came Sumati. From Sumati came Bhūtajyoti, and from Bhūtajyoti came Vasu.

PURPORT

Here it is said, *kṣatraṁ brahma-bhūyaṁ gataṁ kṣitau:* although the Dhārṣṭas belonged to the *kṣatriya* caste, they were able to convert themselves into *brāhmaṇas.* This gives clear evidence supporting the following statement by Nārada (*Bhāg.* 7.11.35):

yasya yal lakṣaṇaṁ proktaṁ
puṁso varṇābhivyañjakam
yad anyatrāpi dṛśyeta
tat tenaiva vinirdiśet

If the qualities of one group are found in the men of another, those men should be recognized by their qualities, by their symptoms, not by the caste of the family in which they were born. Birth is not at all important; it is one's qualities that are stressed in all Vedic literature.

TEXT 18

वसोः प्रतीकस्तत्पुत्र ओघवानोघवत्पिता ।
कन्या चौघवती नाम सुदर्शन उवाह ताम् ॥१८॥

vasoḥ pratīkas tat-putra
oghavān oghavat-pitā
kanyā caughavatī nāma
sudarśana uvāha tām

vasoḥ—of Vasu; *pratīkaḥ*—named Pratīka; *tat-putraḥ*—his son; *oghavān*—named Oghavān; *oghavat-pitā*—who was the father of Oghavān; *kanyā*—his daughter; *ca*—also; *oghavatī*—Oghavatī; *nāma*—by the name; *sudarśanaḥ*—Sudarśana; *uvāha*—married; *tām*—that daughter (Oghavatī).

TRANSLATION

The son of Vasu was Pratīka, whose son was Oghavān. Oghavān's son was also known as Oghavān, and his daughter was Oghavatī. Sudarśana married that daughter.

TEXT 19

चित्रसेनो नरिष्यन्ताद्दक्षस्तस्य सुतोऽभवत् ।
तस्य मीढ्वांस्ततः पूर्ण इन्द्रसेनस्तु तत्सुतः ॥१९॥

citraseno nariṣyantād
ṛkṣas tasya suto 'bhavat
tasya mīḍhvāṁs tataḥ pūrṇa
indrasenas tu tat-sutaḥ

citrasenaḥ—one named Citrasena; *nariṣyantāt*—from Nariṣyanta, another son of Manu; *ṛkṣaḥ*—Ṛkṣa; *tasya*—of Citrasena; *sutaḥ*—the son; *abhavat*—became; *tasya*—of him (Ṛkṣa); *mīḍhvān*—Mīḍhvān; *tataḥ*—from him (Mīḍhvān); *pūrṇaḥ*—Pūrṇa; *indrasenaḥ*—Indrasena; *tu*—but; *tat-sutaḥ*—the son of him (Pūrṇa).

TRANSLATION

From Nariṣyanta came a son named Citrasena and from him a son named Ṛkṣa. From Ṛkṣa came Mīḍhvān, from Mīḍhvān came Pūrṇa, and from Pūrṇa came Indrasena.

TEXT 20

वीतिहोत्रस्त्विन्द्रसेनात् तस्य सत्यश्रवा अभूत् ।
उरुश्रवाः सुतस्तस्य देवदत्तस्ततोऽभवत् ॥२०॥

vītihotras tv indrasenāt
tasya satyaśravā abhūt
uruśravāḥ sutas tasya
devadattas tato 'bhavat

vītihotraḥ—Vītihotra; *tu*—but; *indrasenāt*—from Indrasena; *tasya*—of Vītihotra; *satyaśravāḥ*—known by the name Satyaśravā; *abhūt*—there was; *uruśravāḥ*—Uruśravā; *sutaḥ*—was the son; *tasya*—of him (Satyaśravā); *devadattaḥ*—Devadatta; *tataḥ*—from Uruśravā; *abhavat*—there was.

TRANSLATION

From Indrasena came Vītihotra, from Vītihotra came Satyaśravā, from Satyaśravā came the son named Uruśravā, and from Uruśravā came Devadatta.

TEXT 21

ततोऽग्निवेश्यो भगवानग्निः स्वयमभूत् सुतः ।
कानीन इति विख्यातो जातूकर्ण्यो महानृषिः ॥२१॥

tato 'gniveśyo bhagavān
agniḥ svayam abhūt sutaḥ
kānīna iti vikhyāto
jātūkarṇyo mahān ṛṣiḥ

tataḥ—from Devadatta; *agniveśyaḥ*—a son named Agniveśya; *bhagavān*—the most powerful; *agniḥ*—the fire-god; *svayam*—personally; *abhūt*—became; *sutaḥ*—the son; *kānīnaḥ*—Kānīna; *iti*—thus; *vikhyātaḥ*—was celebrated; *jātūkarṇyaḥ*—Jātūkarṇya; *mahān ṛṣiḥ*—the great saintly person.

TRANSLATION

From Devadatta came a son known as Agniveśya, who was the fire-god Agni himself. This son, who was a celebrated saint, was well known as Kānīna and Jātūkarṇya.

PURPORT

Agniveśya was also known as Kānīna and Jātūkarṇya.

TEXT 22

ततो ब्रह्मकुलं जातमाग्निवेश्यायनं नृप ।
नरिष्यन्तान्वयः प्रोक्तो दिष्टवंशमतः शृणु ॥२२॥

tato brahma-kulaṁ jātam
āgniveśyāyanaṁ nṛpa
nariṣyantānvayaḥ prokto
diṣṭa-vaṁśam ataḥ śṛṇu

tataḥ—from Agniveśya; *brahma-kulam*—a dynasty of *brāhmaṇas;* *jātam*—was generated; *āgniveśyāyanam*—known as Āgniveśyāyana; *nṛpa*—O King Parīkṣit; *nariṣyanta*—of Nariṣyanta; *anvayaḥ*—descendants; *proktaḥ*—have been explained; *diṣṭa-vaṁśam*—the dynasty of Diṣṭa; *ataḥ*—hereafter; *śṛṇu*—hear.

TRANSLATION

O King, from Agniveśya came a brahminical dynasty known as Āgniveśyāyana. Now that I have described the descendants of Nariṣyanta, let me describe the descendants of Diṣṭa. Please hear from me.

TEXTS 23–24

नाभागो दिष्टपुत्रोऽन्यः कर्मणा वैश्यतां गतः ।
भलन्दनः सुतस्तस्य वत्सप्रीतिर्भलन्दनात् ॥२३॥
वत्सप्रीतेः सुतः प्रांशुस्तत्सुतं प्रमतिं विदुः ।
खनित्रः प्रमतेस्तस्माच्चाक्षुषोऽथ विविंशतिः ॥२४॥

nābhāgo diṣṭa-putro 'nyaḥ
karmaṇā vaiśyatāṁ gataḥ
bhalandanaḥ sutas tasya
vatsaprītir bhalandanāt

vatsaprīteḥ sutaḥ prāṁśus
tat-sutaṁ pramatiṁ viduḥ
khanitraḥ pramates tasmāc
cākṣuṣo 'tha viviṁśatiḥ

nābhāgaḥ—by the name Nābhāga; *diṣṭa-putraḥ*—the son of Diṣṭa; *anyaḥ*—another; *karmaṇā*—by occupation; *vaiśyatām*—the order of the *vaiśyas; gataḥ*—achieved; *bhalandanaḥ*—by the name Bhalandana; *sutaḥ*—son; *tasya*—of him (Nābhāga); *vatsaprītiḥ*—by the name Vatsaprīti; *bhalandanāt*—from Bhalandana; *vatsaprīteḥ*—from Vatsaprīti; *sutaḥ*—the son; *prāṁśuḥ*—was named Prāṁśu; *tat-sutam*—the son of him (Prāṁśu); *pramatim*—was named Pramati; *viduḥ*—you should understand; *khanitraḥ*—was named Khanitra; *pramateḥ*—from Pramati; *tasmāt*—from him (Khanitra); *cākṣuṣaḥ*—was named Cākṣuṣa; *atha*—thus (from Cākṣuṣa); *viviṁśatiḥ*—the son named Viviṁśati.

TRANSLATION

Diṣṭa had a son by the name Nābhāga. This Nābhāga, who was different from the Nābhāga described later, became a vaiśya by occupational duty. The son of Nābhāga was known as Bhalandana, the son of Bhalandana was Vatsaprīti, and his son was Prāṁśu. Prāṁśu's son was Pramati, Pramati's son was Khanitra, Khanitra's son was Cākṣuṣa, and his son was Viviṁśati.

PURPORT

From Manu, one son became a *kṣatriya*, another a *brāhmaṇa*, and another a *vaiśya*. This confirms the statement by Nārada Muni, *yasya yal lakṣaṇaṁ proktaṁ puṁso varṇābhivyañjakam* (*Bhāg.* 7.11.35). One should always remember that *brāhmaṇas*, *kṣatriyas* and *vaiśyas* should never be regarded as members of a caste by birth. A *brāhmaṇa* may be changed into a *kṣatriya*, and a *kṣatriya* into a *brāhmaṇa*. Similarly, a *brāhmaṇa* or *kṣatriya* may be changed into a *vaiśya*, and a *vaiśya* into a *brāhmaṇa* or *kṣatriya*. This is confirmed in *Bhagavad-gītā* (*cātur-varṇyaṁ mayā sṛṣṭaṁ guṇa-karma-vibhāgaśaḥ*). So one is a *brāhmaṇa*, *kṣatriya* or *vaiśya* never by birth, but by quality. There is a great need of *brāhmaṇas*. Therefore, in the Kṛṣṇa consciousness movement, we are trying to train some *brāhmaṇas* to guide human society. Because at present there is a scarcity of *brāhmaṇas*, the brain of human society is lost. Because practically everyone is a *śūdra*, no one at the present moment can guide the members of society to the proper path by which to achieve perfection in life.

TEXT 25

विविंशतिसुतो रम्भः खनीनेत्रोऽस्य धार्मिकः ।
करन्धमो महाराज तस्यासीदात्मजो नृप ॥२५॥

viviṁśateḥ suto rambhaḥ
khanīnetro 'sya dhārmikaḥ
karandhamo mahārāja
tasyāsīd ātmajo nṛpa

viviṁśateḥ—from Viviṁśati; *sutaḥ*—the son; *rambhaḥ*—named Rambha; *khanīnetraḥ*—named Khanīnetra; *asya*—of Rambha;

dhārmikaḥ—very religious; *karandhamaḥ*—named Karandhama; *mahārāja*—O King; *tasya*—of him (Khanīnetra); *āsīt*—was; *ātmajaḥ*—the son; *nṛpa*—O King.

TRANSLATION

The son of Viviṁśati was Rambha, whose son was the great and religious King Khanīnetra. O King, the son of Khanīnetra was King Karandhama.

TEXT 26

तस्यावीक्षित् सुतो यस्य मरुत्तश्चक्रवर्त्यभूत् ।
संवर्तोऽयाजयद् यं वै महायोग्यङ्गिरःसुतः ॥२६॥

tasyāvīkṣit suto yasya
maruttaś cakravarty abhūt
saṁvarto 'yājayad yaṁ vai
mahā-yogy aṅgiraḥ-sutaḥ

tasya—of him (Karandhama); *avīkṣit*—named Avīkṣit; *sutaḥ*—the son; *yasya*—of whom (Avīkṣit); *maruttaḥ*—(the son) named Marutta; *cakravartī*—the emperor; *abhūt*—became; *saṁvartaḥ*—Saṁvarta; *ayājayat*—engaged in performing sacrifice; *yam*—unto whom (Marutta); *vai*—indeed; *mahā-yogī*—the great mystic; *aṅgiraḥ-sutaḥ*—the son of Aṅgirā.

TRANSLATION

From Karandhama came a son named Avīkṣit, and from Avīkṣit a son named Marutta, who was the emperor. The great mystic Saṁvarta, the son of Aṅgirā, engaged Marutta in performing a sacrifice [yajña].

TEXT 27

मरुत्तस्य यथा यज्ञो न तथान्योऽस्ति कश्चन ।
सर्वं हिरण्मयं त्वासीद् यत् किञ्चिच्चास्य शोभनम् ॥२७॥

maruttasya yathā yajño
na tathānyo 'sti kaścana

sarvaṁ hiraṇmayaṁ tv āsīd
yat kiñcic cāsya śobhanam

maruttasya—of Marutta; *yathā*—as; *yajñaḥ*—performance of sacrifice; *na*—not; *tathā*—like that; *anyaḥ*—any other; *asti*—there is; *kaścana*—anything; *sarvam*—everything; *hiraṇ-mayam*—made of gold; *tu*—indeed; *āsīt*—there was; *yat kiñcit*—whatever he had; *ca*—and; *asya*—of Marutta; *śobhanam*—extremely beautiful.

TRANSLATION

The sacrificial paraphernalia of King Marutta was extremely beautiful, for everything was made of gold. Indeed, no other sacrifice could compare to his.

TEXT 28

अमाद्यदिन्द्रः सोमेन दक्षिणाभिर्द्विजातयः ।
मरुतः परिवेष्टारो विश्वेदेवाः सभासदः ॥२८॥

amādyad indraḥ somena
dakṣiṇābhir dvijātayaḥ
marutaḥ pariveṣṭāro
viśvedevāḥ sabhā-sadaḥ

amādyat—became intoxicated; *indraḥ*—the King of heaven, Lord Indra; *somena*—by drinking the intoxicant *soma-rasa; dakṣiṇābhiḥ*—by receiving sufficient contributions; *dvijātayaḥ*—the brahminical group; *marutaḥ*—the airs; *pariveṣṭāraḥ*—offering the foodstuffs; *viśvedevāḥ*—universal demigods; *sabhā-sadaḥ*—members of the assembly.

TRANSLATION

In that sacrifice, King Indra became intoxicated by drinking a large quantity of soma-rasa. The brāhmaṇas received ample contributions, and therefore they were satisfied. For that sacrifice, the various demigods who control the winds offered foodstuffs, and the Viśvedevas were members of the assembly.

PURPORT

Because of the *yajña* performed by Marutta, everyone was pleased, especially the *brāhmaṇas* and *kṣatriyas*. *Brāhmaṇas* are interested in receiving contributions as priests, and *kṣatriyas* are interested in drinking. All of them, therefore, were satisfied with their different engagements.

TEXT 29

मरुत्तस्य दमः पुत्रस्तस्यासीद् राज्यवर्धनः ।
सुधृतिस्तत्सुतो जज्ञे सौधृतेयो नरः सुतः ॥२९॥

maruttasya damaḥ putras
tasyāsīd rājyavardhanaḥ
sudhṛtis tat-suto jajñe
saudhṛteyo naraḥ sutaḥ

maruttasya—of Marutta; *damaḥ*—(was named) Dama; *putraḥ*—the son; *tasya*—of him (Dama); *āsīt*—there was; *rājya-vardhanaḥ*—named Rājyavardhana, or one who can expand the kingdom; *sudhṛtiḥ*—was named Sudhṛti; *tat-sutaḥ*—the son of him (Rājyavardhana); *jajñe*—was born; *saudhṛteyaḥ*—from Sudhṛti; *naraḥ*—named Nara; *sutaḥ*—the son.

TRANSLATION

Marutta's son was Dama, Dama's son was Rājyavardhana, Rājyavardhana's son was Sudhṛti, and his son was Nara.

TEXT 30

तत्सुतः केवलस्तस्माद् धुन्धुमान् वेगवांस्ततः ।
बन्धुस्तस्याभवद् यस्य तृणबिन्दुर्महीपतिः ॥३०॥

tat-sutaḥ kevalas tasmād
dhundhumān vegavāṁs tataḥ
budhas tasyābhavad yasya
tṛṇabindur mahīpatiḥ

tat-sutaḥ—the son of him (Nara); *kevalaḥ*—was named Kevala; *tasmāt*—from him (Kevala); *dhundhumān*—a son was born named Dhundhumān; *vegavān*—named Vegavān; *tataḥ*—from him (Dhundhumān); *budhaḥ*—named Budha; *tasya*—of him (Vegavān); *abhavat*—there was; *yasya*—of whom (Budha); *tṛṇabinduḥ*—a son named Tṛṇabindu; *mahīpatiḥ*—the king.

TRANSLATION

The son of Nara was Kevala, and his son was Dhundhumān, whose son was Vegavān. Vegavān's son was Budha, and Budha's son was Tṛṇabindu, who became the king of this earth.

TEXT 31

तं भेजेऽलम्बुषा देवी भजनीयगुणालयम् ।
वराप्सरा यतः पुत्राः कन्या चेलविलाभवत् ॥३१॥

taṁ bheje 'lambuṣā devī
bhajanīya-guṇālayam
varāpsarā yataḥ putrāḥ
kanyā celavilābhavat

tam—him (Tṛṇabindu); *bheje*—accepted as husband; *alambuṣā*—the girl Alambuṣā; *devī*—goddess; *bhajanīya*—worthy of accepting; *guṇa-ālayam*—the reservoir of all good qualities; *vara-apsarāḥ*—the best of the Apsarās; *yataḥ*—from whom (Tṛṇabindu); *putrāḥ*—some sons; *kanyā*—a daughter; *ca*—and; *ilavilā*—named Ilavilā; *abhavat*—was born.

TRANSLATION

The best of the Apsarās, the highly qualified girl named Alambuṣā, accepted the similarly qualified Tṛṇabindu as her husband. She gave birth to a few sons and a daughter known as Ilavilā.

TEXT 32

यस्यामुत्पादयामास विश्रवा धनदं सुतम् ।
प्रादाय विद्यां परमामृषिर्योगेश्वरः पितुः ॥३२॥

yasyām utpādayām āsa
viśravā dhanadaṁ sutam
prādāya vidyāṁ paramām
ṛṣir yogeśvaraḥ pituḥ

yasyām—in whom (Ilavilā); *utpādayām āsa*—gave birth; *viśravāḥ*—Viśravā; *dhana-dam*—Kuvera, or one who gives money; *sutam*—to a son; *prādāya*—after receiving; *vidyām*—absolute knowledge; *paramām*—supreme; *ṛṣiḥ*—the great saintly person; *yoga-īśvaraḥ*—master of mystic *yoga; pituḥ*—from his father.

TRANSLATION

After the great saint Viśravā, the master of mystic yoga, received absolute knowledge from his father, he begot in the womb of Ilavilā the greatly celebrated son known as Kuvera, the giver of money.

TEXT 33

विशालः शून्यबन्धुश्च धूम्रकेतुश्च तत्सुताः ।
विशालो वंशकृद् राजा वैशालीं निर्ममे पुरीम् ॥३३॥

viśālaḥ śūnyabandhuś ca
dhūmraketuś ca tat-sutāḥ
viśālo vaṁśa-kṛd rājā
vaiśālīṁ nirmame purīm

viśālaḥ—named Viśāla; *śūnyabandhuḥ*—named Śūnyabandhu; *ca*—also; *dhūmraketuḥ*—named Dhūmraketu; *ca*—also; *tat-sutāḥ*—the sons of Tṛṇabindu; *viśālaḥ*—among the three, King Viśāla; *vaṁśa-kṛt*—made a dynasty; *rājā*—the king; *vaiśālīm*—by the name Vaiśālī; *nirmame*—constructed; *purīm*—a palace.

TRANSLATION

Tṛṇabindu had three sons, named Viśāla, Śūnyabandhu and Dhūmraketu. Among these three, Viśāla created a dynasty and constructed a palace called Vaiśālī.

TEXT 34

हेमचन्द्रः सुतस्तस्य धूम्राक्षस्तस्य चात्मजः ।
तत्पुत्रात् संयमादासीत् कृशाश्वः सहदेवजः ॥३४॥

hemacandraḥ sutas tasya
dhūmrākṣas tasya cātmajaḥ
tat-putrāt saṁyamād āsīt
kṛśāśvaḥ saha-devajaḥ

hemacandraḥ—was named Hemacandra; *sutaḥ*—the son; *tasya*—of him (Viśāla); *dhūmrākṣaḥ*—was named Dhūmrākṣa; *tasya*—of him (Hemacandra); *ca*—also; *ātmajaḥ*—the son; *tat-putrāt*—from the son of him (Dhūmrākṣa); *saṁyamāt*—from he who was named Saṁyama; *āsīt*—there was; *kṛśāśvaḥ*—Kṛśāśva; *saha*—along with; *devajaḥ*—Devaja.

TRANSLATION

The son of Viśāla was known as Hemacandra, his son was Dhūmrākṣa, and his son was Saṁyama, whose sons were Devaja and Kṛśāśva.

TEXTS 35–36

कृशाश्वात् सोमदत्तोऽभूद् योऽश्वमेधैरिडस्पतिम् ।
इष्ट्वा पुरुषमापाग्र्यां गतिं योगेश्वराश्रिताम् ॥३५॥
सौमदत्तिस्तु सुमतिस्तत्पुत्रो जनमेजयः ।
एते वैशालभूपालास्तृणबिन्दोर्यशोधराः ॥३६॥

kṛśāśvāt somadatto 'bhūd
yo 'śvamedhair iḍaspatim
iṣṭvā puruṣam āpāgryāṁ
gatiṁ yogeśvarāśritām

saumadattis tu sumatis
tat-putro janamejayaḥ
ete vaiśāla-bhūpālās
tṛṇabindor yaśodharāḥ

kṛśāśvāt—from Kṛśvāśva; *somadattaḥ*—a son named Somadatta; *abhūt*—there was; *yaḥ*—he who (Somadatta); *aśvamedhaiḥ*—by the performance of *aśvamedha* sacrifices; *iḍaspatim*—unto Lord Viṣṇu; *iṣṭvā*—after worshiping; *puruṣam*—Lord Viṣṇu; *āpa*—achieved; *agryām*—the best of all; *gatim*—the destination; *yogeśvara-āśritām*—the place occupied by great mystic *yogīs; saumadattiḥ*—the son of Somadatta; *tu*—but; *sumatiḥ*—a son named Sumati; *tat-putraḥ*—the son of him (Sumati); *janamejayaḥ*—was named Janamejaya; *ete*—all of them; *vaiśāla-bhūpālāḥ*—the kings in the dynasty of Vaiśāla; *tṛṇabindoḥ yaśaḥ-dharāḥ*—continued the fame of King Tṛṇabindu.

TRANSLATION

The son of Kṛśāśva was Somadatta, who performed aśvamedha sacrifices and thus satisfied the Supreme Personality of Godhead, Viṣṇu. By worshiping the Supreme Lord, he achieved the most exalted post, a residence on the planet to which great mystic yogīs are elevated. The son of Somadatta was Sumati, whose son was Janamejaya. All these kings appearing in the dynasty of Viśāla properly maintained the celebrated position of King Tṛṇabindu.

Thus end the Bhaktivedanta purports of the Ninth Canto, Second Chapter, of the Śrīmad-Bhāgavatam, *entitled "The Dynasties of the Sons of Manu."*

CHAPTER THREE

The Marriage of Sukanyā and Cyavana Muni

This chapter describes the dynasty of Śaryāti, another son of Manu, and also tells about Sukanyā and Revatī.

Devajña Śaryāti gave instructions about what to do in the ritualistic ceremony observed on the second day of the *yajña* of the Aṅgirasas. One day, Śaryāti, along with his daughter, known as Sukanyā, went to the *āśrama* of Cyavana Muni. There Sukanyā saw two glowing substances within a hole of earthworms, and by chance she pierced those two glowing substances. As soon as she did this, blood began to ooze from that hole. Consequently, King Śaryāti and his companions suffered from constipation and inability to pass urine. When the King asked why circumstances had suddenly changed, he found that Sukanyā was the cause of this misfortune. Then they all offered prayers to Cyavana Muni just to satisfy him according to his own desire, and Devajña Śaryāti offered his daughter to Cyavana Muni, who was a very old man.

When the heavenly physicians the Aśvinī-kumāra brothers once visited Cyavana Muni, the *muni* requested them to give him back his youth. These two physicians took Cyavana Muni to a particular lake, in which they bathed and regained full youth. After this, Sukanyā could not distinguish her husband. She then surrendered unto the Aśvinī-kumāras, who were very satisfied with her chastity and who therefore introduced her again to her husband. Cyavana Muni then engaged King Śaryāti in performing the *soma-yajña* and gave the Aśvinī-kumāras the privilege to drink *soma-rasa.* The King of heaven, Lord Indra, became very angry at this, but he could do no harm to Śaryāti. Henceforward, the Aśvinī-kumāra physicians were able to share in the *soma-rasa.*

Śaryāti later had three sons, named Uttānabarhi, Ānarta and Bhūriṣeṇa. Ānarta had one son, whose name was Revata. Revata had one hundred sons, of whom the eldest was Kakudmī. Kakudmī was advised by Lord Brahmā to offer his beautiful daughter, Revatī, to Baladeva, who belongs to the *viṣṇu-tattva* category. After doing this, Kakudmī retired from family life and entered the forest of Badarikāśrama to execute austerities and penances.

TEXT 1

श्रीशुक उवाच
शर्यातिर्मानवो राजा ब्रह्मिष्ठः सम्बभूव ह ।
यो वा अङ्गिरसां सत्रे द्वितीयमहरूचिवान् ॥ १ ॥

śrī-śuka uvāca
śaryātir mānavo rājā
brahmiṣṭhaḥ sambabhūva ha
yo vā aṅgirasāṁ satre
dvitīyam ahar ūcivān

śrī-śukaḥ uvāca—Śrī Śukadeva Gosvāmī said; *śaryātiḥ*—the king named Śaryāti; *mānavaḥ*—the son of Manu; *rājā*—ruler; *brahmiṣṭhaḥ*—completely in awareness of Vedic knowledge; *sambabhūva ha*—so he became; *yaḥ*—one who; *vā*—either; *aṅgirasām*—of the descendants of Aṅgirā; *satre*—in the arena of sacrifice; *dvitīyam ahaḥ*—the functions to be performed on the second day; *ūcivān*—narrated.

TRANSLATION

Śrī Śukadeva Gosvāmī continued: O King, Śaryāti, another son of Manu, was a ruler completely aware of Vedic knowledge. He gave instructions about the functions for the second day of the yajña to be performed by the descendants of Aṅgirā.

TEXT 2

सुकन्या नाम तस्यासीत् कन्या कमललोचना ।
तया सार्धं वनगतो ह्यगमच्च्यवनाश्रमम् ॥ २ ॥

sukanyā nāma tasyāsīt
kanyā kamala-locanā
tayā sārdhaṁ vana-gato
hy agamac cyavanāśramam

sukanyā—Sukanyā; *nāma*—by name; *tasya*—of him (Śaryāti); *āsīt*—there was; *kanyā*—a daughter; *kamala-locanā*—lotus-eyed; *tayā sārdham*—with her; *vana-gataḥ*—having entered the forest; *hi*—indeed; *agamat*—he went; *cyavana-āśramam*—to the *āśrama* cottage of Cyavana Muni.

TRANSLATION

Śaryāti had a beautiful lotus-eyed daughter named Sukanyā, with whom he went to the forest to see the āśrama of Cyavana Muni.

TEXT 3

सा सखीभिः परिवृता विचिन्वन्त्यङ्घ्रिपान् वने ।
वल्मीकरन्ध्रे ददृशे खद्योते इव ज्योतिषी ॥ ३ ॥

sā sakhībhiḥ parivṛtā
vicinvanty aṅghripān vane
valmīka-randhre dadṛśe
khadyote iva jyotiṣī

sā—that Sukanyā; *sakhībhiḥ*—by her friends; *parivṛtā*—surrounded; *vicinvantī*—collecting; *aṅghripān*—fruits and flowers from the trees; *vane*—in the forest; *valmīka-randhre*—in the hole of an earthworm; *dadṛśe*—observed; *khadyote*—two luminaries; *iva*—like; *jyotiṣī*—two shining things.

TRANSLATION

While that Sukanyā, surrounded by her friends, was collecting various types of fruits from the trees in the forest, she saw within the hole of an earthworm two things glowing like luminaries.

TEXT 4

ते दैवचोदिता बाला ज्योतिषी कण्टकेन वै ।
अविध्यन्मुग्धभावेन सुस्रावासृक् ततो बहिः॥ ४ ॥

te daiva-coditā bālā
jyotiṣī kaṇṭakena vai
avidhyan mugdha-bhāvena
susrāvāsṛk tato bahiḥ

te—those two; *daiva-coditā*—as if impelled by providence; *bālā*—that young daughter; *jyotiṣī*—two glowworms within the hole of the earthworm; *kaṇṭakena*—with a thorn; *vai*—indeed; *avidhyat*—pierced; *mugdha-bhāvena*—as if without knowledge; *susrāva*—came out; *asṛk*—blood; *tataḥ*—from there; *bahiḥ*—outside.

TRANSLATION

As if induced by providence, the girl ignorantly pierced those two glowworms with a thorn, and when they were pierced, blood began to ooze out of them.

TEXT 5

शकृन्मूत्रनिरोधोऽभूत् सैनिकानां च तत्क्षणात् ।
राजर्षिस्तमुपालक्ष्य पुरुषान् विस्मितोऽब्रवीत् ॥ ५ ॥

śakṛn-mūtra-nirodho 'bhūt
sainikānāṁ ca tat-kṣaṇāt
rājarṣis tam upālakṣya
puruṣān vismito 'bravīt

śakṛt—of stool; *mūtra*—and of urine; *nirodhaḥ*—stoppage; *abhūt*—so became; *sainikānām*—of all the soldiers; *ca*—and; *tat-kṣaṇāt*—immediately; *rājarṣiḥ*—the King; *tam upālakṣya*—seeing the incident; *puruṣān*—to his men; *vismitaḥ*—being surprised; *abravīt*—began to speak.

TRANSLATION

Thereupon, all the soldiers of Śaryāti were immediately obstructed from passing urine and stool. Upon perceiving this, Śaryāti spoke to his associates in surprise.

TEXT 6

अप्यभद्रं न युष्माभिर्भार्गवस्य विचेष्टितम् ।
व्यक्तं केनापि नस्तस्य कृतमाश्रमदूषणम् ॥ ६ ॥

apy abhadraṁ na yuṣmābhir
bhārgavasya viceṣṭitam
vyaktaṁ kenāpi nas tasya
kṛtam āśrama-dūṣaṇam

api—alas; *abhadram*—something mischievous; *naḥ*—among us; *yuṣmābhiḥ*—by ourselves; *bhārgavasya*—of Cyavana Muni; *viceṣṭitam*—has been attempted; *vyaktam*—now it is clear; *kena api*—by someone; *naḥ*—among ourselves; *tasya*—of him (Cyavana Muni); *kṛtam*—has been done; *āśrama-dūṣaṇam*—pollution of the *āśrama.*

TRANSLATION

How strange it is that one of us has attempted to do something wrong to Cyavana Muni, the son of Bhṛgu. It certainly appears that someone among us has polluted this āśrama.

TEXT 7

सुकन्या प्राह पितरं भीता किञ्चित् कृतं मया ।
द्वे ज्योतिषी अजानन्त्या निर्भिन्ने कण्टकेन वै ॥ ७ ॥

sukanyā prāha pitaraṁ
bhītā kiñcit kṛtaṁ mayā
dve jyotiṣī ajānantyā
nirbhinne kaṇṭakena vai

sukanyā—the girl Sukanyā; *prāha*—said; *pitaram*—unto her father; *bhītā*—being afraid; *kiñcit*—something; *kṛtam*—has been done; *mayā*—by me; *dve*—two; *jyotiṣī*—luminous objects; *ajānantyā*—because of ignorance; *nirbhinne*—have been pierced; *kaṇṭakena*—with a thorn; *vai*—indeed.

TRANSLATION

Being very much afraid, the girl Sukanyā said to her father: I have done something wrong, for I have ignorantly pierced these two luminous substances with a thorn.

TEXT 8

दुहितुस्तद् वचः श्रुत्वा शर्यातिर्जातसाध्वसः ।
मुनिं प्रसादयामास वल्मीकान्तर्हितं शनैः ॥ ८ ॥

duhitus tad vacaḥ śrutvā
śaryātir jāta-sādhvasaḥ
munim̐ prasādayām āsa
valmīkāntarhitam̐ śanaiḥ

duhituḥ—of his daughter; *tat vacaḥ*—that statement; *śrutvā*—after hearing; *śaryātiḥ*—King Śaryāti; *jāta-sādhvasaḥ*—becoming afraid; *munim*—unto Cyavana Muni; *prasādayām āsa*—tried to appease; *valmīka-antarhitam*—who was sitting within the hole of the earthworm; *śanaiḥ*—gradually.

TRANSLATION

After hearing this statement by his daughter, King Śaryāti was very much afraid. In various ways, he tried to appease Cyavana Muni, for it was he who sat within the hole of the earthworm.

TEXT 9

तदभिप्रायमाज्ञाय प्रादाद् दुहितरं मुनेः ।
कृच्छ्रान्मुक्तस्तमामन्त्र्य पुरं प्रायात् समाहितः ॥ ९ ॥

tad-abhiprāyam ājñāya
prādād duhitaram̐ muneḥ
kṛcchrān muktas tam āmantrya
puram̐ prāyāt samāhitaḥ

tat—of Cyavana Muni; *abhiprāyam*—the purpose; *ājñāya*—understanding; *prādāt*—delivered; *duhitaram*—his daughter; *muneḥ*—unto

Cyavana Muni; *kṛcchrāt*—with great difficulty; *muktaḥ*—released; *tam*—the *muni; āmantrya*—taking permission; *puram*—to his own place; *prāyāt*—went away; *samāhitaḥ*—being very contemplative.

TRANSLATION

King Śaryāti, being very contemplative and thus understanding Cyavana Muni's purpose, gave his daughter in charity to the sage. Thus released from danger with great difficulty, he took permission from Cyavana Muni and returned home.

PURPORT

The King, after hearing the statement of his daughter, certainly told the great sage Cyavana Muni everything about how his daughter had ignorantly committed such an offense. The *muni*, however, inquired from the King whether the daughter was married. In this way, the King, understanding the purpose of the great sage Cyavana Muni (*tad-abhiprāyam ājñāya*), immediately gave the *muni* his daughter in charity and escaped the danger of being cursed. Thus with the permission of the great sage the King returned home.

TEXT 10

सुकन्या च्यवनं प्राप्य पतिं परमकोपनम् ।
प्रीणयामास चित्तज्ञा अप्रमत्तानुवृत्तिभिः ॥१०॥

sukanyā cyavanaṁ prāpya
patiṁ parama-kopanam
prīṇayām āsa citta-jñā
apramattānuvṛttibhiḥ

sukanyā—the girl named Sukanyā, the daughter of King Śaryāti; *cyavanam*—the great sage Cyavana Muni; *prāpya*—after obtaining; *patim*—as her husband; *parama-kopanam*—who was always very angry; *prīṇayām āsa*—she satisfied him; *citta-jñā*—understanding the mind of her husband; *apramattā anuvṛttibhiḥ*—by executing services without being bewildered.

TRANSLATION

Cyavana Muni was very irritable, but since Sukanyā had gotten him as her husband, she dealt with him carefully, according to his mood. Knowing his mind, she performed service to him without being bewildered.

PURPORT

This is an indication of the relationship between husband and wife. A great personality like Cyavana Muni has the temperament of always wanting to be in a superior position. Such a person cannot submit to anyone. Therefore, Cyavana Muni had an irritable temperament. His wife, Sukanyā, could understand his attitude, and under the circumstances she treated him accordingly. If any wife wants to be happy with her husband, she must try to understand her husband's temperament and please him. This is victory for a woman. Even in the dealings of Lord Kṛṣṇa with His different queens, it has been seen that although the queens were the daughters of great kings, they placed themselves before Lord Kṛṣṇa as His maidservants. However great a woman may be, she must place herself before her husband in this way; that is to say, she must be ready to carry out her husband's orders and please him in all circumstances. Then her life will be successful. When the wife becomes as irritable as the husband, their life at home is sure to be disturbed or ultimately completely broken. In the modern day, the wife is never submissive, and therefore home life is broken even by slight incidents. Either the wife or the husband may take advantage of the divorce laws. According to the Vedic law, however, there is no such thing as divorce laws, and a woman must be trained to be submissive to the will of her husband. Westerners contend that this is a slave mentality for the wife, but factually it is not; it is the tactic by which a woman can conquer the heart of her husband, however irritable or cruel he may be. In this case we clearly see that although Cyavana Muni was not young but indeed old enough to be Sukanyā's grandfather and was also very irritable, Sukanyā, the beautiful young daughter of a king, submitted herself to her old husband and tried to please him in all respects. Thus she was a faithful and chaste wife.

TEXT 11

कस्यचित् त्वथ कालस्य नासत्यावाश्रमागतौ ।
तौ पूजयित्वा प्रोवाच वयो मे दत्तमीश्वरौ ॥११॥

kasyacit tv atha kālasya
nāsatyāv āśramāgatau
tau pūjayitvā provāca
vayo me dattam īśvarau

kasyacit—after some (time); *tu*—but; *atha*—in this way; *kālasya*—time having passed; *nāsatyau*—the two Aśvinī-kumāras; *āśrama*—that place of Cyavana Muni; *āgatau*—reached; *tau*—unto those two; *pūjayitvā*—offering respectful obeisances; *provāca*—said; *vayaḥ*—youth; *me*—unto me; *dattam*—please give; *īśvarau*—because you two are able to do so.

TRANSLATION

Thereafter, some time having passed, the Aśvinī-kumāra brothers, the heavenly physicians, happened to come to Cyavana Muni's āśrama. After offering them respectful obeisances, Cyavana Muni requested them to give him youthful life, for they were able to do so.

PURPORT

The heavenly physicians like the Aśvinī-kumāras could give youthful life even to one who was advanced in age. Indeed, great *yogīs*, with their mystic powers, can even bring a dead body back to life if the structure of the body is in order. We have already discussed this in connection with Bali Mahārāja's soldiers and their treatment by Śukrācārya. Modern medical science has not yet discovered how to bring a dead body back to life or bring youthful energy to an old body, but from these verses we can understand that such treatment is possible if one is able to take knowledge from the Vedic information. The Aśvinī-kumāras were expert in *Āyur-veda*, as was Dhanvantari. In every department of material science, there is a perfection to be achieved, and to achieve it one must consult the Vedic literature. The highest perfection is to become a devotee of the Lord. To attain this perfection, one must consult *Śrīmad-Bhāgavatam*, which is understood to be the ripe fruit of the Vedic desire tree (*nigama-kalpa-taror galitaṁ phalam*).

TEXT 12

ग्रहं ग्रहीष्ये सोमस्य यज्ञे वामप्यसोमपोः ।
क्रियतां मे वयो रूपं प्रमदानां यदीप्सितम् ॥१२॥

grahaṁ grahīṣye somasya
yajñe vām apy asoma-poḥ
kriyatāṁ me vayo-rūpaṁ
pramadānāṁ yad īpsitam

graham—a full pot; *grahīṣye*—I shall give; *somasya*—of *soma-rasa;* *yajñe*—in sacrifice; *vām*—of both of you; *api*—although; *asoma-poḥ*—of you two, who are not eligible to drink *soma-rasa; kriyatām*—just execute; *me*—my; *vayaḥ*—young age; *rūpam*—beauty of a young man; *pramadānām*—of women as a class; *yat*—which is; *īpsitam*—desirable.

TRANSLATION

Cyavana Muni said: Although you are ineligible to drink soma-rasa in sacrifices, I promise to give you a full pot of it. Kindly arrange beauty and youth for me, because they are attractive to young women.

TEXT 13

बाढमित्यूचतुर्विप्रमभिनन्द्य भिषक्तमौ ।
निमज्जतां भवानस्मिन् ह्रदे सिद्धविनिर्मिते ॥१३॥

bāḍham ity ūcatur vipram
abhinandya bhiṣaktamau
nimajjatāṁ bhavān asmin
hrade siddha-vinirmite

bāḍham—yes, we shall act; *iti*—thus; *ūcatuḥ*—they both replied, accepting the proposal of Cyavana; *vipram*—unto the *brāhmaṇa*

(Cyavana Muni); *abhinandya*—congratulating him; *bhiṣak-tamau*—the two great physicians, the Aśvinī-kumāras; *nimajjatām*—just dive; *bhavān*—yourself; *asmin*—in this; *hrade*—lake; *siddha-vinirmite*—which is especially meant for all kinds of perfection.

TRANSLATION

The great physicians, the Aśvinī-kumāras, very gladly accepted Cyavana Muni's proposal. Thus they told the brāhmaṇa, "Just dive into this lake of successful life." [One who bathes in this lake has his desires fulfilled.]

TEXT 14

इत्युक्तो जरया ग्रस्तदेहो धमनिसन्ततः ।
ह्रदं प्रवेशितोऽश्विभ्यां वलीपलितविग्रहः ॥१४॥

ity ukto jarayā grasta-
deho dhamani-santataḥ
hradaṁ praveśito 'śvibhyāṁ
valī-palita-vigrahaḥ

iti uktaḥ—thus being addressed; *jarayā*—by old age and invalidity; *grasta-dehaḥ*—the body being so diseased; *dhamani-santataḥ*—whose veins were visible everywhere on the body; *hradam*—the lake; *praveśitaḥ*—entered; *aśvibhyām*—helped by the Aśvinī-kumāras; *valī-palita-vigrahaḥ*—whose body had loose skin and white hair.

TRANSLATION

After saying this, the Aśvinī-kumāras caught hold of Cyavana Muni, who was an old, diseased invalid with loose skin, white hair, and veins visible all over his body, and all three of them entered the lake.

PURPORT

Cyavana Muni was so old that he could not enter the lake alone. Thus the Aśvinī-kumāras caught hold of his body, and the three of them entered the lake.

TEXT 15

पुरुषास्त्रय उत्तस्थुरपीव्या वनिताप्रियाः ।
पद्मस्रजः कुण्डलिनस्तुल्यरूपाः सुवाससः ॥१५॥

puruṣās traya uttasthur
apīvyā vanitā-priyāḥ
padma-srajaḥ kuṇḍalinas
tulya-rūpāḥ suvāsasaḥ

puruṣāḥ—men; *trayaḥ*—three; *uttasthuḥ*—arose (from the lake); *apīvyāḥ*—extremely beautiful; *vanitā-priyāḥ*—as a man becomes very attractive to women; *padma-srajaḥ*—decorated with garlands of lotuses; *kuṇḍalinaḥ*—with earrings; *tulya-rūpāḥ*—all of them had the same bodily features; *su-vāsasaḥ*—very nicely dressed.

TRANSLATION

Thereafter, three men with very beautiful bodily features emerged from the lake. They were nicely dressed and decorated with earrings and garlands of lotuses. All of them were of the same standard of beauty.

TEXT 16

तान् निरीक्ष्य वरारोहा सरूपान् सूर्यवर्चसः ।
अजानती पतिं साध्वी अश्विनौ शरणं ययौ ॥१६॥

tān nirīkṣya varārohā
sarūpān sūrya-varcasaḥ
ajānatī patiṁ sādhvī
aśvinau śaraṇaṁ yayau

tān—unto them; *nirīkṣya*—after observing; *vara-ārohā*—that beautiful Sukanyā; *sa-rūpān*—all of them equally beautiful; *sūrya-varcasaḥ*—with a bodily effulgence like the effulgence of the sun; *ajānatī*—not knowing; *patim*—her husband; *sādhvī*—that chaste woman; *aśvinau*—unto the Aśvinī-kumāras; *śaraṇam*—shelter; *yayau*—took.

TRANSLATION

The chaste and very beautiful Sukanyā could not distinguish her husband from the two Aśvinī-kumāras, for they were equally beautiful. Not understanding who her real husband was, she took shelter of the Aśvinī-kumāras.

PURPORT

Sukanyā could have selected any one of them as her husband, for one could not distinguish among them, but because she was chaste, she took shelter of the Aśvinī-kumāras so that they could inform her who her actual husband was. A chaste woman will never accept any man other than her husband, even if there be someone equally as handsome and qualified.

TEXT 17

दर्शयित्वा पतिं तस्यै पातिव्रत्येन तोषितौ ।
ऋषिमामन्त्र्य ययतुर्विमानेन त्रिविष्टपम् ॥१७॥

darśayitvā patiṁ tasyai
pāti-vratyena toṣitau
ṛṣim āmantrya yayatur
vimānena triviṣṭapam

darśayitvā—after showing; *patim*—her husband; *tasyai*—unto Sukanyā; *pāti-vratyena*—because of her strong faith in her husband; *toṣitau*—being very pleased with her; *ṛṣim*—unto Cyavana Muni; *āmantrya*—taking his permission; *yayatuḥ*—they went away; *vimānena*—taking their own airplane; *triviṣṭapam*—to the heavenly planets.

TRANSLATION

The Aśvinī-kumāras were very pleased to see Sukanyā's chastity and faithfulness. Thus they showed her Cyavana Muni, her husband, and after taking permission from him, they returned to the heavenly planets in their plane.

TEXT 18

यक्ष्यमाणोऽथ शर्यातिश्च्यवनस्याश्रमं गतः ।
ददर्श दुहितुः पार्श्वे पुरुषं सूर्यवर्चसम् ॥१८॥

yakṣyamāṇo 'tha śaryātiś
cyavanasyāśramaṁ gataḥ
dadarśa duhituḥ pārśve
puruṣaṁ sūrya-varcasam

yakṣyamāṇaḥ—desiring to perform a *yajña; atha*—thus; *śaryātiḥ*—King Śaryāti; *cyavanasya*—of Cyavana Muni; *āśramam*—to the residence; *gataḥ*—having gone; *dadarśa*—he saw; *duhituḥ*—of his daughter; *pārśve*—by the side; *puruṣam*—a man; *sūrya-varcasam*—beautiful and effulgent like the sun.

TRANSLATION

Thereafter, King Śaryāti, desiring to perform a sacrifice, went to the residence of Cyavana Muni. There he saw by the side of his daughter a very beautiful young man, as bright as the sun.

TEXT 19

राजा दुहितरं प्राह कृतपादाभिवन्दनाम् ।
आशिषश्चाप्रयुञ्जानो नातिप्रीतिमना इव ॥१९॥

rājā duhitaraṁ prāha
kṛta-pādābhivandanām
āśiṣaś cāprayuñjāno
nātiprīti-manā iva

rājā—the King (Śaryāti); *duhitaram*—unto the daughter; *prāha*—said; *kṛta-pāda-abhivandanām*—who had already finished offering respectful obeisances to her father; *āśiṣaḥ*—blessings upon her; *ca*—and; *aprayuñjānaḥ*—without offering to the daughter; *na*—not; *atiprīti-manāḥ*—very much pleased; *iva*—like that.

TRANSLATION

After receiving obeisances from his daughter, the King, instead of offering blessings to her, appeared very displeased and spoke as follows.

TEXT 20

चिकीर्षितं ते किमिदं पतिस्त्वया
प्रलम्भितो लोकनमस्कृतो मुनिः ।
यत् त्वं जराग्रस्तमसत्यसम्मतं
विहाय जारं भजसेऽमुमध्वगम् ॥२०॥

cikīrṣitaṁ te kim idaṁ patis tvayā
pralambhito loka-namaskṛto muniḥ
yat tvaṁ jarā-grastam asaty asammataṁ
vihāya jāraṁ bhajase 'mum adhvagam

cikīrṣitam—which you desire to do; *te*—of you; *kim idam*—what is this; *patiḥ*—your husband; *tvayā*—by you; *pralambhitaḥ*—has been cheated; *loka-namaskṛtaḥ*—who is honored by all people; *muniḥ*—a great sage; *yat*—because; *tvam*—you; *jarā-grastam*—very old and invalid; *asati*—O unchaste daughter; *asammatam*—not very attractive; *vihāya*—giving up; *jāram*—paramour; *bhajase*—you have accepted; *amum*—this man; *adhvagam*—comparable to a street beggar.

TRANSLATION

O unchaste girl, what is this that you have desired to do? You have cheated the most respectable husband, who is honored by everyone, for I see that because he was old, diseased and therefore unattractive, you have left his company to accept as your husband this young man, who appears to be a beggar from the street.

PURPORT

This shows the values of Vedic culture. According to the circumstances, Sukanyā had been given a husband who was too old to be compatible with her. Because Cyavana Muni was diseased and very old, he was certainly unfit for the beautiful daughter of King Śaryāti.

Nonetheless, her father expected her to be faithful to her husband. When he suddenly saw that his daughter had accepted someone else, even though the man was young and handsome, he immediately chastised her as *asatī*, unchaste, because he assumed that she had accepted another man in the presence of her husband. According to Vedic culture, even if a young woman is given an old husband, she must respectfully serve him. This is chastity. It is not that because she dislikes her husband she may give him up and accept another. This is against Vedic culture. According to Vedic culture, a woman must accept the husband given to her by her parents and remain chaste and faithful to him. Therefore King Śaryāti was surprised to see a young man by the side of Sukanyā.

TEXT 21

कथं मतिस्तेऽवगतान्यथा सतां
कुलप्रसूते कुलदूषणं त्विदम् ।
बिभर्षि जारं यदपत्रपा कुलं
पितुश्च भर्तुश्च नयस्यधस्तमः ॥२१॥

kathaṁ matis te 'vagatānyathā satāṁ
kula-prasūte kula-dūṣaṇaṁ tv idam
bibharṣi jāraṁ yad apatrapā kulaṁ
pituś ca bhartuś ca nayasy adhas tamaḥ

katham—how; *matiḥ te*—your consciousness; *avagatā*—has gone down; *anyathā*—otherwise; *satām*—of the most respectable; *kula-prasūte*—O my daughter, born in the family; *kula-dūṣaṇam*—who are the degradation of the family; *tu*—but; *idam*—this; *bibharṣi*—you are maintaining; *jāram*—a paramour; *yat*—as it is; *apatrapā*—without shame; *kulam*—the dynasty; *pituḥ*—of your father; *ca*—and; *bhartuḥ*—of your husband; *ca*—and; *nayasi*—you are bringing down; *adhaḥ tamaḥ*—downward into darkness or hell.

TRANSLATION

O my daughter, who were born in a respectable family, how have you degraded your consciousness in this way? How is it that

you are shamelessly maintaining a paramour? You will thus degrade the dynasties of both your father and your husband to hellish life.

PURPORT

It is quite clear that according to Vedic culture a woman who accepts a paramour or second husband in the presence of the husband she has married is certainly responsible for the degradation of her father's family and the family of her husband. The rules of Vedic culture in this regard are strictly observed in the respectable families of *brāhmaṇas, kṣatriyas* and *vaiśyas* even today; only the *śūdras* are degraded in this matter. For a woman of the *brāhmaṇa, kṣatriya* or *vaiśya* class to accept another husband in the presence of the husband she has married, or to file for divorce or accept a boyfriend or paramour, is unacceptable in the Vedic culture. Therefore King Śaryāti, who did not know the real facts of Cyavana Muni's transformation, was surprised to see the behavior of his daughter.

TEXT 22

एवं ब्रुवाणं पितरं स्मयमाना शुचिस्मिता ।
उवाच तात जामाता तवैष भृगुनन्दनः ॥२२॥

evaṁ bruvāṇaṁ pitaraṁ
smayamānā śuci-smitā
uvāca tāta jāmātā
tavaiṣa bhṛgu-nandanaḥ

evam—in this way; *bruvāṇam*—who was talking and chastising her; *pitaram*—unto her father; *smayamānā*—smiling (because she was chaste); *śuci-smitā*—laughingly; *uvāca*—replied; *tāta*—O my dear father; *jāmātā*—son-in-law; *tava*—your; *eṣaḥ*—this young man; *bhṛgu-nandanaḥ*—is Cyavana Muni (and no one else).

TRANSLATION

Sukanyā, however, being very proud of her chastity, smiled upon hearing the rebukes of her father. She smilingly told him,

"My dear father, this young man by my side is your actual son-in-law, the great sage Cyavana, who was born in the family of Bhṛgu."

PURPORT

Although the father chastised the daughter, assuming that she had accepted another husband, the daughter knew that she was completely honest and chaste, and therefore she was smiling. When she explained that her husband, Cyavana Muni, had now been transformed into a young man, she was very proud of her chastity, and thus she smiled as she talked with her father.

TEXT 23

शशंस पित्रे तत् सर्वं वयोरूपाभिलम्भनम् ।
विस्मितः परमप्रीतस्तनयां परिषस्वजे ॥२३॥

śaśaṁsa pitre tat sarvaṁ
vayo-rūpābhilambhanam
vismitaḥ parama-prītas
tanayāṁ pariṣasvaje

śaśaṁsa—she described; *pitre*—unto her father; *tat*—that; *sarvam*—everything; *vayaḥ*—of the change of age; *rūpa*—and of beauty; *abhilambhanam*—how there was achievement (by her husband); *vismitaḥ*—being surprised; *parama-prītaḥ*—was extremely pleased; *tanayām*—unto his daughter; *pariṣasvaje*—embraced with pleasure.

TRANSLATION

Thus Sukanyā explained how her husband had received the beautiful body of a young man. When the King heard this he was very surprised, and in great pleasure he embraced his beloved daughter.

TEXT 24

सोमेन याजयन् वीरं ग्रहं सोमस्य चाग्रहीत् ।
असोमपोरप्यश्विनोश्च्यवनः स्वेन तेजसा ॥२४॥

somena yājayan vīraṁ
grahaṁ somasya cāgrahīt
asoma-por apy aśvinoś
cyavanaḥ svena tejasā

somena—with the *soma; yājayan*—causing to perform the sacrifice; *vīram*—the King (Śaryāti); *graham*—the full pot; *somasya*—of the *soma-rasa; ca*—also; *agrahīt*—delivered; *asoma-poḥ*—who were not allowed to drink the *soma-rasa; api*—although; *aśvinoḥ*—of the Aśvinī-kumāras; *cyavanaḥ*—Cyavana Muni; *svena*—his own; *tejasā*—by prowess.

TRANSLATION

Cyavana Muni, by his own prowess, enabled King Śaryāti to perform the soma-yajña. The muni offered a full pot of soma-rasa to the Aśvinī-kumāras, although they were unfit to drink it.

TEXT 25

हन्तुं तमाददे वज्रं सद्योमन्युरमर्षितः ।
सवज्रं स्तम्भयामास भुजमिन्द्रस्य भार्गवः ॥२५॥

hantuṁ tam ādade vajraṁ
sadyo manyur amarṣitaḥ
savajraṁ stambhayām āsa
bhujam indrasya bhārgavaḥ

hantum—to kill; *tam*—him (Cyavana); *ādade*—Indra took up; *vajram*—his thunderbolt; *sadyaḥ*—immediately; *manyuḥ*—because of great anger, without consideration; *amarṣitaḥ*—being very much perturbed; *sa-vajram*—with the thunderbolt; *stambhayām āsa*—paralyzed; *bhujam*—the arm; *indrasya*—of Indra; *bhārgavaḥ*—Cyavana Muni, the descendant of Bhṛgu.

TRANSLATION

King Indra, being perturbed and angry, wanted to kill Cyavana Muni, and therefore he impetuously took up his thunderbolt. But

Cyavana Muni, by his powers, paralyzed Indra's arm that held the thunderbolt.

TEXT 26

अन्वजानंस्ततः सर्वे ग्रहं सोमस्य चाश्विनोः ।
भिषजाविति यत् पूर्वं सोमाहुत्या बहिष्कृतौ ॥२६॥

anvajānaṁs tataḥ sarve
grahaṁ somasya cāśvinoḥ
bhiṣajāv iti yat pūrvaṁ
somāhutyā bahiṣ-kṛtau

anvajānan—with their permission; *tataḥ*—thereafter; *sarve*—all the demigods; *graham*—a full pot; *somasya*—of *soma-rasa; ca*—also; *aśvinoḥ*—of the Aśvinī-kumāras; *bhiṣajau*—although only physicians; *iti*—thus; *yat*—because; *pūrvam*—before this; *soma-āhutyā*—with a share in the *soma-yajña; bahiḥ-kṛtau*—who had been disallowed or excluded.

TRANSLATION

Although the Aśvinī-kumāras were only physicians and were therefore excluded from drinking soma-rasa in sacrifices, the demigods agreed to allow them henceforward to drink it.

TEXT 27

उत्तानबर्हिरानर्तो भूरिषेण इति त्रयः ।
शर्यातेरभवन् पुत्रा आनर्ताद् रेवतोऽभवत् ॥२७॥

uttānabarhir ānarto
bhūriṣeṇa iti trayaḥ
śaryāter abhavan putrā
ānartād revato 'bhavat

uttānabarhiḥ—Uttānabarhi; *ānartaḥ*—Ānarta; *bhūriṣeṇaḥ*—Bhūriṣeṇa; *iti*—thus; *trayaḥ*—three; *śaryāteḥ*—of King Śaryāti; *abhavan*—were begotten; *putrāḥ*—sons; *ānartāt*—from Ānarta; *revataḥ*—Revata; *abhavat*—was born.

TRANSLATION

King Śaryāti begot three sons, named Uttānabarhi, Ānarta and Bhūriṣeṇa. From Ānarta came a son named Revata.

TEXT 28

सोऽन्तःसमुद्रे नगरीं विनिर्माय कुशस्थलीम् ।
आस्थितोऽभुङ्क्त विषयानानर्तादीनरिन्दम ।
तस्य पुत्रशतं जज्ञे ककुद्मिज्येष्ठमुत्तमम् ॥२८॥

so 'ntaḥ-samudre nagarīṁ
vinirmāya kuśasthalīm
āsthito 'bhuṅkta viṣayān
ānartādīn arindama
tasya putra-śataṁ jajñe
kakudmi-jyeṣṭham uttamam

saḥ—Revata; *antaḥ-samudre*—in the depths of the ocean; *nagarīm*—a town; *vinirmāya*—after constructing; *kuśasthalīm*—named Kuśasthalī; *āsthitaḥ*—lived there; *abhuṅkta*—enjoyed material happiness; *viṣayān*—kingdoms; *ānarta-ādīn*—Ānarta and others; *arim-dama*—O Mahārāja Parīkṣit, subduer of enemies; *tasya*—his; *putra-śatam*—one hundred sons; *jajñe*—were born; *kakudmi-jyeṣṭham*—of whom the eldest was Kakudmī; *uttamam*—most powerful and opulent.

TRANSLATION

O Mahārāja Parīkṣit, subduer of enemies, this Revata constructed a kingdom known as Kuśasthalī in the depths of the ocean. There he lived and ruled such tracts of land as Ānarta, etc. He had one hundred very nice sons, of whom the eldest was Kakudmī.

TEXT 29

ककुद्मी रेवतीं कन्यां स्वामादाय विभुं गतः ।
पुत्र्या वरं परिप्रष्टुं ब्रह्मलोकमपावृतम् ॥२९॥

kakudmī revatīṁ kanyāṁ
svām ādāya vibhuṁ gataḥ
putryā varaṁ paripraṣṭuṁ
brahmalokam apāvṛtam

kakudmī—King Kakudmī; *revatīm*—named Revatī; *kanyām*—the daughter of Kakudmī; *svām*—his own; *ādāya*—taking; *vibhum*—before Lord Brahmā; *gataḥ*—he went; *putryāḥ*—of his daughter; *varam*—a husband; *paripraṣṭum*—to inquire about; *brahmalokam*—Brahmaloka; *apāvṛtam*—transcendental to the three qualities.

TRANSLATION

Taking his own daughter, Revatī, Kakudmī went to Lord Brahmā in Brahmaloka, which is transcendental to the three modes of material nature, and inquired about a husband for her.

PURPORT

It appears that Brahmaloka, the abode of Lord Brahmā, is also transcendental, above the three modes of material nature (*apāvṛtam*).

TEXT 30

आवर्तमाने गान्धर्वे स्थितोऽलब्धक्षणः क्षणम् ।
तदन्त आद्यमानम्य स्वाभिप्रायं न्यवेदयत् ॥३०॥

āvartamāne gāndharve
sthito 'labdha-kṣaṇaḥ kṣaṇam
tad-anta ādyam ānamya
svābhiprāyaṁ nyavedayat

āvartamāne—because of being engaged; *gāndharve*—in hearing songs from the Gandharvas; *sthitaḥ*—situated; *alabdha-kṣaṇaḥ*—there was no time to talk; *kṣaṇam*—even a moment; *tat-ante*—when it ended; *ādyam*—unto the original teacher of the universe (Lord Brahmā); *ānamya*—after offering obeisances; *sva-abhiprāyam*—his own desire; *nyavedayat*—Kakudmī submitted.

TRANSLATION

When Kakudmī arrived there, Lord Brahmā was engaged in hearing musical performances by the Gandharvas and had not a moment to talk with him. Therefore Kakudmī waited, and at the end of the musical performances he offered his obeisances to Lord Brahmā and thus submitted his long-standing desire.

TEXT 31

तच्छ्रुत्वा भगवान् ब्रह्मा प्रहस्य तमुवाच ह ।
अहो राजन् निरुद्धास्ते कालेन हृदि ये कृताः ॥३१॥

tac chrutvā bhagavān brahmā
prahasya tam uvāca ha
aho rājan niruddhās te
kālena hṛdi ye kṛtāḥ

tat—that; *śrutvā*—hearing; *bhagavān*—the most powerful; *brahmā*—Lord Brahmā; *prahasya*—after laughing; *tam*—unto King Kakudmī; *uvāca ha*—said; *aho*—alas; *rājan*—O King; *niruddhāḥ*—all gone; *te*—all of them; *kālena*—by the course of time; *hṛdi*—within the core of the heart; *ye*—all of them; *kṛtāḥ*—who have been decided upon for acceptance as your son-in-law.

TRANSLATION

After hearing his words, Lord Brahmā, who is most powerful, laughed loudly and said to Kakudmī: O King, all those whom you may have decided within the core of your heart to accept as your son-in-law have passed away in the course of time.

TEXT 32

तत्पुत्रपौत्रनप्तॄणां गोत्राणि च न शृण्महे ।
कालोऽभियातस्त्रिणवचतुर्युगविकल्पितः ॥३२॥

tat putra-pautra-naptṝṇāṁ
gotrāṇi ca na śṛṇmahe

kālo 'bhiyātas tri-ṇava-
catur-yuga-vikalpitaḥ

tat—there; *putra*—of the sons; *pautra*—of the grandsons; *naptṝṇām*—and of the descendants; *gotrāṇi*—the family dynasties; *ca*—also; *na*—not; *śṛṇmahe*—we do hear of; *kālaḥ*—time; *abhiyātaḥ*—have passed; *tri*—three; *nava*—nine; *catur-yuga*—four *yugas* (Satya, Tretā, Dvāpara and Kali); *vikalpitaḥ*—thus measured.

TRANSLATION

Twenty-seven catur-yugas have already passed. Those upon whom you may have decided are now gone, and so are their sons, grandsons and other descendants. You cannot even hear about their names.

PURPORT

During Lord Brahmā's day, fourteen Manus or one thousand *mahā-yugas* pass away. Brahmā informed King Kakudmī that twenty-seven *mahā-yugas*, each consisting of the four periods Satya, Tretā, Dvāpara and Kali, had already passed. All the kings and other great personalities born in those *yugas* had now departed from memory into obscurity. This is the way of time as it moves through past, present and future.

TEXT 33

तद् गच्छ देवदेवांशो बलदेवो महाबलः ।
कन्यारत्नमिदं राजन् नररत्नाय देहि भोः ॥३३॥

tad gaccha deva-devāṁśo
baladevo mahā-balaḥ
kanyā-ratnam idaṁ rājan
nara-ratnāya dehi bhoḥ

tat—therefore; *gaccha*—you go; *deva-deva-aṁśaḥ*—whose plenary portion is Lord Viṣṇu; *baladevaḥ*—known as Baladeva; *mahā-balaḥ*—the supreme powerful; *kanyā-ratnam*—your beautiful daughter; *idam*—this; *rājan*—O King; *nara-ratnāya*—unto the Supreme Personality of Godhead, who is always youthful; *dehi*—just give to Him (in charity); *bhoḥ*—O King.

TRANSLATION

O King, leave here and offer your daughter to Lord Baladeva, who is still present. He is most powerful. Indeed, He is the Supreme Personality of Godhead, whose plenary portion is Lord Viṣṇu. Your daughter is fit to be given to Him in charity.

TEXT 34

भुवो भारावताराय भगवान् भूतभावनः ।
अवतीर्णो निजांशेन पुण्यश्रवणकीर्तनः ॥३४॥

bhuvo bhārāvatārāya
bhagavān bhūta-bhāvanaḥ
avatīrṇo nijāṁśena
puṇya-śravaṇa-kīrtanaḥ

bhuvaḥ—of the world; *bhāra-avatārāya*—to lessen the burden; *bhagavān*—the Supreme Personality of Godhead; *bhūta-bhāvanaḥ*—always the well-wisher of all the living entities; *avatīrṇaḥ*—now He has descended; *nija-aṁśena*—with all the paraphernalia that is part of Him; *puṇya-śravaṇa-kīrtanaḥ*—He is simply worshiped by hearing and chanting, by which one becomes purified.

TRANSLATION

Lord Baladeva is the Supreme Personality of Godhead. One who hears and chants about Him is purified. Because He is always the well-wisher of all living entities, He has descended with all His paraphernalia to purify the entire world and lessen its burden.

TEXT 35

इत्यादिष्टोऽभिवन्द्याजं नृपः स्वपुरमागतः ।
त्यक्तं पुण्यजनत्रासाद् भ्रातृभिर्दिक्ष्ववस्थितैः ॥३५॥

ity ādiṣṭo 'bhivandyājaṁ
nṛpaḥ sva-puram āgataḥ
tyaktaṁ puṇya-jana-trāsād
bhrātṛbhir dikṣv avasthitaiḥ

iti—thus; *ādiṣṭaḥ*—being ordered by Lord Brahmā; *abhivandya*—after offering obeisances; *ajam*—unto Lord Brahmā; *nṛpaḥ*—the King; *sva-puram*—to his own residence; *āgataḥ*—returned; *tyaktam*—which was vacant; *puṇya-jana*—of higher living entities; *trāsāt*—because of their fear; *bhrātṛbhiḥ*—by his brothers; *dikṣu*—in different directions; *avasthitaiḥ*—who were residing.

TRANSLATION

Having received this order from Lord Brahmā, Kakudmī offered obeisances unto him and returned to his own residence. He then saw that his residence was vacant, having been abandoned by his brothers and other relatives, who were living in all directions because of fear of such higher living beings as the Yakṣas.

TEXT 36

सुतां दत्त्वानवद्याङ्गीं बलाय बलशालिने ।
बदर्याख्यं गतो राजा तप्तुं नारायणाश्रमम् ॥३६॥

sutāṁ dattvānavadyāṅgīṁ
balāya bala-śāline
badary-ākhyaṁ gato rājā
taptuṁ nārāyaṇāśramam

sutām—his daughter; *dattvā*—after delivering; *anavadya-aṅgīm*—having a perfect body; *balāya*—unto Lord Baladeva; *bala-śāline*—unto the most powerful, the supreme powerful; *badarī-ākhyam*—named Badarikāśrama; *gataḥ*—he went; *rājā*—the King; *taptum*—to perform austerities; *nārāyaṇa-āśramam*—to the place of Nara-Nārāyaṇa.

TRANSLATION

Thereafter, the King gave his most beautiful daughter in charity to the supremely powerful Baladeva and then retired from worldly life and went to Badarikāśrama to please Nara-Nārāyaṇa.

Thus end the Bhaktivedanta purports of the Ninth Canto, Third Chapter, of the Śrīmad-Bhāgavatam, *entitled "The Marriage of Sukanyā and Cyavana Muni."*

CHAPTER FOUR

Ambarīṣa Mahārāja Offended by Durvāsā Muni

This chapter describes the history of Mahārāja Nabhaga, of his son Nābhāga, and of Mahārāja Ambarīṣa.

The son of Manu was Nabhaga, and his son Nābhāga lived for many years in the *gurukula.* In Nābhāga's absence, his brothers did not consider his share of the kingdom, but instead divided the property among themselves. When Nābhāga returned home, his brothers bestowed upon him their father as his share, but when Nābhāga went to his father and told him about the dealings of the brothers, his father informed him that this was cheating and advised him that for his livelihood he should go to the sacrificial arena and describe two *mantras* to be chanted there. Nābhāga executed the order of his father, and thus Aṅgirā and other great saintly persons gave him all the money collected in that sacrifice. To test Nābhāga, Lord Śiva challenged his claim to the wealth, but when Lord Śiva was satisfied by Nābhāga's behavior, Lord Śiva offered him all the riches.

From Nābhāga was born Ambarīṣa, the most powerful and celebrated devotee. Mahārāja Ambarīṣa was the emperor of the entire world, but he considered his opulence temporary. Indeed, knowing that such material opulence is the cause of downfall into conditional life, he was unattached to this opulence. He engaged his senses and mind in the service of the Lord. This process is called *yukta-vairāgya,* or feasible renunciation, which is quite suitable for worship of the Supreme Personality of Godhead. Because Mahārāja Ambarīṣa, as the emperor, was immensely opulent, he performed devotional service with great opulence, and therefore, despite his wealth, he had no attachment to his wife, children or kingdom. He constantly engaged his senses and mind in the service of the Lord. Therefore, to say nothing of enjoying material opulence, he never desired even liberation.

Once Mahārāja Ambarīṣa was worshiping the Supreme Personality of Godhead in Vṛndāvana, observing the vow of Dvādaśī. On Dvādaśī, the day after Ekādaśī, when he was about to break his Ekādaśī fast, the great mystic *yogī* Durvāsā appeared in his house and became his guest. King Ambarīṣa respectfully received Durvāsā Muni, and Durvāsā Muni, after accepting his invitation to eat there, went to bathe in the Yamunā River at noontime. Because he was absorbed in *samādhi*, he did not come back very soon. Mahārāja Ambarīṣa, however, upon seeing that the time to break the fast was passing, drank a little water, in accordance with the advice of learned *brāhmaṇas*, just to observe the formality of breaking the fast. By mystic power, Durvāsā Muni could understand that this had happened, and he was very angry. When he returned he began to chastise Mahārāja Ambarīṣa, but he was not satisfied, and finally he created from his hair a demon appearing like the fire of death. The Supreme Personality of Godhead, however, is always the protector of His devotee, and to protect Mahārāja Ambarīṣa, He sent His disc, the Sudarśana *cakra*, which immediately vanquished the fiery demon and then pursued Durvāsā, who was so envious of Mahārāja Ambarīṣa. Durvāsā fled to Brahmaloka, Śivaloka and all the other higher planets, but he could not protect himself from the wrath of the Sudarśana *cakra*. Finally he went to the spiritual world and surrendered to Lord Nārāyaṇa, but Lord Nārāyaṇa could not excuse a person who had offended a Vaiṣṇava. To be excused from such an offense, one must submit to the Vaiṣṇava whom he has offended. There is no other way to be excused. Thus Lord Nārāyaṇa advised Durvāsā to return to Mahārāja Ambarīṣa and beg his pardon.

TEXT 1

श्रीशुक उवाच

नाभागो नभगापत्यं यं ततं भ्रातरः कविम् ।
यविष्ठं व्यभजन् दायं ब्रह्मचारिणमागतम् ॥ १ ॥

śrī-śuka uvāca
nābhāgo nabhagāpatyaṁ
yaṁ tataṁ bhrātaraḥ kavim
yaviṣṭhaṁ vyabhajan dāyaṁ
brahmacāriṇam āgatam

śrī-śukaḥ uvāca—Śrī Śukadeva Gosvāmī said; *nābhāgaḥ*—Nābhāga; *nabhaga-apatyam*—was the son of Mahārāja Nabhaga; *yam*—unto whom; *tatam*—the father; *bhrātaraḥ*—the elder brothers; *kavim*—the learned; *yaviṣṭham*—the youngest; *vyabhajan*—divided; *dāyam*—the property; *brahmacāriṇam*—having accepted the life of a *brahmacārī* perpetually (*naiṣṭhika*); *āgatam*—returned.

TRANSLATION

Śukadeva Gosvāmī said: The son of Nabhaga named Nābhāga lived for a long time at the place of his spiritual master. Therefore, his brothers thought that he was not going to become a gṛhastha and would not return. Consequently, without providing a share for him, they divided the property of their father among themselves. When Nābhāga returned from the place of his spiritual master, they gave him their father as his share.

PURPORT

There are two kinds of *brahmacārīs.* One may return home, marry and become a householder, whereas the other, known as *bṛhad-vrata,* takes a vow to remain a *brahmacārī* perpetually. The *bṛhad-vrata brahmacārī* does not return from the place of the spiritual master; he stays there, and later he directly takes *sannyāsa.* Because Nābhāga did not return from the place of his spiritual master, his brothers thought that he had taken *bṛhadvrata-brahmacarya.* Therefore, they did not preserve his share, and when he returned they gave him their father as his share.

TEXT 2

भ्रातरोऽभाङ्क्त किं मह्यं भजाम पितरं तव ।
त्वां ममार्यास्तताभाङ्क्षुर्मा पुत्रक तदादृथाः ॥ २ ॥

bhrātaro 'bhāṅkta kiṁ mahyaṁ
bhajāma pitaraṁ tava
tvāṁ mamāryās tatābhāṅkṣur
mā putraka tad ādṛthāḥ

bhrātaraḥ—O my brothers; *abhāṅkta*—have you given as the share of our father's property; *kim*—what; *mahyam*—unto me; *bhajāma*—we allot; *pitaram*—the father himself; *tava*—as your share; *tvām*—you; *mama*—unto me; *āryāḥ*—my elder brothers; *tata*—O my father; *abhāṅkṣuḥ*—have given the share; *mā*—do not; *putraka*—O my dear son; *tat*—to this statement; *ādṛthāḥ*—give any importance.

TRANSLATION

Nābhāga inquired, "My dear brothers, what have you given to me as my share of our father's property?" His elder brothers answered, "We have kept our father as your share." But when Nābhāga went to his father and said, "My dear father, my elder brothers have given you as my share of property," the father replied, "My dear son, do not rely upon their cheating words. I am not your property."

TEXT 3

इमे अङ्गिरसः सत्रमासतेऽद्य सुमेधसः ।
षष्ठं षष्ठमुपेत्याहः कवे मुह्यन्ति कर्मणि ॥ ३ ॥

ime aṅgirasaḥ satram
āsate 'dya sumedhasaḥ
ṣaṣṭhaṁ ṣaṣṭham upetyāhaḥ
kave muhyanti karmaṇi

ime—all these; *aṅgirasaḥ*—descendants of the dynasty of Aṅgirā; *satram*—sacrifice; *āsate*—are performing; *adya*—today; *sumedhasaḥ*—who are all very intelligent; *ṣaṣṭham*—sixth; *ṣaṣṭham*—sixth; *upetya*—after achieving; *ahaḥ*—day; *kave*—O best of learned men; *muhyanti*—become bewildered; *karmaṇi*—in discharging fruitive activities.

TRANSLATION

Nābhāga's father said: All the descendants of Aṅgirā are now going to perform a great sacrifice, but although they are very intelligent, on every sixth day they will be bewildered in performing sacrifice and will make mistakes in their daily duties.

PURPORT

Nābhāga was very simple hearted. Therefore when he went to his father, the father, in compassion for his son, suggested that as a means of livelihood Nābhāga could go to the descendants of Aṅgirā and take advantage of their misgivings in performing *yajña.*

TEXTS 4–5

तांस्त्वं शंसय सूक्ते द्वे वैश्वदेवे महात्मनः ।
ते स्वर्यन्तो धनं सत्रपरिशेषणमात्मनः ॥ ४ ॥
दास्यन्ति तेऽथ तानर्च्छ तथा स कृतवान् यथा ।
तस्मै दत्त्वा ययुः स्वर्गं ते सत्रपरिशेषणम् ॥ ५ ॥

tāṁs tvaṁ śaṁsaya sūkte dve
vaiśvadeve mahātmanaḥ
te svar yanto dhanaṁ satra-
pariśeṣitam ātmanaḥ

dāsyanti te 'tha tān arccha
tathā sa kṛtavān yathā
tasmai dattvā yayuḥ svargaṁ
te satra-pariśeṣaṇam

tān—to all of them; *tvam*—yourself; *śaṁsaya*—describe; *sūkte*—Vedic hymns; *dve*—two; *vaiśvadeve*—in connection with Vaiśvadeva, the Supreme Personality of Godhead; *mahātmanaḥ*—to all of those great souls; *te*—they; *svaḥ yantaḥ*—while going to their respective destinations in the heavenly planets; *dhanam*—the wealth; *satra-pariśeṣitam*—which remains after the end of the *yajña; ātmanaḥ*—their own property; *dāsyanti*—will deliver; *te*—unto you; *atha*—therefore; *tān*—to them; *arccha*—go there; *tathā*—in that way (according to his father's orders); *saḥ*—he (Nābhāga); *kṛtavān*—executed; *yathā*—as advised by his father; *tasmai*—unto him; *dattvā*—after giving; *yayuḥ*—went; *svargam*—to the heavenly planets; *te*—all of them; *satra-pariśeṣaṇam*—remnants of *yajña.*

TRANSLATION

Nābhāga's father continued: "Go to those great souls and describe two Vedic hymns pertaining to Vaiśvadeva. When the great sages have completed the sacrifice and are going to the heavenly planets, they will give you the remnants of the money they have received from the sacrifice. Therefore, go there immediately." Thus Nābhāga acted exactly according to the advice of his father, and the great sages of the Aṅgirā dynasty gave him all their wealth and then went to the heavenly planets.

TEXT 6

तं कश्चित् स्वीकरिष्यन्तं पुरुषः कृष्णदर्शनः ।
उवाचोत्तरतोऽभ्येत्य ममेदं वास्तुकं वसु ॥ ६ ॥

taṁ kaścit svīkariṣyantaṁ
puruṣaḥ kṛṣṇa-darśanaḥ
uvācottarato 'bhyetya
mamedaṁ vāstukaṁ vasu

tam—unto Nābhāga; *kaścit*—someone; *svīkariṣyantam*—while accepting the riches given by the great sages; *puruṣaḥ*—a person; *kṛṣṇa-darśanaḥ*—black-looking; *uvāca*—said; *uttarataḥ*—from the north; *abhyetya*—coming; *mama*—my; *idam*—these; *vāstukam*—remnants of the sacrifice; *vasu*—all the riches.

TRANSLATION

Thereafter, while Nābhāga was accepting the riches, a black-looking person from the north came to him and said, "All the wealth from this sacrificial arena belongs to me."

TEXT 7

ममेदमृषिभिर्दत्तमिति तर्हि स्म मानवः ।
स्यान्नौ ते पितरि प्रश्नः पृष्टवान् पितरं यथा ॥ ७ ॥

mamedam ṛṣibhir dattam
iti tarhi sma mānavaḥ

syān nau te pitari praśnaḥ
pṛṣṭavān pitaraṁ yathā

mama—my; *idam*—all these; *ṛṣibhiḥ*—by the great saintly persons; *dattam*—have been delivered; *iti*—thus; *tarhi*—therefore; *sma*—indeed; *mānavaḥ*—Nābhāga; *syāt*—let there be; *nau*—of ourselves; *te*—your; *pitari*—unto the father; *praśnaḥ*—an inquiry; *pṛṣṭavān*—he also inquired; *pitaram*—from his father; *yathā*—as requested.

TRANSLATION

Nābhāga then said, "These riches belong to me. The great saintly persons have delivered them to me." When Nābhāga said this, the black-looking person replied, "Let us go to your father and ask him to settle our disagreement." In accordance with this, Nābhāga inquired from his father.

TEXT 8

यज्ञवास्तुगतं सर्वमुच्छिष्टमृषयः क्वचित् ।
चक्रुर्हि भागं रुद्राय स देवः सर्वमर्हति ॥ ८ ॥

yajña-vāstu-gataṁ sarvam
ucchiṣṭam ṛṣayaḥ kvacit
cakrur hi bhāgaṁ rudrāya
sa devaḥ sarvam arhati

yajña-vāstu-gatam—things belonging to the sacrificial arena; *sarvam*—everything; *ucchiṣṭam*—remnants; *ṛṣayaḥ*—the great sages; *kvacit*—sometimes, in the Dakṣa-yajña; *cakruḥ*—did so; *hi*—indeed; *bhāgam*—share; *rudrāya*—unto Lord Śiva; *saḥ*—that; *devaḥ*—demigod; *sarvam*—everything; *arhati*—deserves.

TRANSLATION

The father of Nābhāga said: Whatever the great sages sacrificed in the arena of the Dakṣa-yajña, they offered to Lord Śiva as his share. Therefore, everything in the sacrificial arena certainly belongs to Lord Śiva.

TEXT 9

नाभागस्तं प्रणम्याह तवेश किल वास्तुकम् ।
इत्याह मे पिता ब्रह्मञ्छिरसा त्वां प्रसादये ॥ ९ ॥

nābhāgas taṁ praṇamyāha
taveśa kila vāstukam
ity āha me pitā brahmañ
chirasā tvāṁ prasādaye

nābhāgaḥ—Nābhāga; *tam*—unto him (Lord Śiva); *praṇamya*—offering obeisances; *āha*—said; *tava*—yours; *īśa*—O lord; *kila*—certainly; *vāstukam*—everything in the arena of sacrifice; *iti*—thus; *āha*—said; *me*—my; *pitā*—father; *brahman*—O *brāhmaṇa; śirasā*—bowing my head; *tvām*—unto you; *prasādaye*—I am begging your mercy.

TRANSLATION

Thereupon, after offering obeisances to Lord Śiva, Nābhāga said: O worshipable lord, everything in this arena of sacrifice is yours. This is the assertion of my father. Now, with great respect, I bow my head before you, begging your mercy.

TEXT 10

यत् ते पितावदद् धर्मं त्वं च सत्यं प्रभाषसे ।
ददामि ते मन्त्रदृशो ज्ञानं ब्रह्म सनातनम् ॥१०॥

yat te pitāvadad dharmaṁ
tvaṁ ca satyaṁ prabhāṣase
dadāmi te mantra-dṛśo
jñānaṁ brahma sanātanam

yat—whatever; *te*—your; *pitā*—father; *avadat*—explained; *dharmam*—truth; *tvam ca*—you also; *satyam*—truth; *prabhāṣase*—are speaking; *dadāmi*—I shall give; *te*—unto you; *mantra-dṛśaḥ*—who know the science of *mantra; jñānam*—knowledge; *brahma*—transcendental; *sanātanam*—eternal.

TRANSLATION

Lord Śiva said: Whatever your father has said is the truth, and you also are speaking the same truth. Therefore, I, who know the Vedic mantras, shall explain transcendental knowledge to you.

TEXT 11

गृहाण द्रविणं दत्तं मत्सत्रपरिशेषितम् ।
इत्युक्त्वान्तर्हितो रुद्रो भगवान् धर्मवत्सलः ॥११॥

gṛhāṇa draviṇaṁ dattaṁ
mat-satra-pariśeṣitam
ity uktvāntarhito rudro
bhagavān dharma-vatsalaḥ

gṛhāṇa—please take now; *draviṇam*—all the wealth; *dattam*—is given (to you by me); *mat-satra-pariśeṣitam*—the remnants of the sacrifice executed on my behalf; *iti uktvā*—after speaking like this; *antarhitaḥ*—disappeared; *rudraḥ*—Lord Śiva; *bhagavān*—the most powerful demigod; *dharma-vatsalaḥ*—adherent to the principles of religion.

TRANSLATION

Lord Śiva said, "Now you may take all the wealth remaining from the sacrifice, for I give it to you." After saying this, Lord Śiva, who is most adherent to the religious principles, disappeared from that place.

TEXT 12

य एतत् संस्मरेत् प्रातः सायं च सुसमाहितः ।
कविर्भवति मन्त्रज्ञो गतिं चैव तथात्मनः ॥१२॥

ya etat saṁsmaret prātaḥ
sāyaṁ ca susamāhitaḥ
kavir bhavati mantra-jño
gatiṁ caiva tathātmanaḥ

yaḥ—anyone who; *etat*—about this incident; *saṁsmaret*—may remember; *prātaḥ*—in the morning; *sāyam ca*—and in the evening; *su-samāhitaḥ*—with great attention; *kaviḥ*—learned; *bhavati*—becomes; *mantra-jñaḥ*—well aware of all Vedic *mantras; gatim*—the destination; *ca*—also; *eva*—indeed; *tathā ātmanaḥ*—like that of the self-realized soul.

TRANSLATION

If one hears and chants or remembers this narration in the morning and evening with great attention, he certainly becomes learned, experienced in understanding the Vedic hymns, and expert in self-realization.

TEXT 13

नाभागादम्बरीषोऽभून्महाभागवतः कृती ।
नास्पृशद् ब्रह्मशापोऽपि यं न प्रतिहतः क्वचित् ॥१३॥

nābhāgād ambarīṣo 'bhūn
mahā-bhāgavataḥ kṛtī
nāspṛśad brahma-śāpo 'pi
yaṁ na pratihataḥ kvacit

nābhāgāt—from Nābhāga; *ambarīṣaḥ*—Mahārāja Ambarīṣa; *abhūt*—took birth; *mahā-bhāgavataḥ*—the most exalted devotee; *kṛtī*—very celebrated; *na aspṛśat*—could not touch; *brahma-śāpaḥ api*—even the curse of a *brāhmaṇa; yam*—unto whom (Ambarīṣa Mahārāja); *na*—neither; *pratihataḥ*—failed; *kvacit*—at any time.

TRANSLATION

From Nābhāga, Mahārāja Ambarīṣa took birth. Mahārāja Ambarīṣa was an exalted devotee, celebrated for his great merits. Although he was cursed by an infallible brāhmaṇa, the curse could not touch him.

TEXT 14

श्रीराजोवाच
भगवञ्छ्रोतुमिच्छामि राजर्षेस्तस्य धीमतः ।
न प्राभूद् यत्र निर्मुक्तो ब्रह्मदण्डो दुरत्ययः ॥१४॥

śrī-rājovāca
bhagavañ chrotum icchāmi
rājarṣes tasya dhīmataḥ
na prābhūd yatra nirmukto
brahma-daṇḍo duratyayaḥ

śrī-rājā uvāca—King Parīkṣit inquired; *bhagavan*—O great *brāhmaṇa; śrotum icchāmi*—I wish to hear (from you); *rājarṣeḥ*—of the great King Ambarīṣa; *tasya*—of him; *dhīmataḥ*—who was such a greatly sober personality; *na*—not; *prābhūt*—could act; *yatra*—upon whom (Mahārāja Ambarīṣa); *nirmuktaḥ*—being released; *brahma-daṇḍaḥ*—the curse of a *brāhmaṇa; duratyayaḥ*—which is insurmountable.

TRANSLATION

King Parīkṣit inquired: O great personality, Mahārāja Ambarīṣa was certainly most exalted and meritorious in character. I wish to hear about him. How surprising it is that the curse of a brāhmaṇa, which is insurmountable, could not act upon him.

TEXTS 15–16

श्रीशुक उवाच
अम्बरीषो महाभागः सप्तद्वीपवतीं महीम् ।
अव्ययां च श्रियं लब्ध्वा विभवं चातुलं भुवि ॥१५॥
मेनेऽतिदुर्लभं पुंसां सर्वं तत् स्वप्नसंस्तुतम् ।
विद्वान् विभवनिर्वाणं तमो विशति यत् पुमान् ॥१६॥

śrī-śuka uvāca
ambarīṣo mahā-bhāgaḥ
sapta-dvīpavatīṁ mahīm
avyayāṁ ca śriyaṁ labdhvā
vibhavaṁ cātulaṁ bhuvi

mene 'tidurlabhaṁ puṁsāṁ
sarvaṁ tat svapna-saṁstutam
vidvān vibhava-nirvāṇaṁ
tamo viśati yat pumān

śrī-śukaḥ uvāca—Śrī Śukadeva Gosvāmī said; *ambarīṣaḥ*—King Ambarīṣa; *mahā-bhāgaḥ*—the greatly fortunate king; *sapta-dvīpa-vatīm*—consisting of seven islands; *mahīm*—the whole world; *avyayām ca*—and inexhaustible; *śriyam*—beauty; *labdhvā*—after achieving; *vibhavam ca*—and opulences; *atulam*—unlimited; *bhuvi*—in this earth; *mene*—he decided; *ati-durlabham*—which is rarely obtained; *puṁ-sām*—of many persons; *sarvam*—everything (he had obtained); *tat*—that which; *svapna-saṁstutam*—as if imagined in a dream; *vidvān*—completely understanding; *vibhava-nirvāṇam*—the annihilation of that opulence; *tamaḥ*—ignorance; *viśati*—fallen into; *yat*—because of which; *pumān*—a person.

TRANSLATION

Śukadeva Gosvāmī said: Mahārāja Ambarīṣa, the most fortunate personality, achieved the rule of the entire world, consisting of seven islands, and achieved inexhaustible, unlimited opulence and prosperity on earth. Although such a position is rarely obtained, Mahārāja Ambarīṣa did not care for it at all, for he knew very well that all such opulence is material. Like that which is imagined in a dream, such opulence will ultimately be destroyed. The King knew that any nondevotee who attains such opulence merges increasingly into material nature's mode of darkness.

PURPORT

For a devotee material opulence is insignificant, whereas for a non-devotee material opulence is the cause of increasing bondage, for a devotee knows that anything material is temporary, whereas a nondevotee regards the temporary so-called happiness as everything and forgets the path of self-realization. Thus for the nondevotee material opulence is a disqualification for spiritual advancement.

TEXT 17

वासुदेवे भगवति तद्भक्तेषु च साधुषु ।
प्राप्तो भावं परं विश्वं येनेदं लोष्ट्रवत् स्मृतम् ॥ १७ ॥

vāsudeve bhagavati
tad-bhakteṣu ca sādhuṣu
prāpto bhāvaṁ paraṁ viśvaṁ
yenedaṁ loṣṭravat smṛtam

vāsudeve—unto the all-pervading Supreme Personality; *bhagavati*—unto the Supreme Personality of Godhead; *tat-bhakteṣu*—unto His devotees; *ca*—also; *sādhuṣu*—unto the saintly persons; *prāptaḥ*—one who has achieved; *bhāvam*—reverence and devotion; *param*—transcendental; *viśvam*—the whole material universe; *yena*—by which (spiritual consciousness); *idam*—this; *loṣṭra-vat*—as insignificant as a piece of stone; *smṛtam*—is accepted (by such devotees).

TRANSLATION

Mahārāja Ambarīṣa was a great devotee of the Supreme Personality of Godhead, Vāsudeva, and of the saintly persons who are the Lord's devotees. Because of this devotion, he thought of the entire universe as being as insignificant as a piece of stone.

TEXTS 18–20

स वै मनः कृष्णपदारविन्दयो-
र्वचांसि वैकुण्ठगुणानुवर्णने ।
करौ हरेर्मन्दिरमार्जनादिषु
श्रुतिं चकाराच्युतसत्कथोदये ॥१८॥

मुकुन्दलिङ्गालयदर्शने दृशौ
तद्भृत्यगात्रस्पर्शेऽङ्गसङ्गमम् ।
घ्राणं च तत्पादसरोजसौरभे
श्रीमत्तुलस्या रसनां तदर्पिते ॥१९॥
पादौ हरेः क्षेत्रपदानुसर्पणे
शिरो हृषीकेशपदाभिवन्दने ।
कामं च दास्ये न तु कामकाम्यया
यथोत्तमश्लोकजनाश्रया रतिः ॥२०॥

sa vai manaḥ kṛṣṇa-padāravindayor
vacāṁsi vaikuṇṭha-guṇānuvarṇane
karau harer mandira-mārjanādiṣu
śrutiṁ cakārācyuta-sat-kathodaye

mukunda-liṅgālaya-darśane dṛśau
tad-bhṛtya-gātra-sparśe 'ṅga-saṅgamam
ghrāṇaṁ ca tat-pāda-saroja-saurabhe
śrīmat-tulasyā rasanāṁ tad-arpite

pādau hareḥ kṣetra-padānusarpaṇe
śiro hṛṣīkeśa-padābhivandane
kāmaṁ ca dāsye na tu kāma-kāmyayā
yathottamaśloka-janāśrayā ratiḥ

saḥ—he (Mahārāja Ambarīṣa); *vai*—indeed; *manaḥ*—his mind; *kṛṣṇa-pada-aravindayoḥ*—(fixed) upon the two lotus feet of Lord Kṛṣṇa; *vacāṁsi*—his words; *vaikuṇṭha-guṇa-anuvarṇane*—describing the glories of Kṛṣṇa; *karau*—his two hands; *hareḥ mandira-mārjana-ādiṣu*—in activities like cleansing the temple of Hari, the Supreme Personality of Godhead; *śrutim*—his ear; *cakāra*—engaged; *acyuta*—of or about Kṛṣṇa, who never falls down; *sat-kathā-udaye*—in hearing the transcendental narrations; *mukunda-liṅga-ālaya-darśane*—in seeing the Deity and temples and holy *dhāmas* of Mukunda; *dṛśau*—his two eyes; *tat-bhṛtya*—of the servants of Kṛṣṇa; *gātra-sparśe*—in touching the bodies; *aṅga-saṅgamam*—contact of his body; *ghrāṇam ca*—and his sense of smell; *tat-pāda*—of His lotus feet; *saroja*—of the lotus flower; *saurabhe*—in (smelling) the fragrance; *śrīmat-tulasyāḥ*—of the *tulasī* leaves; *rasanām*—his tongue; *tat-arpite*—in the *prasāda* offered to the Lord; *pādau*—his two legs; *hareḥ*—of the Personality of Godhead; *kṣetra*—holy places like the temple or Vṛndāvana and Dvārakā; *pada-anusarpaṇe*—walking to those places; *śiraḥ*—the head; *hṛṣīkeśa*—of Kṛṣṇa, the master of the senses; *pada-abhivandane*—in offering obeisances to the lotus feet; *kāmam ca*—and his desires; *dāsye*—in being engaged as a servant; *na*—not; *tu*—indeed; *kāma-kāmyayā*—with a desire for sense gratificaiton; *yathā*—as; *uttamaśloka-jana-āśrayā*—if one takes shelter of a devotee such as Prahlāda; *ratiḥ*—attachment.

TRANSLATION

Mahārāja Ambarīṣa always engaged his mind in meditating upon the lotus feet of Kṛṣṇa, his words in describing the glories of the Lord, his hands in cleansing the Lord's temple, and his ears in hearing the words spoken by Kṛṣṇa or about Kṛṣṇa. He engaged his eyes in seeing the Deity of Kṛṣṇa, Kṛṣṇa's temples and Kṛṣṇa's places like Mathurā and Vṛndāvana, he engaged his sense of touch in touching the bodies of the Lord's devotees, he engaged his sense of smell in smelling the fragrance of tulasī offered to the Lord, and he engaged his tongue in tasting the Lord's prasāda. He engaged his legs in walking to the holy places and temples of the Lord, his head in bowing down before the Lord, and all his desires in serving the Lord, twenty-four hours a day. Indeed, Mahārāja Ambarīṣa never desired anything for his own sense gratification. He engaged all his senses in devotional service, in various engagements related to the Lord. This is the way to increase attachment for the Lord and be completely free from all material desires.

PURPORT

In *Bhagavad-gītā* (7.1) the Lord recommends, *mayy āsakta-manāḥ pārtha yogaṁ yuñjan mad-āśrayaḥ*. This indicates that one must execute devotional service under the guidance of a devotee or directly under the guidance of the Supreme Personality of Godhead. It is not possible, however, to train oneself without guidance from the spiritual master. Therefore, according to the instructions of Śrīla Rūpa Gosvāmī, the first business of a devotee is to accept a bona fide spiritual master who can train him to engage his various senses in rendering transcendental service to the Lord. The Lord also says in *Bhagavad-gītā* (7.1), *asaṁśayaṁ samagraṁ māṁ yathā jñāsyasi tac chṛṇu.* In other words, if one wants to understand the Supreme Personality of Godhead in completeness, one must follow the prescriptions given by Kṛṣṇa by following in the footsteps of Mahārāja Ambarīṣa. It is said, *hṛṣīkeṇa hṛṣīkeśa-sevanaṁ bhaktir ucyate: bhakti* means to engage the senses in the service of the master of the senses, Kṛṣṇa, who is called Hṛṣīkeśa or Acyuta. These words are used in these verses. *Acyuta-sat-kathodaye, hṛṣīkeśa-padābhivandane.* The words Acyuta and Hṛṣīkeśa are also used in *Bhagavad-gītā. Bhagavad-gītā* is *kṛṣṇa-kathā* spoken directly by Kṛṣṇa, and *Śrīmad-Bhāgavatam* is also *kṛṣṇa-kathā* because everything described in the *Bhāgavatam* is in relationship with Kṛṣṇa.

TEXT 21

एवं सदा कर्मकलापमात्मनः
परेऽधियज्ञे भगवत्यधोक्षजे ।
सर्वात्मभावं विदधन्महीमिमां
तन्निष्ठविप्राभिहितः शशास ह ॥२१॥

evaṁ sadā karma-kalāpam ātmanaḥ
pare 'dhiyajñe bhagavaty adhokṣaje
sarvātma-bhāvaṁ vidadhan mahīm imāṁ
tan-niṣṭha-viprābhihitaḥ śaśāsa ha

evam—thus (living a devotional life); *sadā*—always; *karma-kalāpam*—the prescribed occupational duties as a *kṣatriya* king; *ātmanaḥ*—of himself, personally (the head of the state); *pare*—unto the supreme transcendence; *adhiyajñe*—unto the supreme proprietor, the supreme enjoyer; *bhagavati*—unto the Supreme Personality of Godhead; *adhokṣaje*—unto He who is beyond material sense perception; *sarva-ātma-bhāvam*—all different varieties of devotional service;

vidadhat—executing, offering; *mahīm*—the planet earth; *imām*—this; *tat-niṣṭha*—who are faithful devotees of the Lord; *vipra*—by such *brāhmaṇas; abhihitaḥ*—directed; *śaśāsa*—ruled; *ha*—in the past.

TRANSLATION

In performing his prescribed duties as king, Mahārāja Ambarīṣa always offered the results of his royal activities to the Supreme Personality of Godhead, Kṛṣṇa, who is the enjoyer of everything and is beyond the perception of material senses. He certainly took advice from brāhmaṇas who were faithful devotees of the Lord, and thus he ruled the planet earth without difficulty.

PURPORT

As stated in *Bhagavad-gītā* (5.29):

bhoktāraṁ yajña-tapasāṁ
sarva-loka-maheśvaram
suhṛdaṁ sarva-bhūtānāṁ
jñātvā māṁ śāntim ṛcchati

People are very much anxious to live in peace and prosperity in this material world, and here in *Bhagavad-gītā* the peace formula is given personally by the Supreme Personality of Godhead: everyone should understand that Kṛṣṇa, the Supreme Personality of Godhead, is the ultimate proprietor of all the planets and is therefore the enjoyer of all activities, political, social, cultural, religious, economic and so on. The Lord has given perfect advice in *Bhagavad-gītā*, and Ambarīṣa Mahārāja, as the ideal executive head, ruled the entire world as a Vaiṣṇava, taking advice from Vaiṣṇava *brāhmaṇas.* The *śāstras* enjoin that even though a *brāhmaṇa* may be well versed in the occupational brahminical duties and may be very learned in Vedic knowledge, he cannot give advice as a *guru* until he is a Vaiṣṇava.

ṣaṭ-karma-nipuṇo vipro
mantra-tantra-viśāradaḥ
avaiṣṇavo gurur na syād
vaiṣṇavaḥ śva-paco guruḥ

Therefore, as indicated here by the words *tan-niṣṭha-viprābhihitaḥ*, Mahārāja Ambarīṣa took advice from *brāhmaṇas* who were pure devotees of the Lord, for ordinary *brāhmaṇas* who are merely learned scholars or experts in performing ritualistic ceremonies are not competent to give advice.

In modern times, there are legislative assemblies whose members are authorized to make laws for the welfare of the state, but according to this description of the kingdom of Mahārāja Ambarīṣa, the country or the world should be ruled by a chief executive whose advisors are all devotee *brāhmaṇas*. Such advisors or members of the legislative assembly should not be professional politicians, nor should they be selected by the ignorant public. Rather, they should be appointed by the king. When the king, the executive head of the state, is a devotee and he follows the instructions of devotee *brāhmaṇas* in ruling the country, everyone will be peaceful and prosperous. When the king and his advisors are perfect devotees, nothing can be wrong in the state. All the citizens should become devotees of the Lord, and then their good character will automatically follow.

yasyāsti bhaktir bhagavaty akiñcanā
sarvair guṇais tatra samāsate surāḥ
harāv abhaktasya kuto mahad-guṇā
manorathenāsati dhāvato bahiḥ

"One who has unflinching devotion for the Personality of Godhead has all the good qualities of the demigods. But one who is not a devotee of the Lord has only material qualifications that are of little value. This is because he is hovering on the mental plane and is certain to be attracted by the glaring material energy." (*Bhāg.* 5.18.12) Citizens under the guidance of a Kṛṣṇa conscious king will become devotees, and then there will be no need to enact new laws every day to reform the way of life in the state. If the citizens are trained to become devotees, they will automatically become peaceful and honest, and if they are guided by a devoted king advised by devotees, the state will not be in the material world but in the spiritual world. All the states of the world should therefore follow the ideal of the rule or administration of Mahārāja Ambarīṣa, as described here.

TEXT 22

ईजेऽश्वमेधैरधियज्ञमीश्वरं
महाविभूत्योपचिताङ्गदक्षिणैः ।
ततैर्वसिष्ठासितगौतमादिभि-
र्धन्वन्यभिस्रोतमसौ सरस्वतीम् ॥२२॥

īje 'śvamedhair adhiyajñam īśvaraṁ
mahā-vibhūtyopacitāṅga-dakṣiṇaiḥ
tatair vasiṣṭhāsita-gautamādibhir
dhanvany abhisrotam asau sarasvatīm

īje—worshiped; *aśvamedhaiḥ*—by performing the horse sacrifice *yajñas; adhiyajñam*—to satisfy the master of all *yajñas; īśvaram*—the Supreme Personality of Godhead; *mahā-vibhūtyā*—with great opulence; *upacita-aṅga-dakṣiṇaiḥ*—with all prescribed paraphernalia and contributions of *dakṣiṇā* to the *brāhmaṇas; tataiḥ*—executed; *vasiṣṭha-asita-gautama-ādibhiḥ*—by such *brāhmaṇas* as Vasiṣṭha, Asita and Gautama; *dhanvani*—in the desert; *abhisrotam*—inundated by the water of the river; *asau*—Mahārāja Ambarīṣa; *sarasvatīm*—on the bank of the Sarasvatī.

TRANSLATION

In desert countries where there flowed the River Sarasvatī, Mahārāja Ambarīṣa performed great sacrifices like the aśvamedha-yajña and thus satisfied the master of all yajñas, the Supreme Personality of Godhead. Such sacrifices were performed with great opulence and suitable paraphernalia and with contributions of dakṣiṇā to the brāhmaṇas, who were supervised by great personalities like Vasiṣṭha, Asita and Gautama, representing the king, the performer of the sacrifices.

PURPORT

When one performs ritualistic sacrifices as prescribed in the *Vedas*, one needs expert *brāhmaṇas* known as *yājñika-brāhmaṇas*. In Kali-yuga, however, there is a scarcity of such *brāhmaṇas*. Therefore in

Kali-yuga the sacrifice recommended in *śāstra* is *saṅkīrtana-yajña* (*yajñaiḥ saṅkīrtana-prāyair yajanti hi sumedhasaḥ*). Instead of spending money unnecessarily on performing *yajñas* impossible to perform in this age of Kali because of the scarcity of *yājñika-brāhmaṇas*, one who is intelligent performs *saṅkīrtana-yajña.* Without properly performed *yajñas* to satisfy the Supreme Personality of Godhead, there will be scarcity of rain (*yajñād bhavati parjanyaḥ*). Therefore the performance of *yajña* is essential. Without *yajña* there will be a scarcity of rain, and because of this scarcity, no food grains will be produced, and there will be famines. It is the duty of the king, therefore, to perform different types of *yajñas*, such as the *aśvamedha-yajña*, to maintain the production of food grains. *Annād bhavanti bhūtāni.* Without food grains, both men and animals will starve. Therefore *yajña* is necessary for the state to perform because by *yajña* the people in general will be fed sumptuously. The *brāhmaṇas* and *yājñika* priests should be sufficiently paid for their expert service. This payment is called *dakṣiṇā.* Ambarīṣa Mahārāja, as the head of the state, performed all these *yajñas* through great personalities like Vasiṣṭha, Gautama and Asita. Personally, however, he was engaged in devotional service, as mentioned before (*sa vai manaḥ kṛṣṇa-padāravindayoḥ*). The king or head of state must see that things go on well under proper guidance, and he must be an ideal devotee, as exemplified by Mahārāja Ambarīṣa. It is the duty of the king to see that food grains are produced even in desert countries, what to speak of elsewhere.

TEXT 23

यस्य क्रतुषु गीर्वाणैः सदस्या ऋत्विजो जनाः ।
तुल्यरूपाश्चानिमिषा व्यदृश्यन्त सुवाससः ॥२३॥

yasya kratuṣu gīrvāṇaiḥ
sadasyā ṛtvijo janāḥ
tulya-rūpāś cānimiṣā
vyadṛśyanta suvāsasaḥ

yasya—of whom (Mahārāja Ambarīṣa); *kratuṣu*—in sacrifices (performed by him); *gīrvāṇaiḥ*—with the demigods; *sadasyāḥ*—members for executing the sacrifice; *ṛtvijaḥ*—the priests; *janāḥ*—and other expert men; *tulya-rūpāḥ*—appearing exactly like; *ca*—and; *animiṣāḥ*—

with unblinking eyes like those of the demigods; *vyadṛśyanta*—being seen; *su-vāsasaḥ*—well dressed with valuable garments.

TRANSLATION

In the sacrifice arranged by Mahārāja Ambarīṣa, the members of the assembly and the priests [especially hotā, udgātā, brahmā and adhvaryu] were gorgeously dressed, and they all looked exactly like demigods. They eagerly saw to the proper performance of the yajña.

TEXT 24

स्वर्गो न प्रार्थितो यस्य मनुजैरमरप्रियः ।
शृण्वद्भिरुपगायद्भिरुत्तमश्लोकचेष्टितम् ॥२४॥

svargo na prārthito yasya
manujair amara-priyaḥ
śṛṇvadbhir upagāyadbhir
uttamaśloka-ceṣṭitam

svargaḥ—life in the heavenly planets; *na*—not; *prārthitaḥ*—a subject for aspiration; *yasya*—of whom (Ambarīṣa Mahārāja); *manujaiḥ*—by the citizens; *amara-priyaḥ*—very dear even to the demigods; *śṛṇvadbhiḥ*—who were accustomed to hear; *upagāyadbhiḥ*—and accustomed to chant; *uttamaśloka*—of the Supreme Personality of Godhead; *ceṣṭitam*—about the glorious activities.

TRANSLATION

The citizens of the state of Mahārāja Ambarīṣa were accustomed to chanting and hearing about the glorious activities of the Personality of Godhead. Thus they never aspired to be elevated to the heavenly planets, which are extremely dear even to the demigods.

PURPORT

A pure devotee who has been trained in the practice of chanting and hearing the holy name of the Lord and His fame, qualities, form, paraphernalia and so on is never interested in elevation to the heavenly planets, even though such places are extremely dear even to the demigods.

nārāyaṇa-parāḥ sarve
na kutaścana bibhyati
svargāpavarga-narakeṣv
api tulyārtha-darśinaḥ

"Devotees solely engaged in the devotional service of the Supreme Personality of Godhead, Nārāyaṇa, never fear any condition of life. The heavenly planets, liberation and the hellish planets are all the same to a devotee." (*Bhāg.* 6.17.28) A devotee is always situated in the spiritual world. Therefore he does not desire anything. He is known as *akāma*, or desireless, because he has nothing to desire except to render transcendental loving service to the Supreme Personality of Godhead. Because Mahārāja Ambarīṣa was a most exalted devotee of the Lord, he trained his subjects in such a way that the citizens in his state were not interested in anything material, including even the happiness of the heavenly planets.

TEXT 25

संवर्धयन्ति यत् कामाः स्वाराज्यपरिभाविताः ।
दुर्लभा नापि सिद्धानां मुकुन्दं हृदि पश्यतः ॥२५॥

saṁvardhayanti yat kāmāḥ
svārājya-paribhāvitāḥ
durlabhā nāpi siddhānāṁ
mukundaṁ hṛdi paśyataḥ

saṁvardhayanti—increase happiness; *yat*—because; *kāmāḥ*—such aspirations; *svā-rājya*—situated in his own constitutional position of rendering service to the Lord; *paribhāvitāḥ*—saturated with such aspirations; *durlabhāḥ*—very rarely obtained; *na*—not; *api*—also; *siddhānām*—of the great mystics; *mukundam*—Kṛṣṇa, the Supreme

Personality of Godhead; *hṛdi*—within the core of the heart; *paśyataḥ*—persons always accustomed to seeing Him.

TRANSLATION

Those who are saturated with the transcendental happiness of rendering service to the Supreme Personality of Godhead are uninterested even in the achievements of great mystics, for such achievements do not enhance the transcendental bliss felt by a devotee who always thinks of Kṛṣṇa within the core of his heart.

PURPORT

A pure devotee is uninterested not only in elevation to the higher planetary systems but even in the perfections of mystic *yoga.* Real perfection is devotional service. The happiness derived from merging in the impersonal Brahman and the happiness derived from the eight perfections of mystic *yoga* (*aṇimā, laghimā, prāpti* and so on) do not give any pleasure to the devotee. As stated by Śrīla Prabodhānanda Sarasvatī:

kaivalyaṁ narakāyate tridaśa-pūr ākāśa-puṣpāyate
durdāntendriya-kāla-sarpa-paṭalī protkhāta-daṁṣṭrāyate
viśvaṁ pūrṇa-sukhāyate vidhi-mahendrādiś ca kīṭāyate
yat kāruṇya-kaṭākṣa-vaibhavavatāṁ taṁ gauram eva stumaḥ
(*Caitanya-candrāmṛta* 5)

When a devotee has achieved the position of rendering transcendental loving service to the Lord through the mercy of Lord Caitanya, he thinks the impersonal Brahman to be no better than hell, and he regards material happiness in the heavenly planets to be like a will-o'-the-wisp. As far as the perfection of mystic powers is concerned, a devotee compares it to a venomous snake with no teeth. A mystic *yogī* is especially concerned with controlling the senses, but because the senses of a devotee are engaged in the service of the Lord (*hṛṣīkeṇa hṛṣīkeśa-sevanaṁ bhaktir ucyate*) there is no need for separate control of the senses. For those who are materially engaged, control of the senses is required, but a devotee's senses are all engaged in the service of the Lord, which means that they are already controlled. *Paraṁ dṛṣṭvā nivartate* (Bg. 2.59). A devotee's senses are not attracted by material enjoyment. And even though the material world is full of misery, the devotee considers this material world to be also spiritual because everything is engaged in the service of the Lord. The difference between the spiritual world and material world is the mentality of service. *Nirbandhaḥ kṛṣṇa-sambandhe yuktaṁ vairāgyam ucyate.* When there is no mentality of service to the Supreme Personality of Godhead, one's activities are material.

prāpañci-katayā buddhyā
hari-sambandhi-vastunaḥ
mumukṣubhiḥ parityāgo
vairāgyaṁ phalgu kathyate
(*Bhakti-rasāmṛta-sindhu* 1.2.256)

That which is not engaged in the service of the Lord is material, and nothing thus engaged should be given up. In the construction of a high skyscraper and the construction of a temple, there may be the same enthusiasm, but the endeavors are different, for one is material and the other spiritual. Spiritual activities should not be confused with material activities and given up. Nothing connected with Hari, the Supreme Personality of Godhead, is material. A devotee who considers all this is always situated in spiritual activities, and therefore he is no longer attracted by material activities (*paraṁ dṛṣṭvā nivartate*).

TEXT 26

स इत्थं भक्तियोगेन तपोयुक्तेन पार्थिवः ।
स्वधर्मेण हरिं प्रीणन् सर्वान् कामाञ्छनैर्जहौ ॥२६॥

sa itthaṁ bhakti-yogena
tapo-yuktena pārthivaḥ
sva-dharmeṇa hariṁ prīṇan
sarvān kāmān śanair jahau

saḥ—he (Ambarīṣa Mahārāja); *ittham*—in this way; *bhakti-yogena*—by performing transcendental loving service to the Lord; *tapaḥ-*

yuktena—which is simultaneously the best process of austerity; *pārthivaḥ*—the King; *sva-dharmeṇa*—by his constitutional activities; *harim*—unto the Supreme Lord; *prīṇan*—satisfying; *sarvān*—all varieties of; *kāmān*—material desires; *śanaiḥ*—gradually; *jahau*—gave up.

TRANSLATION

The king of this planet, Mahārāja Ambarīṣa, thus performed devotional service to the Lord and in this endeavor practiced severe austerity. Always satisfying the Supreme Personality of Godhead by his constitutional activities, he gradually gave up all material desires.

PURPORT

Severe austerities in the practice of devotional service are of many varieties. For example, in worshiping the Deity in the temple there are certainly laborious activities. *Śrī-vigrahārādhana-nitya-nānā-śṛṅgāra-tan-mandira-mārjanādau.* One must decorate the Deity, cleanse the temple, bring water from the Ganges and Yamunā, continue the routine work, perform *ārati* many times, prepare first-class food for the Deity, prepare dresses and so on. In this way, one must constantly be engaged in various activities, and the hard labor involved is certainly an austerity. Similarly, the hard labor involved in preaching, preparing literature, preaching to atheistic men and distributing literature door to door is of course an austerity (*tapo-yuktena*). *Tapo divyaṁ putrakā.* Such austerity is necessary. *Yena sattvaṁ śuddhyet.* By such austerity in devotional service, one is purified of material existence (*kāmān śanair jahau*). Indeed, such austerity leads one to the constitutional position of devotional service. In this way one can give up material desires, and as soon as one is freed from material desires, he is free from the repetition of birth and death, old age and disease.

TEXT 27

गृहेषु दारेषु सुतेषु बन्धुषु
द्विपोत्तमस्यन्दनवाजिवस्तुषु ।

अक्षय्यरत्नाभरणाम्बरादि-
ष्वनन्तकोशेष्वकरोदसन्मतिम् ॥२७॥

gṛheṣu dāreṣu suteṣu bandhuṣu
dvipottama-syandana-vāji-vastuṣu
akṣayya-ratnābharaṇāmbarādiṣv
ananta-kośeṣv akarod asan-matim

gṛheṣu—in the homes; *dāreṣu*—in wives; *suteṣu*—in children; *bandhuṣu*—in friends and relatives; *dvipa-uttama*—in the best of powerful elephants; *syandana*—in nice chariots; *vāji*—in first-class horses; *vastuṣu*—in all such things; *akṣayya*—whose value never decreases; *ratna*—in jewels; *ābharaṇa*—in ornaments; *ambara-ādiṣu*—in such dresses and ornaments; *ananta-kośeṣu*—in an inexhaustible treasury; *akarot*—accepted; *asat-matim*—no attachment.

TRANSLATION

Mahārāja Ambarīṣa gave up all attachment to household affairs, wives, children, friends and relatives, to the best of powerful elephants, to beautiful chariots, carts, horses and inexhaustible jewels, and to ornaments, garments and an inexhaustible treasury. He gave up attachment to all of them, regarding them as temporary and material.

PURPORT

Anāsaktasya viṣayān yathārham upayuñjataḥ. Material possessions can be accepted as far as they can be used in devotional service. *Ānukūlyena kṛṣṇānuśīlanam. Ānukūlyasya saṅkalpaḥ prātikūlyasya varjanam.* In preaching, many things considered material are needed. A devotee should not have any attachment for such material involvements as house, wife, children, friends and cars. Mahārāja Ambarīṣa, for example, had all such things, but he was not attached to them. This is the effect of *bhakti-yoga. Bhaktiḥ pareśānubhavo viraktir anyatra ca* (*Bhāg.* 11.2.42). One who is advanced in devotional service has no attachment for material things for sense enjoyment, but for preaching, to spread the glories of the Lord, he accepts such things without attachment. *Anāsaktasya viṣayān yathārham upayuñjataḥ.* Everything can be used to the extent that it can be engaged in Kṛṣṇa's service.

TEXT 28

तस्मा अदाद्धरिश्चक्रं प्रत्यनीकभयावहम् ।
एकान्तभक्तिभावेन प्रीतो भक्ताभिरक्षणम् ॥२८॥

tasmā adād dhariś cakraṁ
pratyanīka-bhayāvaham
ekānta-bhakti-bhāvena
prīto bhaktābhirakṣaṇam

tasmai—unto him (Ambarīṣa Mahārāja); *adāt*—gave; *hariḥ*—the Supreme Personality of Godhead; *cakram*—His disc; *pratyanīka-bhaya-āvaham*—the Lord's disc, which was extremely fearful to the enemies of the Lord and His devotees; *ekānta-bhakti-bhāvena*—because of his performing unalloyed devotional service; *prītaḥ*—the Lord being so pleased; *bhakta-abhirakṣaṇam*—for the protection of His devotees.

TRANSLATION

Being very pleased by the unalloyed devotion of Mahārāja Ambarīṣa, the Supreme Personality of Godhead gave the King His disc, which is fearful to enemies and which always protects the devotee from enemies and adversities.

PURPORT

A devotee, being always engaged in the service of the Lord, may not be expert in self-defense, but because a devotee fully depends on the lotus feet of the Supreme Personality of Godhead, he is always sure of protection by the Lord. Prahlāda Mahārāja said:

naivodvije para duratyaya-vaitaraṇyās
tvad-vīrya-gāyana-mahāmṛta-magna-cittaḥ
(*Bhāg.* 7.9.43)

A devotee is always merged in the ocean of the transcendental bliss of rendering service to the Lord. Therefore he is not at all afraid of any adverse situation in the material world. The Lord also promises, *kaunteya pratijānīhi na me bhaktaḥ praṇaśyati:* "O Arjuna, you may declare to the world that the devotees of the Lord are never vanquished." (Bg. 9.31) For the protection of the devotees, Kṛṣṇa's disc, the Sudarśana *cakra,* is always ready. This disc is extremely fearful to the nondevotees (*pratyanīka-bhayāvaham*). Therefore although Mahārāja Ambarīṣa was fully engaged in devotional service, his kingdom was free of all fear of adversity.

TEXT 29

आरिराधयिषुः कृष्णं महिष्या तुल्यशीलया ।
युक्तः सांवत्सरं वीरो दधार द्वादशीव्रतम् ॥२९॥

ārirādhayiṣuḥ kṛṣṇaṁ
mahiṣyā tulya-śīlayā
yuktaḥ sāṁvatsaraṁ vīro
dadhāra dvādaśī-vratam

ārirādhayiṣuḥ—aspiring to worship; *kṛṣṇam*—the Supreme Lord, Kṛṣṇa; *mahiṣyā*—with his queen; *tulya-śīlayā*—who was equally as qualified as Mahārāja Ambarīṣa; *yuktaḥ*—together; *sāṁvatsaram*—for one year; *vīraḥ*—the King; *dadhāra*—accepted; *dvādaśī-vratam*—the vow for observing Ekādaśī and Dvādaśī.

TRANSLATION

To worship Lord Kṛṣṇa, Mahārāja Ambarīṣa, along with his queen, who was equally qualified, observed the vow of Ekādaśī and Dvādaśī for one year.

PURPORT

To observe Ekādaśī-vrata and Dvādaśī-vrata means to please the Supreme Personality of Godhead. Those interested in advancing in Kṛṣṇa consciousness must observe Ekādaśī-vrata regularly. Mahārāja Ambarīṣa's queen was equally as qualified as the King. Therefore it was possible for Mahārāja Ambarīṣa to engage his life in household affairs. In this regard, the word *tulya-śīlayā* is very significant. Unless a wife is equally as qualified as her husband, household affairs are very difficult to continue. Cāṇakya Paṇḍita advises that a person in such a situation should immediately give up household life and become a *vānaprastha* or *sannyāsī:*

mātā yasya gṛhe nāsti
bhāryā cāpriya-vādinī
araṇyaṁ tena gantavyaṁ
yathāraṇyaṁ tathā gṛham

A person who has no mother at home and whose wife is not agreeable with him should immediately go away to the forest. Because human life is meant for spiritual advancement only, one's wife must be helpful in this endeavor. Otherwise there is no need of household life.

TEXT 30

व्रतान्ते कार्तिके मासि त्रिरात्रं समुपोषितः ।
स्नातः कदाचित्कालिन्द्यां हरिं मधुवनेऽर्चयत् ॥३०॥

vratānte kārtike māsi
tri-rātraṁ samupoṣitaḥ
snātaḥ kadācit kālindyāṁ
hariṁ madhuvane 'rcayat

vrata-ante—at the end of observing the vow; *kārtike*—in the month of Kārtika (October–November); *māsi*—in that month; *tri-rātram*—for three nights; *samupoṣitaḥ*—after completely observing the fast; *snātaḥ*—after bathing; *kadācit*—once upon a time; *kālindyām*—on the bank of the Yamunā; *harim*—unto the Supreme Personality of Godhead; *madhuvane*—in that part of the Vṛndāvana area known as Madhuvana; *arcayat*—worshiped the Lord.

TRANSLATION

In the month of Kārtika, after observing that vow for one year, after observing a fast for three nights and after bathing in the Yamunā, Mahārāja Ambarīṣa worshiped the Supreme Personality of Godhead, Hari, in Madhuvana.

TEXTS 31–32

महाभिषेकविधिना सर्वोपस्करसम्पदा ।
अभिषिच्याम्बराकल्पैर्गन्धमाल्यार्हणादिभिः ॥३१॥
तद्गतान्तरभावेन पूजयामास केशवम् ।
ब्राह्मणांश्च महाभागान् सिद्धार्थानपि भक्तितः ॥३२॥

mahābhiṣeka-vidhinā
sarvopaskara-sampadā
abhiṣicyāmbarākalpair
gandha-mālyārhaṇādibhiḥ

tad-gatāntara-bhāvena
pūjayām āsa keśavam
brāhmaṇāṁś ca mahā-bhāgān
siddhārthān api bhaktitaḥ

mahā-abhiṣeka-vidhinā—by the regulative principles for bathing the Deity; *sarva-upaskara-sampadā*—by all the paraphernalia for worshiping the Deity; *abhiṣicya*—after bathing; *ambara-ākalpaiḥ*—with nice clothing and ornaments; *gandha-mālya*—with fragrant flower garlands; *arhaṇa-ādibhiḥ*—and with other paraphernalia to worship the Deity; *tat-gata-antara-bhāvena*—his mind saturated with devotional service; *pūjayām āsa*—he worshiped; *keśavam*—unto Kṛṣṇa; *brāhmaṇān ca*—and the *brāhmaṇas; mahā-bhāgān*—who were greatly fortunate; *siddha-arthān*—self-satisfied, without waiting for any worship; *api*—even; *bhaktitaḥ*—with great devotion.

TRANSLATION

Following the regulative principles of mahābhiṣeka, Mahārāja Ambarīṣa performed the bathing ceremony for the Deity of Lord Kṛṣṇa with all paraphernalia, and then he dressed the Deity with fine clothing, ornaments, fragrant flower garlands and other paraphernalia for worship of the Lord. With attention and devotion, he worshiped Kṛṣṇa and all the greatly fortunate brāhmaṇas who were free from material desires.

TEXTS 33–35

गवां रुक्मविषाणीनां रूप्याङ्घ्रीणां सुवाससाम् ।
पयःशीलवयोरूपवत्सोपस्करसम्पदाम् ॥३३॥
प्राहिणोत् साधुविप्रेभ्यो गृहेषु न्यर्बुदानिषट् ।
भोजयित्वा द्विजानग्रे स्वाद्वन्नं गुणवत्तमम् ॥३४॥
लब्धकामैरनुज्ञातः पारणायोपचक्रमे ।
तस्य तर्ह्यतिथिः साक्षाद् दुर्वासा भगवानभूत ॥३५॥

gavāṁ rukma-viṣāṇīnāṁ
rūpyāṅghrīṇāṁ suvāsasām
payaḥśīla-vayo-rūpa-
vatsopaskara-sampadām

prāhiṇot sādhu-viprebhyo
gṛheṣu nyarbudāni ṣaṭ
bhojayitvā dvijān agre
svādv annaṁ guṇavattamam

labdha-kāmair anujñātaḥ
pāraṇāyopacakrame
tasya tarhy atithiḥ sākṣād
durvāsā bhagavān abhūt

gavām—cows; *rukma-viṣāṇīnām*—whose horns were covered with gold plate; *rūpya-aṅghrīṇām*—whose hooves were covered with silver plate; *su-vāsasām*—very nicely decorated with garments; *payaḥ-śīla*—with full milk bags; *vayaḥ*—young; *rūpa*—beautiful; *vatsa-upaskara-sampadām*—with nice calves; *prāhiṇot*—gave in charity; *sādhu-viprebhyaḥ*—unto the *brāhmaṇas* and saintly persons; *gṛheṣu*—(who arrived) in his house; *nyarbudāni*—ten crores (one hundred million); *ṣaṭ*—six times; *bhojayitvā*—feeding them; *dvijān agre*—first the *brāhmaṇas; svādu annam*—very tasteful eatables; *guṇavat-tamam*—highly delicious; *labdha-kāmaiḥ*—by those *brāhmaṇas*, being fully satisfied; *anujñātaḥ*—by their permission; *pāraṇāya*—for completing the Dvādaśī; *upacakrame*—was just about to observe the final ceremony; *tasya*—of him (Ambarīṣa); *tarhi*—immediately; *atithiḥ*—unwanted or uncalled-for guest; *sākṣāt*—directly; *durvāsāḥ*—the great mystic Durvāsā; *bhagavān*—very powerful; *abhūt*—appeared on the scene as a guest.

TRANSLATION

Thereafter, Mahārāja Ambarīṣa satisfied all the guests who arrived at his house, especially the brāhmaṇas. He gave in charity sixty crores of cows whose horns were covered with gold plate and whose hooves were covered with silver plate. All the cows were well decorated with garments and had full milk bags. They were mild-natured, young and beautiful and were accompanied by their calves. After giving these cows, the King first sumptuously fed all the brāhmaṇas, and when they were fully satisfied, he was about to observe the end of Ekādaśī, with their permission, by breaking the fast. Exactly at that time, however, Durvāsā Muni, the great and powerful mystic, appeared on the scene as an uninvited guest.

TEXT 36

तमानर्चातिथिं भूपः प्रत्युत्थानासनार्हणैः ।
ययाचेऽभ्यवहाराय पादमूलमुपागतः ॥३६॥

tam ānarcātithiṁ bhūpaḥ
pratyutthānāsanārhaṇaiḥ
yayāce 'bhyavahārāya
pāda-mūlam upāgataḥ

tam—unto him (Durvāsā); *ānarca*—worshiped; *atithim*—although an uninvited guest; *bhūpaḥ*—the King (Ambarīṣa); *pratyutthāna*—by standing up; *āsana*—by offering a seat; *arhaṇaiḥ*—and by paraphernalia for worship; *yayāce*—requested; *abhyavahārāya*—for eating; *pāda-mūlam*—at the root of his feet; *upāgataḥ*—fell down.

TRANSLATION

After standing up to receive Durvāsā Muni, King Ambarīṣa offered him a seat and paraphernalia of worship. Then, sitting at his feet, the King requested the great sage to eat.

TEXT 37

प्रतिनन्द्य स तां याच्ञां कर्तुमावश्यकं गतः ।
निममज्ज बृहद् ध्यायन् कालिन्दीसलिले शुभे ॥३७॥

pratinandya sa tāṁ yācñāṁ
kartum āvaśyakaṁ gataḥ
nimamajja bṛhad dhyāyan
kālindī-salile śubhe

pratinandya—gladly accepting; *saḥ*—Durvāsā Muni; *tām*—that; *yācñām*—request; *kartum*—to perform; *āvaśyakam*—the necessary ritualistic ceremonies; *gataḥ*—went; *nimamajja*—dipped his body in the water; *bṛhat*—the Supreme Brahman; *dhyāyan*—meditating on; *kālindī*—of the Yamunā; *salile*—in the water; *śubhe*—very auspicious.

TRANSLATION

Durvāsā Muni gladly accepted the request of Mahārāja Ambarīṣa, but to perform the regulative ritualistic ceremonies he went to the River Yamunā. There he dipped into the water of the auspicious Yamunā and meditated upon the impersonal Brahman.

TEXT 38

मुहूर्तार्धावशिष्टायां द्वादश्यां पारणं प्रति ।
चिन्तयामास धर्मज्ञो द्विजैस्तद्धर्मसङ्कटे ॥३८॥

muhūrtārdhāvaśiṣṭāyāṁ
dvādaśyāṁ pāraṇaṁ prati
cintayām āsa dharma-jño
dvijais tad-dharma-saṅkaṭe

muhūrta-ardha-avaśiṣṭāyām—was remaining only for half a moment; *dvādaśyām*—when the Dvādaśī day; *pāraṇam*—the breaking of the fast; *prati*—to observe; *cintayām āsa*—began to think about; *dharma-jñaḥ*—one who knows the principles of religion; *dvijaiḥ*—by the *brāhmaṇas; tat-dharma*—concerning that religious principle; *saṅkaṭe*—in such a dangerous condition.

TRANSLATION

In the meantime, only a muhūrta of the Dvādaśī day was left on which to break the fast. Consequently, it was imperative that the fast be broken immediately. In this dangerous situation, the King consulted learned brāhmaṇas.

TEXTS 39–40

ब्राह्मणातिक्रमे दोषो द्वादश्यां यदपारणे ।
यत्कृत्वा साधु मे भूयादधर्मो वा न मां स्पृशेत् ॥३९॥
अम्भसा केवलेनाथ करिष्ये व्रतपारणम् ।
आहुरब्भक्षणं विप्रा ह्यशितं नाशितं च तत् ॥४०॥

brāhmaṇātikrame doṣo
dvādaśyāṁ yad apāraṇe
yat kṛtvā sādhu me bhūyād
adharmo vā na māṁ spṛśet

ambhasā kevalenātha
kariṣye vrata-pāraṇam
āhur ab-bhakṣaṇaṁ viprā
hy aśitaṁ nāśitaṁ ca tat

brāhmaṇa-atikrame—in surpassing the rules of respect to the *brāhmaṇas; doṣaḥ*—there is a fault; *dvādaśyām*—on the Dvādaśī day; *yat*—because; *apāraṇe*—in not breaking the fast in due time; *yat kṛtvā*—after doing which action; *sādhu*—what is auspicious; *me*—unto me; *bhūyāt*—may so become; *adharmaḥ*—what is irreligious; *vā*—either; *na*—not; *mām*—unto me; *spṛśet*—may touch; *ambhasā*—by water; *kevalena*—only; *atha*—therefore; *kariṣye*—I shall execute; *vrata-pāraṇam*—the completion of the vow; *āhuḥ*—said; *ap-bhakṣaṇam*—drinking water; *viprāḥ*—O *brāhmaṇas; hi*—indeed; *aśitam*—eating; *na aśitam ca*—as well as not eating; *tat*—such an action.

TRANSLATION

The King said: "To transgress the laws of respectful behavior toward the brāhmaṇas is certainly a great offense. On the other

hand, if one does not observe the breaking of the fast within the time of Dvādaśī, there is a flaw in one's observance of the vow. Therefore, O brāhmaṇas, if you think that it will be auspicious and not irreligious, I shall break the fast by drinking water." In this way, after consulting with the brāhmaṇas, the King reached this decision, for according to brahminical opinion, drinking water may be accepted as eating and also as not eating.

PURPORT

When Mahārāja Ambarīṣa, in his dilemma, consulted the *brāhmaṇas* about whether he should break the fast or wait for Durvāsā Muni, apparently they could not give a definite answer about what to do. A Vaiṣṇava, however, is the most intelligent personality. Therefore Mahārāja Ambarīṣa himself decided, in the presence of the *brāhmaṇas,* that he would drink a little water, for this would confirm that the fast was broken but would not transgress the laws for receiving a *brāhmaṇa.* In the *Vedas* it is said, *apo 'śnāti tan naivāśitaṁ naivānaśitam.* This Vedic injunction declares that the drinking of water may be accepted as eating or as not eating. Sometimes in our practical experience we see that some political leader adhering to *satyāgraha* will not eat but will drink water. Considering that drinking water would not be eating, Mahārāja Ambarīṣa decided to act in this way.

TEXT 41

इत्यपः प्राश्य राजर्षिश्चिन्तयन् मनसाच्युतम् ।
प्रत्यचष्ट कुरुश्रेष्ठ द्विजागमनमेव सः ॥४१॥

ity apaḥ prāśya rājarṣiś
cintayan manasācyutam
pratyacaṣṭa kuru-śreṣṭha
dvijāgamanam eva saḥ

iti—thus; *apaḥ*—water; *prāśya*—after drinking; *rājarṣiḥ*—the great King Ambarīṣa; *cintayan*—meditating upon; *manasā*—by the mind; *acyutam*—the Supreme Personality of Godhead; *pratyacaṣṭa*—began to wait; *kuru-śreṣṭha*—O best of the Kuru kings; *dvija-āgamanam*—the return of Durvāsā Muni, the great mystic *brāhmaṇa; eva*—indeed; *saḥ*—the King.

TRANSLATION

O best of the Kuru dynasty, after he drank some water, King Ambarīṣa, meditating upon the Supreme Personality of Godhead within his heart, waited for the return of the great mystic Durvāsā Muni.

TEXT 42

दुर्वासा यमुनाकूलात् कृतावश्यक आगतः ।
राज्ञाभिनन्दितस्तस्य बुबुधे चेष्टितं धिया ॥४२॥

durvāsā yamunā-kūlāt
kṛtāvaśyaka āgataḥ
rājñābhinanditas tasya
bubudhe ceṣṭitaṁ dhiyā

durvāsāḥ—the great sage; *yamunā-kūlāt*—from the bank of the River Yamunā; *kṛta*—had been performed; *āvaśyakaḥ*—he by whom the necessary ritualistic ceremonies; *āgataḥ*—returned; *rājñā*—by the King; *abhinanditaḥ*—being well received; *tasya*—his; *bubudhe*—could understand; *ceṣṭitam*—performance; *dhiyā*—by intelligence.

TRANSLATION

After executing the ritualistic ceremonies to be performed at noon, Durvāsā returned from the bank of the Yamunā. The King received him well, offering all respects, but Durvāsā Muni, by his mystic power, could understand that King Ambarīṣa had drunk water without his permission.

TEXT 43

मन्युना प्रचलद्गात्रो भ्रुकुटीकुटिलाननः ।
बुभुक्षितश्च सुतरां कृताञ्जलिमभाषत ॥४३॥

manyunā pracalad-gātro
bhru-kuṭī-kuṭilānanaḥ
bubhukṣitaś ca sutarāṁ
kṛtāñjalim abhāṣata

manyunā—agitated by great anger; *pracalat-gātraḥ*—his body trembling; *bhru-kuṭī*—by the eyebrows; *kuṭila*—curved; *ānanaḥ*—face; *bubhukṣitaḥ ca*—and hungry at the same time; *sutarām*—very much; *kṛta-añjalim*—to Ambarīṣa Mahārāja, who stood there with folded hands; *abhāṣata*—he addressed.

TRANSLATION

Still hungry, Durvāsā Muni, his body trembling, his face curved and his eyebrows crooked in a frown, angrily spoke as follows to King Ambarīṣa, who stood before him with folded hands.

TEXT 44

अहो अस्य नृशंसस्य श्रियोन्मत्तस्य पश्यत ।
धर्मव्यतिक्रमं विष्णोरभक्तस्येशमानिनः ॥४४॥

aho asya nṛ-śaṁsasya
śriyonmattasya paśyata
dharma-vyatikramaṁ viṣṇor
abhaktasyeśa-māninaḥ

aho—alas; *asya*—of this man; *nṛ-śaṁsasya*—who is so cruel; *śriyā unmattasya*—puffed up because of great opulence; *paśyata*—everyone just see; *dharma-vyatikramam*—the transgression of the regulative principles of religion; *viṣṇoḥ abhaktasya*—who is not a devotee of Lord Viṣṇu; *īśa-māninaḥ*—considering himself the Supreme Lord, independent of everything.

TRANSLATION

Alas, just see the behavior of this cruel man! He is not a devotee of Lord Viṣṇu. Being proud of his material opulence and

his position, he considers himself God. Just see how he has transgressed the laws of religion.

PURPORT

Śrīla Viśvanātha Cakravartī Ṭhākura has diverted the entire meaning of this verse as spoken by Durvāsā Muni. Durvāsā Muni used the word *nṛ-śaṁsasya* to indicate that the King was cruel, but Viśvanātha Cakravartī Ṭhākura interprets it to mean that the King's character was glorified by all the local people. He says that the word *nṛ* means "by all the local people" and that *śaṁsasya* means "of he (Ambarīṣa) whose character was glorified." Similarly, one who is very rich becomes mad because of his wealth and is therefore called *śriyā-unmattasya*, but Śrīla Viśvanātha Cakravartī Ṭhākura interprets these words to mean that although Mahārāja Ambarīṣa was such an opulent king, he was not mad after money, for he had already surpassed the madness of material opulence. Similarly, the word *īśa-māninaḥ* is interpreted to mean that he was so respectful to the Supreme Personality of Godhead that he did not transgress the laws for observing Ekādaśī-pāraṇa, despite the thinking of Durvāsā Muni, for he only took water. In this way, Śrīla Viśvanātha Cakravartī Ṭhākura has supported Ambarīṣa Mahārāja and all his activities.

TEXT 45

यो मामतिथिमायातमातिथ्येन निमन्त्र्य च ।
अदत्त्वा भुक्तवांस्तस्य सद्यस्ते दर्शये फलम् ॥४५॥

yo mām atithim āyātam
ātithyena nimantrya ca
adattvā bhuktavāṁs tasya
sadyas te darśaye phalam

yaḥ—this man who; *mām*—unto me; *atithim*—who, being an uninvited guest; *āyātam*—had come here; *ātithyena*—with the reception of a guest; *nimantrya*—after inviting me; *ca*—also; *adattvā*—without giving (food); *bhuktavān*—has himself eaten; *tasya*—of him; *sadyaḥ*—immediately; *te*—of you; *darśaye*—I shall show; *phalam*—the result.

TRANSLATION

Mahārāja Ambarīṣa, you have invited me to eat as a guest, but instead of feeding me, you yourself have eaten first. Because of your misbehavior, I shall show you something to punish you.

PURPORT

A devotee cannot be defeated by a so-called mystic *yogī*. This will be proved by the failure of Durvāsā Muni's endeavor to chastise Mahārāja Ambarīṣa. *Harāv abhaktasya kuto mahad-guṇāḥ* (*Bhāg.* 5.18.12). One who is not a pure devotee of the Supreme Lord has no good qualifications, however great a mystic, philosopher or fruitive worker he may be. Only a devotee emerges victorious in all circumstances, as will be shown in this incident involving the rivalry between Durvāsā and Mahārāja Ambarīṣa.

TEXT 46

एवं ब्रुवाण उत्कृत्य जटां रोषप्रदीपितः ।
तया स निर्ममे तस्मै कृत्यां कालानलोपमाम् ॥४६॥

evaṁ bruvāṇa utkṛtya
jaṭāṁ roṣa-pradīpitaḥ
tayā sa nirmame tasmai
kṛtyāṁ kālānalopamām

evam—thus; *bruvāṇaḥ*—speaking (Durvāsā Muni); *utkṛtya*—uprooting; *jaṭām*—a bunch of hair; *roṣa-pradīpitaḥ*—being reddish because he was very angry; *tayā*—by that bunch of hair from his head; *saḥ*—Durvāsā Muni; *nirmame*—created; *tasmai*—to punish Mahārāja Ambarīṣa; *kṛtyām*—a demon; *kāla-anala-upamām*—appearing just like the blazing fire of devastation.

TRANSLATION

As Durvāsā Muni said this, his face became red with anger. Uprooting a bunch of hair from his head, he created a demon resembling the blazing fire of devastation to punish Mahārāja Ambarīṣa.

TEXT 47

तामापतन्तीं ज्वलतीमसिहस्तां पदा भुवम् ।
वेपयन्तीं समुद्वीक्ष्य न चचाल पदान्नृपः ॥४७॥

tām āpatantīṁ jvalatīm
asi-hastāṁ padā bhuvam
vepayantīṁ samudvīkṣya
na cacāla padān nṛpaḥ

tām—that (demon); *āpatantīm*—coming forward to attack him; *jvalatīm*—blazing like fire; *asi-hastām*—with a trident in his hand; *padā*—with his footstep; *bhuvam*—the surface of the earth; *vepayantīm*—causing to tremble; *samudvīkṣya*—seeing him perfectly; *na*—not; *cacāla*—moved; *padāt*—from his place; *nṛpaḥ*—the King.

TRANSLATION

Taking a trident in his hand and making the surface of the earth tremble with his footsteps, that blazing creature came before Mahārāja Ambarīṣa. But the King, upon seeing him, was not at all disturbed and did not move even slightly from his position.

PURPORT

Nārāyaṇa-parāḥ sarve na kutaścana bibhyati (*Bhāg.* 6.17.28). A pure devotee of Nārāyaṇa is never afraid of any material danger. There are many examples of devotees such as Prahlāda Mahārāja, who was tortured by his father but was not at all afraid, although he was only a five-year-old boy. Therefore, following the examples of Ambarīṣa Mahārāja and Prahlāda Mahārāja, a devotee should learn how to tolerate all such awkward positions in this world. Devotees are often tortured by non-devotees, yet the pure devotee, depending fully on the mercy of the Supreme Personality of Godhead, is never disturbed by such inimical activities.

TEXT 48

प्राग्दिष्टं भृत्यरक्षायां पुरुषेण महात्मना ।
ददाह कृत्यां तां चक्रं क्रुद्धाहिमिव पावकः ॥४८॥

prāg diṣṭaṁ bhṛtya-rakṣāyāṁ
puruṣeṇa mahātmanā
dadāha kṛtyāṁ tāṁ cakraṁ
kruddhāhim iva pāvakaḥ

prāk diṣṭam—as previously arranged; *bhṛtya-rakṣāyām*—for the protection of his servants; *puruṣeṇa*—by the Supreme Person; *mahā-ātmanā*—by the Supersoul; *dadāha*—burnt to ashes; *kṛtyām*—that created demon; *tām*—him; *cakram*—the disc; *kruddha*—angry; *ahim*—a serpent; *iva*—like; *pāvakaḥ*—fire.

TRANSLATION

As fire in the forest immediately burns to ashes an angry snake, so, by the previous order of the Supreme Personality of Godhead, His disc, the Sudarśana cakra, immediately burnt to ashes the created demon to protect the Lord's devotee.

PURPORT

As a pure devotee, Mahārāja Ambarīṣa, although in such danger, did not move an inch from his position, nor did he request the Supreme Personality of Godhead to give him protection. He was fixed in understanding, and it was certain that he was simply thinking of the Supreme Personality of Godhead in the core of his heart. A devotee is never fearful of his death, for he meditates on the Supreme Personality of Godhead always, not for any material profit, but as his duty. The Lord, however, knows how to protect His devotee. As indicated by the words *prāg diṣṭam,* the Lord knew everything. Therefore, before anything happened, He had already arranged for His *cakra* to protect Mahārāja Ambarīṣa. This protection is offered to a devotee even from the very beginning of his devotional service. *Kaunteya pratijānīhi na me bhaktaḥ praṇaśyati* (Bg. 9.31). If one simply begins devotional service, he is immediately protected by the Supreme Personality of Godhead. This is also confirmed in *Bhagavad-gītā* (18.66): *ahaṁ tvāṁ sarva-pāpebhyo mokṣayiṣyāmi.* Protection begins immediately. The Lord is so kind and merciful that He gives the devotee proper guidance and all protection, and thus the devotee very peacefully makes solid progress in Kṛṣṇa consciousness without outward disturbances. A serpent may be very angry and ready to bite, but the furious snake is helpless when faced by a blazing fire in the forest. Although an enemy of a devotee may be very strong, he is compared to an angry serpent before the fire of devotional service.

TEXT 49

तदभिद्रवदुद्वीक्ष्य स्वप्रयासं च निष्फलम् ।
दुर्वासा दुद्रुवे भीतो दिक्षु प्राणपरीप्सया ॥४९॥

tad-abhidravad udvīkṣya
sva-prayāsaṁ ca niṣphalam
durvāsā dudruve bhīto
dikṣu prāṇa-parīpsayā

tat—of that disc; *abhidravat*—moving toward him; *udvīkṣya*—after seeing; *sva-prayāsam*—his own attempt; *ca*—and; *niṣphalam*—having failed; *durvāsāḥ*—Durvāsā Muni; *dudruve*—began to run; *bhītaḥ*—full of fear; *dikṣu*—in every direction; *prāṇa-parīpsayā*—with a desire to save his life.

TRANSLATION

Upon seeing that his own attempt had failed and that the Sudarśana cakra was moving toward him, Durvāsā Muni became very frightened and began to run in all directions to save his life.

TEXT 50

तमन्वधावद् भगवद्रथाङ्गं
दावाग्निरुद्धूतशिखो यथाहिम् ।
तथानुषक्तं मुनिरीक्षमाणो
गुहां विविक्षुः प्रससार मेरोः ॥५०॥

tam anvadhāvad bhagavad-rathāṅgaṁ
dāvāgnir uddhūta-śikho yathāhim

tathānuṣaktaṁ munir īkṣamāṇo
guhāṁ vivikṣuḥ prasasāra meroḥ

tam—unto Durvāsā; *anvadhāvat*—began to follow; *bhagavat-ratha-aṅgam*—the disc appearing from the wheel of the Lord's chariot; *dāva-agniḥ*—like a forest fire; *uddhūta*—blazing high; *śikhaḥ*—having flames; *yathā ahim*—as it follows a snake; *tathā*—in the same way; *anuṣaktam*—as if touching Durvāsā Muni's back; *muniḥ*—the sage; *īkṣamāṇaḥ*—seeing like that; *guhām*—a cave; *vivikṣuḥ*—wanted to enter; *prasasāra*—began to move quickly; *meroḥ*—of Meru Mountain.

TRANSLATION

As the blazing flames of a forest fire pursue a snake, the disc of the Supreme Personality of Godhead began following Durvāsā Muni. Durvāsā Muni saw that the disc was almost touching his back, and thus he ran very swiftly, desiring to enter a cave of Sumeru Mountain.

TEXT 51

दिशो नभः क्ष्मां विवरान् समुद्रान्
लोकान् सपालांस्त्रिदिवं गतः सः ।
यतो यतो धावति तत्र तत्र
सुदर्शनं दुष्प्रसहं ददर्श ॥५१॥

diśo nabhaḥ kṣmāṁ vivarān samudrān
lokān sapālāṁs tridivaṁ gataḥ saḥ
yato yato dhāvati tatra tatra
sudarśanaṁ duṣprasahaṁ dadarśa

diśaḥ—all directions; *nabhaḥ*—in the sky; *kṣmām*—on the surface of the earth; *vivarān*—within the holes; *samudrān*—within the seas; *lokān*—all places; *sa-pālān*—as well as their rulers; *tridivam*—the heavenly planets; *gataḥ*—gone; *saḥ*—Durvāsā Muni; *yataḥ yataḥ*—wheresoever; *dhāvati*—he went; *tatra tatra*—there, everywhere; *sudarśanam*—the disc of the Lord; *duṣprasaham*—extremely fearful; *dadarśa*—Durvāsā Muni saw.

TRANSLATION

Just to protect himself, Durvāsā Muni fled everywhere, in all directions—in the sky, on the surface of the earth, in caves, in the ocean, on different planets of the rulers of the three worlds, and even on the heavenly planets—but wherever he went he immediately saw following him the unbearable fire of the Sudarśana cakra.

TEXT 52

अलब्धनाथः स सदा कुतश्चित्
संत्रस्तचित्तोऽरणमेषमाणः ।
देवं विरिञ्चं समगाद् विधात-
स्त्राह्यात्मयोनेऽजिततेजसो माम् ॥५२॥

alabdha-nāthaḥ sa sadā kutaścit
santrasta-citto 'raṇam eṣamāṇaḥ
devaṁ viriñcaṁ samagād vidhātas
trāhy ātma-yone 'jita-tejaso mām

alabdha-nāthaḥ—without getting the shelter of a protector; *saḥ*—Durvāsā Muni; *sadā*—always; *kutaścit*—somewhere; *santrasta-cittaḥ*—with a fearful heart; *araṇam*—a person who can give shelter; *eṣamāṇaḥ*—seeking; *devam*—at last to the chief demigod; *viriñcam*—Lord Brahmā; *samagāt*—approached; *vidhātaḥ*—O my lord; *trāhi*—kindly protect; *ātma-yone*—O Lord Brahmā; *ajita-tejasaḥ*—from the fire released by Ajita, the Supreme Personality of Godhead; *mām*—unto me.

TRANSLATION

With a fearful heart, Durvāsā Muni went here and there seeking shelter, but when he could find no shelter, he finally approached Lord Brahmā and said, "O my lord, O Lord Brahmā, kindly protect me from the blazing Sudarśana cakra sent by the Supreme Personality of Godhead."

TEXTS 53–54

श्रीब्रह्मोवाच

स्थानं मदीयं सहविश्वमेतत्
क्रीडावसाने द्विपरार्धसंज्ञे ।
भ्रूभङ्गमात्रेण हि संदिधक्षोः
कालात्मनो यस्य तिरोभविष्यति ॥५३॥
अहं भवो दक्षभृगुप्रधानाः
प्रजेशभूतेशसुरेशमुख्याः ।
सर्वे वयं यन्नियमं प्रपन्ना
मूर्ध्न्यार्पितं लोकहितं वहामः ॥५४॥

śrī-brahmovāca
sthānaṁ madīyaṁ saha-viśvam etat
krīḍāvasāne dvi-parārdha-saṁjñe
bhrū-bhaṅga-mātreṇa hi sandidhakṣoḥ
kālātmano yasya tirobhaviṣyati

ahaṁ bhavo dakṣa-bhṛgu-pradhānāḥ
prajeśa-bhūteśa-sureśa-mukhyāḥ
sarve vayaṁ yan-niyamaṁ prapannā
mūrdhnyārpitaṁ loka-hitaṁ vahāmaḥ

śrī-brahmā uvāca—Lord Brahmā said; *sthānam*—the place where I am; *madīyam*—my residence, Brahmaloka; *saha*—with; *viśvam*—the whole universe; *etat*—this; *krīḍā-avasāne*—at the end of the period for the pastimes of the Supreme Personality of Godhead; *dvi-parārdha-saṁjñe*—the time known as the end of a *dvi-parārdha; bhrū-bhaṅga-mātreṇa*—simply by the flicking of the eyebrows; *hi*—indeed; *sandidhakṣoḥ*—of the Supreme Personality of Godhead, when He desires to burn the whole universe; *kāla-ātmanaḥ*—of the form of destruction; *yasya*—of whom; *tirobhaviṣyati*—will be vanquished; *aham*—I; *bhavaḥ*—Lord Śiva; *dakṣa*—Prajāpati Dakṣa; *bhṛgu*—the great saint Bhṛgu; *pradhānāḥ*—and others headed by them; *prajā-īśa*—the controllers of the *prajās; bhūta-īśa*—the controllers of the living entities; *sura-īśa*—the controllers of the demigods; *mukhyāḥ*—headed by them; *sarve*—all of them; *vayam*—we also; *yat-niyamam*—whose regulative principle; *prapannāḥ*—are surrendered; *mūrdhnyā arpitam*—bowing our heads; *loka-hitam*—for the benefit of all living entities; *vahāmaḥ*—carry out the orders ruling over the living entities.

TRANSLATION

Lord Brahmā said: At the end of the dvi-parārdha, when the pastimes of the Lord come to an end, Lord Viṣṇu, by a flick of His eyebrows, vanquishes the entire universe, including our places of residence. Such personalities as me and Lord Śiva, as well as Dakṣa, Bhṛgu and similar great saints of which they are the head, and also the rulers of the living entities, the rulers of human society and the rulers of the demigods—all of us surrender to that Supreme Personality of Godhead, Lord Viṣṇu, bowing our heads, to carry out His orders for the benefit of all living entities.

PURPORT

In *Bhagavad-gītā* (10.34) it is said, *mṛtyuḥ sarva-haraś cāham:* when the Supreme Personality of Godhead approaches as death, or the supreme controller of time, He takes everything away. In other words, all opulence, prestige and everything we possess is given by the Supreme Lord for some purpose. It is the duty of the surrendered soul to execute the orders of the Supreme. No one can disregard Him. Under the circumstances, Lord Brahmā refused to give shelter to Durvāsā Muni from the powerful Sudarśana *cakra* sent by the Lord.

TEXT 55

प्रत्याख्यातो विरिञ्चेन विष्णुचक्रोपतापितः ।
दुर्वासाः शरणं यातः शर्वं कैलासवासिनम् ॥५५॥

pratyākhyāto viriñcena
viṣṇu-cakropatāpitaḥ

durvāsāḥ śaraṇaṁ yātaḥ
śarvaṁ kailāsa-vāsinam

pratyākhyātaḥ—being refused; *viriñcena*—by Lord Brahmā; *viṣṇu-cakra-upatāpitaḥ*—being scorched by the blazing fire of Lord Viṣṇu's disc; *durvāsāḥ*—the great mystic named Durvāsā; *śaraṇam*—for shelter; *yātaḥ*—went; *śarvam*—unto Lord Śiva; *kailāsa-vāsinam*—the resident of the place known as Kailāsa.

TRANSLATION

When Durvāsā, who was greatly afflicted by the blazing fire of the Sudarśana cakra, was thus refused by Lord Brahmā, he tried to take shelter of Lord Śiva, who always resides on his planet, known as Kailāsa.

TEXT 56

श्रीशङ्कर उवाच
वयं न तात प्रभवाम भूम्नि
यस्मिन् परेऽन्येऽप्यजजीवकोशाः ।
भवन्ति काले न भवन्ति हीदृशाः
सहस्रशो यत्र वयं भ्रमामः ॥५६॥

śrī-śaṅkara uvāca
vayaṁ na tāta prabhavāma bhūmni
yasmin pare 'nye 'py aja-jīva-kośāḥ
bhavanti kāle na bhavanti hīdṛśāḥ
sahasraśo yatra vayaṁ bhramāmaḥ

śrī-śaṅkaraḥ uvāca—Lord Śiva said; *vayam*—we; *na*—not; *tāta*—O my dear son; *prabhavāmaḥ*—sufficiently able; *bhūmni*—unto the great Supreme Personality of Godhead; *yasmin*—in whom; *pare*—in the Transcendence; *anye*—others; *api*—even; *aja*—Lord Brahmā; *jīva*—living entities; *kośāḥ*—the universes; *bhavanti*—can become; *kāle*—in due course of time; *na*—not; *bhavanti*—can become; *hi*—indeed; *īdṛśāḥ*—like this; *sahasraśaḥ*—many thousands and millions; *yatra*—wherein; *vayam*—all of us; *bhramāmaḥ*—are rotating.

TRANSLATION

Lord Śiva said: My dear son, I, Lord Brahmā and the other demigods, who rotate within this universe under the misconception of our greatness, cannot exhibit any power to compete with the Supreme Personality of Godhead, for innumerable universes and their inhabitants come into existence and are annihilated by the simple direction of the Lord.

PURPORT

There are innumerable universes in the material world, and there are innumerable Lord Brahmās, Lord Śivas and other demigods. All of them rotate within this material world under the supreme direction of the Personality of Godhead. Therefore no one is able to compete with the strength of the Lord. Lord Śiva also refused to protect Durvāsā, for Lord Śiva also was under the rays of the Sudarśana *cakra* sent by the Supreme Personality of Godhead.

TEXTS 57–59

अहं सनत्कुमारश्च नारदो भगवानजः ।
कपिलोऽपान्तरतमो देवलो धर्म आसुरिः ॥५७॥
मरीचिप्रमुखाश्चान्ये सिद्धेशाः पारदर्शनाः ।
विदाम न वयं सर्वे यन्मायां माययावृताः ॥५८॥
तस्य विश्वेश्वरस्येदं शस्त्रं दुर्विषहं हि नः ।
तमेवं शरणं याहि हरिस्ते शं विधास्यति ॥५९॥

ahaṁ sanat-kumāraś ca
nārado bhagavān ajaḥ
kapilo 'pāntaratamo
devalo dharma āsuriḥ

marīci-pramukhāś cānye
siddheśāḥ pāra-darśanāḥ

vidāma na vayaṁ sarve
yan-māyāṁ māyayāvṛtāḥ

tasya viśveśvarasyedaṁ
śastraṁ durviṣahaṁ hi naḥ
tam evaṁ śaraṇaṁ yāhi
haris te śaṁ vidhāsyati

aham—I; *sanat-kumāraḥ ca*—and the four Kumāras (Sanaka, Sanātana, Sanat-kumāra and Sananda); *nāradaḥ*—the heavenly sage Nārada; *bhagavān ajaḥ*—the supreme creature of the universe, Lord Brahmā; *kapilaḥ*—the son of Devahūti; *apāntaratamaḥ*—Vyāsadeva; *devalaḥ*—the great sage Devala; *dharmaḥ*—Yamarāja; *āsuriḥ*—the great saint Āsuri; *marīci*—the great saint Marīci; *pramukhāḥ*—headed by; *ca*—also; *anye*—others; *siddha-īśāḥ*—all of them perfect in their knowledge; *pāra-darśanāḥ*—they have seen the end of all knowledge; *vidāmaḥ*—can understand; *na*—not; *vayam*—all of us; *sarve*—totally; *yat-māyām*—the illusory energy of whom; *māyayā*—by that illusory energy; *āvṛtāḥ*—being covered; *tasya*—His; *viśva-īśvarasya*—of the Lord of the universe; *idam*—this; *śastram*—weapon (the disc); *durviṣaham*—even intolerable; *hi*—indeed; *naḥ*—of us; *tam*—to Him; *evam*—therefore; *śaraṇam yāhi*—go to take shelter; *hariḥ*—the Supreme Personality of Godhead; *te*—for you; *śam*—auspiciousness; *vidhāsyati*—certainly will perform.

TRANSLATION

Past, present and future are known to me [Lord Śiva], Sanat-kumāra, Nārada, the most revered Lord Brahmā, Kapila [the son of Devahūti], Apāntaratama [Lord Vyāsadeva], Devala, Yamarāja, Āsuri, Marīci and many saintly persons headed by him, as well as many others who have achieved perfection. Nonetheless, because we are covered by the illusory energy of the Lord, we cannot understand how expansive that illusory energy is. You should simply approach that Supreme Personality of Godhead to get relief, for this Sudarśana cakra is intolerable even to us. Go to

Lord Viṣṇu. He will certainly be kind enough to bestow all good fortune upon you.

TEXT 60

ततो निराशो दुर्वासाः पदं भगवतो ययौ ।
वैकुण्ठाख्यं यदध्यास्ते श्रीनिवासः श्रिया सह ॥६०॥

tato nirāśo durvāsāḥ
padaṁ bhagavato yayau
vaikuṇṭhākhyaṁ yad adhyāste
śrīnivāsaḥ śriyā saha

tataḥ—thereafter; *nirāśaḥ*—disappointed; *durvāsāḥ*—the great mystic Durvāsā; *padam*—to the place; *bhagavataḥ*—of the Supreme Personality of Godhead, Viṣṇu; *yayau*—went; *vaikuṇṭha-ākhyam*—the place known as Vaikuṇṭha; *yat*—wherein; *adhyāste*—lives perpetually; *śrīnivāsaḥ*—Lord Viṣṇu; *śriyā*—with the goddess of fortune; *saha*—with.

TRANSLATION

Thereafter, being disappointed even in taking shelter of Lord Śiva, Durvāsā Muni went to Vaikuṇṭha-dhāma, where the Supreme Personality of Godhead, Nārāyaṇa, resides with His consort, the goddess of fortune.

TEXT 61

संदह्यमानोऽजितशस्त्रवह्निना
तत्पादमूले पतितः सवेपथुः ।
आहाच्युतानन्त सदीप्सित प्रभो
कृतागसं मावहि विश्वभावन ॥६१॥

sandahyamāno 'jita-śastra-vahninā
tat-pāda-mūle patitaḥ savepathuḥ
āhācyutānanta sad-īpsita prabho
kṛtāgasaṁ māvahi viśva-bhāvana

sandahyamānaḥ—being burned by the heat; *ajita-śastra-vahninā*—by the blazing fire of the Supreme Personality of Godhead's weapon; *tat-pāda-mūle*—at His lotus feet; *patitaḥ*—falling down; *sa-vepathuḥ*—with trembling of the body; *āha*—said; *acyuta*—O my Lord, O infallible one; *ananta*—O You of unlimited prowess; *sat-īpsita*—O Lord desired by saintly persons; *prabho*—O Supreme; *kṛta-āgasam*—the greatest offender; *mā*—to me; *avahi*—give protection; *viśva-bhāvana*—O well-wisher of the whole universe.

TRANSLATION

Durvāsā Muni, the great mystic, scorched by the heat of the Sudarśana cakra, fell at the lotus feet of Nārāyaṇa. His body trembling, he spoke as follows: O infallible, unlimited Lord, protector of the entire universe, You are the only desirable objective for all devotees. I am a great offender, my Lord. Please give me protection.

TEXT 62

अजानता ते परमानुभावं
कृतं मयाघं भवतः प्रियाणाम् ।
विधेहि तस्यापचितिं विधात-
र्मुच्येत यन्नाम्न्युदिते नारकोऽपि ॥६२॥

ajānatā te paramānubhāvaṁ
kṛtaṁ mayāghaṁ bhavataḥ priyāṇām
vidhehi tasyāpacitiṁ vidhātar
mucyeta yan-nāmny udite nārako 'pi

ajānatā—without knowledge; *te*—of Your Lordship; *parama-anubhāvam*—the inconceivable prowess; *kṛtam*—has been committed; *mayā*—by me; *agham*—a great offense; *bhavataḥ*—of Your Lordship; *priyāṇām*—at the feet of the devotees; *vidhehi*—now kindly do the needful; *tasya*—of such an offense; *apacitim*—counteraction; *vidhātaḥ*—O supreme controller; *mucyeta*—can be delivered; *yat*—of whose; *nāmni*—when the name; *udite*—is awakened; *nārakaḥ api*—even a person fit for going to hell.

TRANSLATION

O my Lord, O supreme controller, without knowledge of Your unlimited prowess I have offended Your most dear devotee. Very kindly save me from the reaction of this offense. You can do everything, for even if a person is fit for going to hell, You can deliver him simply by awakening within his heart the holy name of Your Lordship.

TEXT 63

श्रीभगवानुवाच
अहं भक्तपराधीनो ह्यस्वतन्त्र इव द्विज ।
साधुभिर्ग्रस्तहृदयो भक्तैर्भक्तजनप्रियः ॥६३॥

śrī-bhagavān uvāca
ahaṁ bhakta-parādhīno
hy asvatantra iva dvija
sādhubhir grasta-hṛdayo
bhaktair bhakta-jana-priyaḥ

śrī-bhagavān uvāca—the Supreme Personality of Godhead said; *aham*—I; *bhakta-parādhīnaḥ*—am dependent on the will of My devotees; *hi*—indeed; *asvatantraḥ*—am not independent; *iva*—exactly like that; *dvija*—O *brāhmaṇa; sādhubhiḥ*—by pure devotees, completely free from all material desires; *grasta-hṛdayaḥ*—My heart is controlled; *bhaktaiḥ*—because they are devotees; *bhakta-jana-priyaḥ*—I am dependent not only on My devotee but also on My devotee's devotee (the devotee's devotee is extremely dear to Me).

TRANSLATION

The Supreme Personality of Godhead said to the brāhmaṇa: I am completely under the control of My devotees. Indeed, I am not at all independent. Because My devotees are completely devoid of material desires, I sit only within the cores of their hearts. What to speak of My devotee, even those who are devotees of My devotee are very dear to Me.

PURPORT

All the great stalwart personalities in the universe, including Lord Brahmā and Lord Śiva, are fully under the control of the Supreme Personality of Godhead, but the Supreme Personality of Godhead is fully under the control of His devotee. Why is this? Because the devotee is *anyābhilāṣitā-śūnya;* in other words, he has no material desires in his heart. His only desire is to think always of the Supreme Personality of Godhead and how to serve Him best. Because of this transcendental qualification, the Supreme Lord is extremely favorable to the devotees—indeed, not only the devotees, but also the devotees of the devotees. Śrīla Narottama dāsa Ṭhākura says, *chāḍiyā vaiṣṇava-sevā nistāra pāyeche kebā:* without being a devotee of a devotee, one cannot be released from material entanglement. Therefore Caitanya Mahāprabhu identified Himself as *gopī-bhartuḥ pada-kamalayor dāsa-dāsānudāsaḥ.* Thus he instructed us to become not directly servants of Kṛṣṇa but servants of the servant of Kṛṣṇa. Devotees like Brahmā, Nārada, Vyāsadeva and Śukadeva Gosvāmī are directly servants of Kṛṣṇa, and one who becomes a servant of Nārada, Vyāsadeva and Śukadeva, like the six Gosvāmīs, is still more devoted. Śrīla Viśvanātha Cakravartī Ṭhākura therefore says, *yasya prasādād bhagavat-prasādaḥ:* if one very sincerely serves the spiritual master, Kṛṣṇa certainly becomes favorable to such a devotee. Following the instructions of a devotee is more valuable than following the instructions of the Supreme Personality of Godhead directly.

TEXT 64

नाहमात्मानमाशासे मद्भक्तैः साधुभिर्विना ।
श्रियं चात्यन्तिकीं ब्रह्मन् येषां गतिरहं परा ॥६४॥

nāham ātmānam āśāse
mad-bhaktaiḥ sādhubhir vinā
śriyaṁ cātyantikīṁ brahman
yeṣāṁ gatir ahaṁ parā

na—not; *aham*—I; *ātmānam*—transcendental bliss; *āśāse*—desire; *mat-bhaktaiḥ*—with My devotees; *sādhubhiḥ*—with the saintly persons; *vinā*—without them; *śriyam*—all My six opulences; *ca*—also;

ātyantikīm—the supreme; *brahman*—O *brāhmaṇa; yeṣām*—of whom; *gatiḥ*—destination; *aham*—I am; *parā*—the ultimate.

TRANSLATION

O best of the brāhmaṇas, without saintly persons for whom I am the only destination, I do not desire to enjoy My transcendental bliss and My supreme opulences.

PURPORT

The Supreme Personality of Godhead is self-sufficient, but to enjoy His transcendental bliss He requires the cooperation of His devotees. In Vṛndāvana, for example, although Lord Kṛṣṇa is full in Himself, He wants the cooperation of His devotees like the cowherd boys and the *gopīs* to increase His transcendental bliss. Such pure devotees, who can increase the pleasure potency of the Supreme Personality of Godhead, are certainly most dear to Him. Not only does the Supreme Personality of Godhead enjoy the company of His devotees, but because He is unlimited He wants to increase His devotees unlimitedly. Thus, He descends to the material world to induce the nondevotees and rebellious living entities to return home, back to Godhead. He requests them to surrender unto Him because, unlimited as He is, He wants to increase His devotees unlimitedly. The Kṛṣṇa consciousness movement is an attempt to increase the number of pure devotees of the Supreme Lord more and more. It is certain that a devotee who helps in this endeavor to satisfy the Supreme Personality of Godhead becomes indirectly a controller of the Supreme Lord. Although the Supreme Lord is full in six opulences, He does not feel transcendental bliss without His devotees. An example that may be cited in this regard is that if a very rich man does not have sons in a family he does not feel happiness. Indeed, sometimes a rich man adopts a son to complete his happiness. The science of transcendental bliss is known to the pure devotee. Therefore the pure devotee is always engaged in increasing the transcendental happiness of the Lord.

TEXT 65

ये दारागारपुत्राप्तप्राणान् वित्तमिमं परम् ।
हित्वा मां शरणं याताः कथं तांस्त्यक्तुमुत्सहे ॥६५॥

ye dārāgāra-putrāpta-
prāṇān vittam imaṁ param
hitvā māṁ śaraṇaṁ yātāḥ
kathaṁ tāṁs tyaktum utsahe

ye—those devotees of Mine who; *dāra*—wife; *agāra*—house; *putra*—children, sons; *āpta*—relatives, society; *prāṇān*—even life; *vittam*—wealth; *imam*—all these; *param*—elevation to the heavenly planets or becoming one by merging into Brahman; *hitvā*—giving up (all these ambitions and paraphernalia); *mām*—unto Me; *śaraṇam*—shelter; *yātāḥ*—having taken; *katham*—how; *tān*—such persons; *tyaktum*—to give them up; *utsahe*—I can be enthusiastic in that way (it is not possible).

TRANSLATION

Since pure devotees give up their homes, wives, children, relatives, riches and even their lives simply to serve Me, without any desire for material improvement in this life or in the next, how can I give up such devotees at any time?

PURPORT

The Supreme Personality of Godhead is worshiped by the words *brahmaṇya-devāya go-brāhmaṇa-hitāya ca.* Thus He is the well-wisher of the *brāhmaṇas.* Durvāsā Muni was certainly a very great *brāhmaṇa,* but because he was a nondevotee, he could not sacrifice everything in devotional service. Great mystic *yogīs* are actually self-interested. The proof is that when Durvāsā Muni created a demon to kill Mahārāja Ambarīṣa, the King stayed fixed in his place, praying to the Supreme Personality of Godhead and depending solely and wholly on Him, whereas when Durvāsā Muni was chased by the Sudarśana *cakra* by the supreme will of the Lord, he was so perturbed that he fled all over the world and tried to take shelter in every nook and corner of the universe. At last, in fear of his life, he approached Lord Brahmā, Lord Śiva and ultimately the Supreme Personality of Godhead. He was so interested in his own body that he wanted to kill the body of a Vaiṣṇava. Therefore, he did not have very good intelligence, and how can an unintelligent person be delivered by the Supreme Personality of Godhead? The Lord certainly tries to give all protection to His devotees who have given up everything for the sake of serving Him.

Another point in this verse is that attachment to *dārāgāra-putrāpta*—home, wife, children, friendship, society and love—is not the way to achieve the favor of the Supreme Personality of Godhead. One who is attached to hearth and home for material pleasure cannot become a pure devotee. Sometimes a pure devotee may have a habit or attraction for wife, children and home but at the same time want to serve the Supreme Lord to the best of his ability. For such a devotee, the Lord makes a special arrangement to take away the objects of his false attachment and thus free him from attachment to wife, home, children, friends and so on. This is special mercy bestowed upon the devotee to bring him back home, back to Godhead.

TEXT 66

मयि निर्बद्धहृदयाः साधवः समदर्शनाः ।
वशे कुर्वन्ति मां भक्त्या सत्स्त्रियः सत्पतिं यथा ॥६६॥

mayi nirbaddha-hṛdayāḥ
sādhavaḥ sama-darśanāḥ
vaśe kurvanti māṁ bhaktyā
sat-striyaḥ sat-patiṁ yathā

mayi—unto Me; *nirbaddha-hṛdayāḥ*—firmly attached in the core of the heart; *sādhavaḥ*—the pure devotees; *sama-darśanāḥ*—who are equal to everyone; *vaśe*—under control; *kurvanti*—they make; *mām*—unto Me; *bhaktyā*—by devotional service; *sat-striyaḥ*—chaste women; *sat-patim*—unto the gentle husband; *yathā*—as.

TRANSLATION

As chaste women bring their gentle husbands under control by service, the pure devotees, who are equal to everyone and completely attached to Me in the core of the heart, bring Me under their full control.

PURPORT

In this verse, the word *sama-darśanāḥ* is significant. The pure devotee is actually equal toward everyone, as confirmed in *Bhagavad-gītā* (18.54): *brahma-bhūtaḥ prasannātmā na śocati na kāṅkṣati/ samaḥ sarveṣu bhūteṣu.* Universal brotherhood is possible when one is a pure devotee (*paṇḍitāḥ sama-darśinaḥ*). A pure devotee is actually learned because he knows his constitutional position, he knows the position of the Supreme Personality of Godhead, and he knows the relationship between the living entity and the Supreme Lord. Thus he has full spiritual knowledge and is automatically liberated (*brahma-bhūtaḥ*). He can therefore see everyone on the spiritual platform. He can comprehend the happiness and distress of all living entities. He understands that what is happiness to him is also happiness to others and that what is distress to him is distressing for others. Therefore he is sympathetic to everyone. As Prahlāda Mahārāja said:

śoce tato vimukha-cetasa indriyārtha-
māyā-sukhāya bharam udvahato vimūḍhān
(*Bhāg.* 7.9.43)

People suffer from material distress because they are not attached to the Supreme Personality of Godhead. A pure devotee's chief concern, therefore, is to raise the ignorant mass of people to the sense of Kṛṣṇa consciousness.

TEXT 67

मत्सेवया प्रतीतं ते सालोक्यादिचतुष्टयम् ।
नेच्छन्ति सेवया पूर्णाः कुतोऽन्यत् कालविप्लुतम् ॥६७॥

mat-sevayā pratītaṁ te
sālokyādi-catuṣṭayam
necchanti sevayā pūrṇāḥ
kuto 'nyat kāla-viplutam

mat-sevayā—by being engaged fully in My transcendental loving service; *pratītam*—automatically achieved; *te*—such pure devotees are fully satisfied; *sālokya-ādi-catuṣṭayam*—the four different types of liberation (*sālokya, sārūpya, sāmīpya* and *sārṣṭi,* what to speak of *sāyujya*); *na*—not; *icchanti*—desire; *sevayā*—simply by devotional service; *pūrṇāḥ*—fully complete; *kutaḥ*—where is the question; *anyat*—other things; *kāla-viplutam*—which are finished in the course of time.

TRANSLATION

My devotees, who are always satisfied to be engaged in My loving service, are not interested even in the four principles of liberation [sālokya, sārūpya, sāmīpya and sārṣṭi], although these are automatically achieved by their service. What then is to be said of such perishable happiness as elevation to the higher planetary systems?

PURPORT

Śrīla Bilvamaṅgala Ṭhākura has estimated the value of liberation as follows:

muktiḥ svayaṁ mukulitāñjaliḥ sevate 'smān
dharmārtha-kāma-gatayaḥ samaya-pratīkṣāḥ

Bilvamaṅgala Ṭhākura realized that if one develops his natural devotional service to the Supreme Personality of Godhead, *mukti* stands before him with folded hands to offer all kinds of service. In other words, the devotee is already liberated. There is no need for him to aspire for different types of liberation. The pure devotee automatically achieves liberation, even without desiring it.

TEXT 68

साधवो हृदयं मह्यं साधूनां हृदयं त्वहम् ।
मदन्यत् ते न जानन्ति नाहं तेभ्यो मनागपि ॥६८॥

sādhavo hṛdayaṁ mahyaṁ
sādhūnāṁ hṛdayaṁ tv aham
mad-anyat te na jānanti
nāhaṁ tebhyo manāg api

sādhavaḥ—the pure devotees; *hṛdayam*—in the core of the heart; *mahyam*—of Me; *sādhūnām*—of the pure devotees also; *hṛdayam*—in the core of the heart; *tu*—indeed; *aham*—I am; *mat-anyat*—anything else but me; *te*—they; *na*—not; *jānanti*—know; *na*—not; *aham*—I; *tebhyaḥ*—than them; *manāk api*—even by a little fraction.

TRANSLATION

The pure devotee is always within the core of My heart, and I am always in the heart of the pure devotee. My devotees do not know anything else but Me, and I do not know anyone else but them.

PURPORT

Since Durvāsā Muni wanted to chastise Mahārāja Ambarīṣa, it is to be understood that he wanted to give pain to the heart of the Supreme Personality of Godhead, for the Lord says, *sādhavo hṛdayaṁ mahyam:* "The pure devotee is always within the core of My heart." The Lord's feelings are like those of a father, who feels pain when his child is in pain. Therefore, offenses at the lotus feet of a devotee are serious. Caitanya Mahāprabhu has very strongly recommended that one not commit any offense at the lotus feet of a devotee. Such offenses are compared to a mad elephant because when a mad elephant enters a garden it causes devastation. Therefore one should be extremely careful not to commit offenses at the lotus feet of a pure devotee. Actually Mahārāja Ambarīṣa was not at all at fault; Durvāsā Muni unnecessarily wanted to chastise him on flimsy grounds. Mahārāja Ambarīṣa wanted to complete the Ekādaśī-pāraṇa as part of devotional service to please the Supreme Personality of Godhead, and therefore he drank a little water. But although Durvāsā Muni was a great mystic *brāhmaṇa*, he did not know what is what. That is the difference between a pure devotee and a so-called learned scholar of Vedic knowledge. The devotees, being always situated in the core of the Lord's heart, surely get all instructions directly from the Lord, as confirmed by the Lord Himself in *Bhagavad-gītā* (10.11):

teṣām evānukampārtham
aham ajñānajaṁ tamaḥ
nāśayāmy ātma-bhāvastho
jñāna-dīpena bhāsvatā

"Out of compassion for them, I, dwelling in their hearts, destroy with the shining lamp of knowledge the darkness born of ignorance." The devotee does not do anything not sanctioned by the Supreme Personality of Godhead. As it is said, *vaiṣṇavera kriyā mudrā vijñeha nā bujhaya.* Even the most learned or experienced person cannot understand the movements of a Vaiṣṇava, a pure devotee. No one, therefore, should criticize a pure Vaiṣṇava. A Vaiṣṇava knows his own business; whatever he does is precisely right because he is always guided by the Supreme Personality of Godhead.

TEXT 69

उपायं कथयिष्यामि तव विप्र शृणुष्व तत् ।
अयं ह्यात्माभिचारस्ते यतस्तं याहि मा चिरम् ।
साधुषु प्रहितं तेजः प्रहर्तुः कुरुतेऽशिवम् ॥६९॥

upāyaṁ kathayiṣyāmi
tava vipra śṛṇuṣva tat
ayaṁ hy ātmābhicāras te
yatas taṁ yāhi mā ciram
sādhuṣu prahitaṁ tejaḥ
prahartuḥ kurute 'śivam

upāyam—the means of protection in this dangerous position; *kathayiṣyāmi*—I shall speak to you; *tava*—of your deliverance from this danger; *vipra*—O *brāhmaṇa; śṛṇuṣva*—just hear from me; *tat*—what I say; *ayam*—this action taken by you; *hi*—indeed; *ātma-abhicāraḥ*—self-envy or envious of yourself (your mind has become your enemy); *te*—for you; *yataḥ*—because of whom; *tam*—to him (Mahārāja Ambarīṣa); *yāhi*—immediately go; *mā ciram*—do not wait even a moment; *sādhuṣu*—unto devotees; *prahitam*—applied; *tejaḥ*—power; *prahartuḥ*—of the executor; *kurute*—does; *aśivam*—inauspiciousness.

TRANSLATION

O brāhmaṇa, let Me now advise you for your own protection. Please hear from Me. By offending Mahārāja Ambarīṣa, you have

acted with self-envy. Therefore you should go to him immediately, without a moment's delay. One's so-called prowess, when employed against the devotee, certainly harms he who employs it. Thus it is the subject, not the object, who is harmed.

PURPORT

A Vaiṣṇava is always an object of envy for nondevotees, even when the nondevotee happens to be his father. To give a practical example, Hiraṇyakaśipu was envious of Prahlāda Mahārāja, but this envy of the devotee was harmful to Hiraṇyakaśipu, not to Prahlāda. Every action taken by Hiraṇyakaśipu against his son Prahlāda Mahārāja was taken very seriously by the Supreme Personality of Godhead, and thus when Hiraṇyakaśipu was on the verge of killing Prahlāda, the Lord personally appeared and killed Hiraṇyakaśipu. Service to a Vaiṣṇava gradually accumulates and becomes an asset for the devotee. Similarly, harmful activities directed against the devotee gradually become the ultimate cause of the performer's falldown. Even such a great *brāhmaṇa* and mystic *yogī* as Durvāsā was in a most dangerous situation because of his offense at the lotus feet of Mahārāja Ambarīṣa, a pure devotee.

TEXT 70

तपो विद्या च विप्राणां निःश्रेयसकरे उभे ।
ते एव दुर्विनीतस्य कल्पेते कर्तुरन्यथा ॥७०॥

tapo vidyā ca viprāṇāṁ
niḥśreyasa-kare ubhe
te eva durvinītasya
kalpete kartur anyathā

tapaḥ—austerities; *vidyā*—knowledge; *ca*—also; *viprāṇām*—of the *brāhmaṇas; niḥśreyasa*—of what is certainly very auspicious for upliftment; *kare*—are causes; *ubhe*—both of them; *te*—such austerity and knowledge; *eva*—indeed; *durvinītasya*—when such a person is an upstart; *kalpete*—become; *kartuḥ*—of the performer; *anyathā*—just the opposite.

TRANSLATION

For a brāhmaṇa, austerity and learning are certainly auspicious, but when acquired by a person who is not gentle, such austerity and learning are most dangerous.

PURPORT

It is said that a jewel is very valuable, but when it is on the hood of a serpent, it is dangerous despite its value. Similarly, when a materialistic nondevotee achieves great success in learning and austerity, that success is dangerous for all of society. So-called learned scientists, for example, invented atomic weapons that are dangerous for all humanity. It is therefore said, *maṇinā bhūṣitaḥ sarpaḥ kim asau na bhayaṅkaraḥ.* A serpent with a jewel on its hood is as dangerous as a serpent without such a jewel. Durvāsā Muni was a very learned *brāhmaṇa* equipped with mystic power, but because he was not a gentleman, he did not know how to use his power. He was therefore extremely dangerous. The Supreme Personality of Godhead is never inclined toward a dangerous person who uses his mystic power for some personal design. By the laws of nature, therefore, such misuse of power is ultimately dangerous not for society but for the person who misuses it.

TEXT 71

ब्रह्मंस्तद् गच्छ भद्रं ते नाभागतनयं नृपम् ।
क्षमापय महाभागं ततः शान्तिर्भविष्यति ॥७१॥

brahmaṁs tad gaccha bhadraṁ te
nābhāga-tanayaṁ nṛpam
kṣamāpaya mahā-bhāgaṁ
tataḥ śāntir bhaviṣyati

brahman—O *brāhmaṇa; tat*—therefore; *gaccha*—you go; *bhadram*—all auspiciousness; *te*—unto you; *nābhāga-tanayam*—to the son of Mahārāja Nābhāga; *nṛpam*—the King (Ambarīṣa); *kṣamāpaya*—just try to pacify him; *mahā-bhāgam*—a great personality, a pure devotee; *tataḥ*—thereafter; *śāntiḥ*—peace; *bhaviṣyati*—there will be.

TRANSLATION

O best of the brāhmaṇas, you should therefore go immediately to King Ambarīṣa, the son of Mahārāja Nābhāga. I wish you all good fortune. If you can satisfy Mahārāja Ambarīṣa, then there will be peace for you.

PURPORT

In this regard, Madhva Muni quotes from the *Garuḍa Purāṇa:*

brahmādi-bhakti-koṭy-aṁśād
aṁśo naivāmbarīṣake
naivanyasya cakrasyāpi
tathāpi harir īśvaraḥ

tātkālikopaceyatvāt
teṣāṁ yaśasa ādirāṭ
brahmādayaś ca tat-kīrtiṁ
vyañjayām āsur uttamām

mohanāya ca daityānāṁ
brahmāde nindanāya ca
anyārthaṁ ca svayaṁ viṣṇur
brahmādyāś ca nirāśiṣaḥ

mānuṣeṣūttamātvāc ca
teṣāṁ bhaktyādibhir guṇaiḥ
brahmāder viṣṇv-adhīnatva-
jñāpanāya ca kevalam

durvāsāś ca svayaṁ rudras
tathāpy anyāyām uktavān
tasyāpy anugrahārthāya
darpa-nāśārtham eva ca

The lesson to be derived from this narration concerning Mahārāja Ambarīṣa and Durvāsā Muni is that all the demigods, including Lord

Brahmā and Lord Śiva, are under the control of Lord Viṣṇu. Therefore, when a Vaiṣṇava is offended, the offender is punished by Viṣṇu, the Supreme Lord. No one can protect such a person, even Lord Brahmā or Lord Śiva.

Thus end the Bhaktivedanta purports of the Ninth Canto, Fourth Chapter, of the Śrīmad-Bhāgavatam, *entitled "Ambarīṣa Mahārāja Offended by Durvāsā Muni."*

CHAPTER FIVE

Durvāsā Muni's Life Spared

In this chapter we find Mahārāja Ambarīṣa offering prayers to the Sudarśana *cakra* and we find how the Sudarśana *cakra* became merciful to Durvāsā Muni.

By the order of the Supreme Personality of Godhead, Viṣṇu, Durvāsā Muni immediately went to Mahārāja Ambarīṣa and fell at his lotus feet. Mahārāja Ambarīṣa, being naturally very humble and meek, felt shy and ashamed because Durvāsā Muni had fallen at his feet, and thus he began to offer prayers to the Sudarśana *cakra* just to save Durvāsā. What is this Sudarśana *cakra?* The Sudarśana *cakra* is the glance of the Supreme Personality of Godhead by which He creates the entire material world. *Sa aikṣata, sa asṛjata.* This is the Vedic version. The Sudarśana *cakra,* which is the origin of creation and is most dear to the Lord, has thousands of spokes. This Sudarśana *cakra* is the killer of the prowess of all other weapons, the killer of darkness, and the manifester of the prowess of devotional service; it is the means of establishing religious principles, and it is the killer of all irreligious activities. Without his mercy, the universe cannot be maintained, and therefore the Sudarśana *cakra* is employed by the Supreme Personality of Godhead. When Mahārāja Ambarīṣa thus prayed that the Sudarśana *cakra* be merciful, the Sudarśana *cakra,* being appeased, refrained from killing Durvāsā Muni, who thus achieved the Sudarśana *cakra's* mercy. Durvāsā Muni thus learned to give up the nasty idea of considering a Vaiṣṇava an ordinary person (*vaiṣṇave jāti-buddhi*). Mahārāja Ambarīṣa belonged to the *kṣatriya* group, and therefore Durvāsā Muni considered him lower than the *brāhmaṇas* and wanted to exercise brahminical power against him. By this incident, everyone should learn how to stop mischievous ideas of neglecting Vaiṣṇavas. After this incident, Mahārāja Ambarīṣa gave Durvāsā Muni sumptuous food to eat, and then the King, who had been standing in the same place for one year without eating anything, also took *prasāda.* Mahārāja Ambarīṣa later divided his property among his sons and went to the bank of the Mānasa-sarovara to execute devotional meditation.

TEXT 1

श्रीशुक उवाच
एवं भगवतादिष्टो दुर्वासाश्चक्रतापितः ।
अम्बरीषमुपावृत्य तत्पादौ दुःखितोऽग्रहीत् ॥ १ ॥

śrī-śuka uvāca
evaṁ bhagavatādiṣṭo
durvāsāś cakra-tāpitaḥ
ambarīṣam upāvṛtya
tat-pādau duḥkhito 'grahīt

śrī-śukaḥ uvāca—Śrī Śukadeva Gosvāmī said; *evam*—in this way; *bhagavatā ādiṣṭaḥ*—being ordered by the Supreme Personality of Godhead; *durvāsāḥ*—the great mystic *yogī* named Durvāsā; *cakra-tāpitaḥ*—being very much harassed by the Sudarśana *cakra; ambarīṣam*—unto Mahārāja Ambarīṣa; *upāvṛtya*—approaching; *tat-pādau*—at his lotus feet; *duḥkhitaḥ*—being very much aggrieved; *agrahīt*—he caught.

TRANSLATION

Śukadeva Gosvāmī said: When thus advised by Lord Viṣṇu, Durvāsā Muni, who was very much harassed by the Sudarśana cakra, immediately approached Mahārāja Ambarīṣa. Being very much aggrieved, the muni fell down and clasped the King's lotus feet.

TEXT 2

तस्य सोद्यममावीक्ष्य पादस्पर्शविलज्जितः ।
अस्तावीत् तद्धरेरस्त्रं कृपया पीडितो भृशम् ॥ २ ॥

tasya sodyamam āvīkṣya
pāda-sparśa-vilajjitaḥ
astāvīt tad dharer astraṁ
kṛpayā pīḍito bhṛśam

tasya—of Durvāsā; *saḥ*—he, Mahārāja Ambarīṣa; *udyamam*—the endeavor; *āvīkṣya*—after seeing; *pāda-sparśa-vilajjitaḥ*—being ashamed because Durvāsā was touching his lotus feet; *astāvīt*—offered prayers; *tat*—to that; *hareḥ astram*—weapon of the Supreme Personality of Godhead; *kṛpayā*—with mercy; *pīḍitaḥ*—aggrieved; *bhṛśam*—very much.

TRANSLATION

When Durvāsā touched his lotus feet, Mahārāja Ambarīṣa was very much ashamed, and when he saw Durvāsā attempting to offer prayers, because of mercy he was aggrieved even more. Thus he immediately began offering prayers to the great weapon of the Supreme Personality of Godhead.

TEXT 3

अम्बरीश उवाच

त्वमग्निर्भगवान् सूर्यस्त्वं सोमो ज्योतिषां पतिः ।
त्वमापस्त्वं क्षितिर्व्योम वायुर्मात्रेन्द्रियाणि च ॥ ३ ॥

ambarīṣa uvāca
tvam agnir bhagavān sūryas
tvaṁ somo jyotiṣāṁ patiḥ
tvam āpas tvaṁ kṣitir vyoma
vāyur mātrendriyāṇi ca

ambarīṣaḥ—Mahārāja Ambarīṣa; *uvāca*—said; *tvam*—you (are); *agniḥ*—the fire; *bhagavān*—the most powerful; *sūryaḥ*—the sun; *tvam*—you (are); *somaḥ*—the moon; *jyotiṣām*—of all the luminaries; *patiḥ*—the master; *tvam*—you (are); *āpaḥ*—water; *tvam*—you (are); *kṣitiḥ*—earth; *vyoma*—sky; *vāyuḥ*—the air; *mātra*—the objects of the senses; *indriyāṇi*—and the senses; *ca*—also.

TRANSLATION

Mahārāja Ambarīṣa said: O Sudarśana cakra, you are fire, you are the most powerful sun, and you are the moon, the master of all luminaries. You are water, earth and sky, you are the air, you are the five sense objects [sound, touch, form, taste and smell], and you are the senses also.

TEXT 4

सुदर्शन नमस्तुभ्यं सहस्राराच्युतप्रिय ।
सर्वास्त्रघातिन् विप्राय स्वस्ति भूया इडस्पते ॥ ४ ॥

sudarśana namas tubhyaṁ
sahasrārācyuta-priya
sarvāstra-ghātin viprāya
svasti bhūyā iḍaspate

sudarśana—O original vision of the Supreme Personality of Godhead; *namaḥ*—respectful obeisances; *tubhyam*—unto you; *sahasra-ara*—O you who have thousands of spokes; *acyuta-priya*—O most favorite of the Supreme Personality of Godhead, Acyuta; *sarva-astra-ghātin*—O destroyer of all weapons; *viprāya*—unto this *brāhmaṇa; svasti*—very auspicious; *bhūyāḥ*—just become; *iḍaspate*—O master of the material world.

TRANSLATION

O most favorite of Acyuta, the Supreme Personality of Godhead, you have thousands of spokes. O master of the material world, destroyer of all weapons, original vision of the Personality of Godhead, I offer my respectful obeisances unto you. Kindly give shelter and be auspicious to this brāhmaṇa.

TEXT 5

त्वं धर्मस्त्वमृतं सत्यं त्वं यज्ञोऽखिलयज्ञभुक् ।
त्वं लोकपालः सर्वात्मा त्वं तेजः पौरुषं परम् ॥ ५ ॥

tvaṁ dharmas tvam ṛtaṁ satyaṁ
tvaṁ yajño 'khila-yajña-bhuk
tvaṁ loka-pālaḥ sarvātmā
tvaṁ tejaḥ pauruṣaṁ param

tvam—you; *dharmaḥ*—religion; *tvam*—you; *ṛtam*—encouraging statements; *satyam*—the ultimate truth; *tvam*—you; *yajñaḥ*—sacrifice;

akhila—universal; *yajña-bhuk*—the enjoyer of the fruits resulting from sacrifice; *tvam*—you; *loka-pālaḥ*—the maintainer of the various planets; *sarva-ātmā*—all-pervading; *tvam*—you; *tejaḥ*—prowess; *pauruṣam*—of the Supreme Personality of Godhead; *param*—transcendental.

TRANSLATION

O Sudarśana wheel, you are religion, you are truth, you are encouraging statements, you are sacrifice, and you are the enjoyer of the fruits of sacrifice. You are the maintainer of the entire universe, and you are the supreme transcendental prowess in the hands of the Supreme Personality of Godhead. You are the original vision of the Lord, and therefore you are known as Sudarśana. Everything has been created by your activities, and therefore you are all-pervading.

PURPORT

The word *sudarśana* means "auspicious vision." From Vedic instructions we understand that this material world is created by the glance of the Supreme Personality of Godhead (*sa aikṣata, sa asṛjata*). The Supreme Personality of Godhead glanced over the *mahat-tattva*, or the total material energy, and when it was agitated, everything came into existence. Western philosophers sometimes think that the original cause of creation was a chunk that exploded. If one thinks of this chunk as the total material energy, the *mahat-tattva*, one can understand that the chunk was agitated by the glance of the Lord, and thus the Lord's glance is the original cause of material creation.

TEXT 6

नमः सुनाभाखिलधर्मसेतवे
ह्यधर्मशीलासुरधूमकेतवे ।
त्रैलोक्यगोपाय विशुद्धवर्चसे
मनोजवायाद्भुतकर्मणे गृणे ॥ ६ ॥

namaḥ sunābhākhila-dharma-setave
hy adharma-śīlāsura-dhūma-ketave

trailokya-gopāya viśuddha-varcase
mano-javāyādbhuta-karmaṇe gṛṇe

namaḥ—all respectful obeisances unto you; *su-nābha*—O you who have an auspicious hub; *akhila-dharma-setave*—whose spokes are considered to be a breech of the entire universe; *hi*—indeed; *adharma-śīla*—who are irreligious; *asura*—for the demons; *dhūma-ketave*—unto you who are like fire or an inauspicious comet; *trailokya*—of the three material worlds; *gopāya*—the maintainer; *viśuddha*—transcendental; *varcase*—whose effulgence; *manaḥ-javāya*—as speedy as the mind; *adbhuta*—wonderful; *karmaṇe*—so active; *gṛṇe*—I simply utter.

TRANSLATION

O Sudarśana, you have a very auspicious hub, and therefore you are the upholder of all religion. You are just like an inauspicious comet for the irreligious demons. Indeed, you are the maintainer of the three worlds, you are full of transcendental effulgence, you are as quick as the mind, and you are able to work wonders. I can simply utter the word "namaḥ," offering all obeisances unto you.

PURPORT

The disc of the Lord is called Sudarśana because he does not discriminate between high and low criminals or demons. Durvāsā Muni was certainly a powerful *brāhmaṇa,* but his acts against the pure devotee Mahārāja Ambarīṣa were no better than the activities of *asuras.* As stated in the *śāstras, dharmaṁ tu sākṣād bhagavat-praṇītam:* the word *dharma* refers to the orders or laws given by the Supreme Personality of Godhead. *Sarva-dharmān parityajya mām ekaṁ śaraṇaṁ vraja:* real *dharma* is surrender unto the Supreme Personality of Godhead. Therefore real *dharma* means *bhakti,* or devotional service to the Lord. The Sudarśana *cakra* is here addressed as *dharma-setave,* the protector of *dharma.* Mahārāja Ambarīṣa was a truly religious person, and consequently for his protection the Sudarśana *cakra* was ready to punish even such a strict *brāhmaṇa* as Durvāsā Muni because he had acted like a demon. There are demons even in the form of *brāhmaṇas.* Therefore the

Sudarśana *cakra* does not discriminate between *brāhmaṇa* demons and *śūdra* demons. Anyone against the Supreme Personality of Godhead and His devotees is called a demon. In the *śāstras* we find many *brāhmaṇas* and *kṣatriyas* who acted as demons and have been described as demons. According to the verdict of the *śāstras*, one has to be understood according to his symptoms. If one is born of a *brāhmaṇa* father but his symptoms are demoniac, he is regarded as a demon. The Sudarśana *cakra* is always concerned with annihilating the demons. Therefore he is described as *adharma-śīlāsura-dhūma-ketave.* Those who are not devotees are called *adharma-śīla.* The Sudarśana *cakra* is just like an inauspicious comet for all such demons.

TEXT 7

त्वत्तेजसा धर्ममयेन संहृतं
तमः प्रकाशश्च दृशो महात्मनाम् ।
दुरत्ययस्ते महिमा गिरां पते
त्वद्रूपमेतत् सदसत् परावरम् ॥ ७ ॥

tvat-tejasā dharma-mayena saṁhṛtaṁ
tamaḥ prakāśaś ca dṛśo mahātmanām
duratyayas te mahimā girāṁ pate
tvad-rūpam etat sad-asat parāvaram

tvat-tejasā—by your effulgence; *dharma-mayena*—which is full of religious principles; *saṁhṛtam*—dissipated; *tamaḥ*—darkness; *prakāśaḥ ca*—illumination also; *dṛśaḥ*—of all directions; *mahā-ātmanām*—of great, learned personalities; *duratyayaḥ*—insurmountable; *te*—your; *mahimā*—glories; *girām pate*—O master of speech; *tvat-rūpam*—your manifestation; *etat*—this; *sat-asat*—manifested and unmanifested; *para-avaram*—superior and inferior.

TRANSLATION

O master of speech, by your effulgence, full of religious principles, the darkness of the world is dissipated, and the knowledge

of learned persons or great souls is manifested. Indeed, no one can surpass your effulgence, for all things, manifested and unmanifested, gross and subtle, superior and inferior, are but various forms of you that are manifested by your effulgence.

PURPORT

Without illumination, nothing can be seen, especially in this material world. The illumination in this world emanates from the effulgence of Sudarśana, the original vision of the Supreme Personality of Godhead. The illuminating principles of the sun, the moon and fire emanate from Sudarśana. Similarly, illumination by knowledge also comes from Sudarśana because with the illumination of Sudarśana one can distinguish one thing from another, the superior from the inferior. Generally people accept a powerful *yogī* like Durvāsā Muni as wonderfully superior, but if such a person is chased by the Sudarśana *cakra*, we can see his real identity and understand how inferior he is because of his dealings with devotees.

TEXT 8

यदा विसृष्टस्त्वमनञ्जनेन वै
बलं प्रविष्टोऽजित दैत्यदानवम् ।
बाहूदरोर्वङ्घ्रिशिरोधराणि
वृश्चन्नजस्रं प्रधने विराजसे ॥ ८ ॥

yadā visṛṣṭas tvam anañjanena vai
balaṁ praviṣṭo 'jita daitya-dānavam
bāhūdarorv-aṅghri-śirodharāṇi
vṛścann ajasraṁ pradhane virājase

yadā—when; *visṛṣṭaḥ*—sent; *tvam*—your good self; *anañjanena*—by the transcendental Supreme Personality of Godhead; *vai*—indeed; *balam*—the soldiers; *praviṣṭaḥ*—entering among; *ajita*—O indefatigable and unconquerable one; *daitya-dānavam*—of the Daityas and Dānavas, the demons; *bāhu*—arms; *udara*—bellies; *ūru*—thighs; *aṅghri*—legs; *śiraḥ-dharāṇi*—necks; *vṛścan*—separating; *ajasram*—incessantly; *pradhane*—in the battlefield; *virājase*—you stay.

TRANSLATION

O indefatigable one, when you are sent by the Supreme Personality of Godhead to enter among the soldiers of the Daityas and the Dānavas, you stay on the battlefield and unendingly separate their arms, bellies, thighs, legs and heads.

TEXT 9

स त्वं जगत्त्राण खलप्रहाणये
निरूपितः सर्वसहो गदाभृता ।
विप्रस्य चास्मत्कुलदैवहेतवे
विधेहि भद्रं तदनुग्रहो हि नः ॥ ९ ॥

sa tvaṁ jagat-trāṇa khala-prahāṇaye
nirūpitaḥ sarva-saho gadā-bhṛtā
viprasya cāsmat-kula-daiva-hetave
vidhehi bhadraṁ tad anugraho hi naḥ

saḥ—that person; *tvam*—your good self; *jagat-trāṇa*—O protector of the whole universe; *khala-prahāṇaye*—in killing the envious enemies; *nirūpitaḥ*—are engaged; *sarva-sahaḥ*—all-powerful; *gadā-bhṛtā*—by the Supreme Personality of Godhead; *viprasya*—of this *brāhmaṇa; ca*—also; *asmat*—our; *kula-daiva-hetave*—for the good fortune of the dynasty; *vidhehi*—kindly do; *bhadram*—all-good; *tat*—that; *anugrahaḥ*—favor; *hi*—indeed; *naḥ*—our.

TRANSLATION

O protector of the universe, you are engaged by the Supreme Personality of Godhead as His all-powerful weapon in killing the envious enemies. For the benefit of our entire dynasty, kindly favor this poor brāhmaṇa. This will certainly be a favor for all of us.

TEXT 10

यद्यस्ति दत्तमिष्टं वा स्वधर्मो वा स्वनुष्ठितः ।
कुलं नो विप्रदैवं चेद् द्विजो भवतु विज्वरः ॥१०॥

yady asti dattam iṣṭaṁ vā
sva-dharmo vā svanuṣṭhitaḥ
kulaṁ no vipra-daivaṁ ced
dvijo bhavatu vijvaraḥ

yadi—if; *asti*—there is; *dattam*—charity; *iṣṭam*—worshiping the Deity; *vā*—either; *sva-dharmaḥ*—occupational duty; *vā*—either; *su-anuṣṭhitaḥ*—perfectly performed; *kulam*—dynasty; *naḥ*—our; *vipra-daivam*—favored by the *brāhmaṇas; cet*—if so; *dvijaḥ*—this *brāhmaṇa; bhavatu*—may become; *vijvaraḥ*—without a burning (from the Sudarśana *cakra*).

TRANSLATION

If our family has given charity to the proper persons, if we have performed ritualistic ceremonies and sacrifices, if we have properly carried out our occupational duties, and if we have been guided by learned brāhmaṇas, I wish, in exchange, that this brāhmaṇa be freed from the burning caused by the Sudarśana cakra.

TEXT 11

यदि नो भगवान् प्रीत एकः सर्वगुणाश्रयः ।
सर्वभूतात्मभावेन द्विजो भवतु विज्वरः ॥११॥

yadi no bhagavān prīta
ekaḥ sarva-guṇāśrayaḥ
sarva-bhūtātma-bhāvena
dvijo bhavatu vijvaraḥ

yadi—if; *naḥ*—unto us; *bhagavān*—the Supreme Personality of Godhead; *prītaḥ*—is satisfied; *ekaḥ*—without any duplicate; *sarva-guṇa-āśrayaḥ*—the reservoir of all transcendental qualities; *sarva-bhūta-ātma-bhāvena*—by a merciful attitude toward all living entities; *dvijaḥ*—this *brāhmaṇa; bhavatu*—may become; *vijvaraḥ*—freed from all burning.

TRANSLATION

If the Supreme Personality of Godhead, who is one without a second, who is the reservoir of all transcendental qualities, and who is the life and soul of all living entities, is pleased with us, we wish that this brāhmaṇa, Durvāsā Muni, be freed from the pain of being burned.

TEXT 12

श्रीशुक उवाच
इति संस्तुवतो राज्ञो विष्णुचक्रं सुदर्शनम् ।
अशाम्यत् सर्वतो विप्रं प्रदहद् राजयाच्ञया ॥१२॥

śrī-śuka uvāca
iti saṁstuvato rājño
viṣṇu-cakraṁ sudarśanam
aśāmyat sarvato vipraṁ
pradahad rāja-yācñayā

śrī-śukaḥ uvāca—Śrī Śukadeva Gosvāmī said; *iti*—thus; *saṁstuvataḥ*—being prayed to; *rājñaḥ*—by the King; *viṣṇu-cakram*—the disc weapon of Lord Viṣṇu; *sudarśanam*—of the name Sudarśana *cakra; aśāmyat*—became no longer disturbing; *sarvataḥ*—in every respect; *vipram*—unto the *brāhmaṇa; pradahat*—causing to burn; *rāja*—of the King; *yācñayā*—by the begging.

TRANSLATION

Śukadeva Gosvāmī continued: When the King offered prayers to the Sudarśana cakra and Lord Viṣṇu, because of his prayers the Sudarśana cakra became peaceful and stopped burning the brāhmaṇa known as Durvāsā Muni.

TEXT 13

स मुक्तोऽस्त्राग्नितापेन दुर्वासाः स्वस्तिमांस्ततः ।
प्रशशंस तमुर्वीशं युञ्जानः परमाशिषः ॥१३॥

sa mukto 'strāgni-tāpena
durvāsāḥ svastimāṁs tataḥ
praśaśaṁsa tam urvīśaṁ
yuñjānaḥ paramāśiṣaḥ

saḥ—he, Durvāsā Muni; *muktaḥ*—being freed; *astra-agni-tāpena*—from the heat of the fire of the Sudarśana *cakra; durvāsāḥ*—the great mystic Durvāsā; *svastimān*—fully satisfied, relieved of the burning; *tataḥ*—then; *praśaśaṁsa*—offered praise; *tam*—unto him; *urvī-īśam*—the King; *yuñjānaḥ*—performing; *parama-āśiṣaḥ*—the highest benedictions.

TRANSLATION

Durvāsā Muni, the greatly powerful mystic, was indeed satisfied when freed from the fire of the Sudarśana cakra. Thus he praised the qualities of Mahārāja Ambarīṣa and offered him the highest benedictions.

TEXT 14

दुर्वासा उवाच
अहो अनन्तदासानां महत्त्वं दृष्टमद्य मे ।
कृतागसोऽपि यद् राजन् मङ्गलानि समीहसे ॥१४॥

durvāsā uvāca
aho ananta-dāsānāṁ
mahattvaṁ dṛṣṭam adya me
kṛtāgaso 'pi yad rājan
maṅgalāni samīhase

durvāsāḥ uvāca—Durvāsā Muni said; *aho*—alas; *ananta-dāsānām*—of the servants of the Supreme Personality of Godhead; *mahattvam*—greatness; *dṛṣṭam*—seen; *adya*—today; *me*—by me; *kṛta-āgasaḥ api*—although I was an offender; *yat*—still; *rājan*—O King; *maṅgalāni*—good fortune; *samīhase*—you are praying for.

TRANSLATION

Durvāsā Muni said: My dear King, today I have experienced the greatness of devotees of the Supreme Personality of Godhead, for

although I have committed an offense, you have prayed for my good fortune.

TEXT 15

दुष्करः को नु साधूनां दुस्त्यजो वा महात्मनाम् ।
यैः संगृहीतो भगवान् सात्वतामृषभो हरिः ॥१५॥

duṣkaraḥ ko nu sādhūnāṁ
dustyajo vā mahātmanām
yaiḥ saṅgṛhīto bhagavān
sātvatām ṛṣabho hariḥ

duṣkaraḥ—difficult to do; *kaḥ*—what; *nu*—indeed; *sādhūnām*—of the devotees; *dustyajaḥ*—impossible to give up; *vā*—either; *mahā-ātmanām*—of the great persons; *yaiḥ*—by which persons; *saṅgṛhītaḥ*—achieved (by devotional service); *bhagavān*—the Supreme Personality of Godhead; *sātvatām*—of the pure devotees; *ṛṣabhaḥ*—the leader; *hariḥ*—the Lord.

TRANSLATION

For those who have achieved the Supreme Personality of Godhead, the master of the pure devotees, what is impossible to do, and what is impossible to give up?

TEXT 16

यन्नामश्रुतिमात्रेण पुमान् भवति निर्मलः ।
तस्य तीर्थपदः किं वा दासानामवशिष्यते ॥१६॥

yan-nāma-śruti-mātreṇa
pumān bhavati nirmalaḥ
tasya tīrtha-padaḥ kiṁ vā
dāsānām avaśiṣyate

yat-nāma—the holy name of the Lord; *śruti-mātreṇa*—simply by hearing; *pumān*—a person; *bhavati*—becomes; *nirmalaḥ*—purified; *tasya*—of Him; *tīrtha-padaḥ*—the Lord, at whose feet are the holy places; *kim vā*—what; *dāsānām*—by the servants; *avaśiṣyate*—remains to be done.

TRANSLATION

What is impossible for the servants of the Lord? By the very hearing of His holy name one is purified.

TEXT 17

राजन्ननुगृहीतोऽहं त्वयातिकरुणात्मना ।
मदघं पृष्ठतः कृत्वा प्राणा यन्मेऽभिरक्षिताः ॥१७॥

rājann anugṛhīto 'haṁ
tvayātikaruṇātmanā
mad-aghaṁ pṛṣṭhataḥ kṛtvā
prāṇā yan me 'bhirakṣitāḥ

rājan—O King; *anugṛhītaḥ*—very much favored; *aham*—I (am); *tvayā*—by you; *ati-karuṇa-ātmanā*—because of your being extremely merciful; *mat-agham*—my offenses; *pṛṣṭhataḥ*—to the back; *kṛtvā*—doing so; *prāṇāḥ*—life; *yat*—that; *me*—my; *abhirakṣitāḥ*—saved.

TRANSLATION

O King, overlooking my offenses, you have saved my life. Thus I am very much obliged to you because you are so merciful.

TEXT 18

राजा तमकृताहारः प्रत्यागमनकाङ्क्षया ।
चरणावुपसंगृह्य प्रसाद्य समभोजयत् ॥१८॥

rājā tam akṛtāhāraḥ
pratyāgamana-kāṅkṣayā
caraṇāv upasaṅgṛhya
prasādya samabhojayat

rājā—the King; *tam*—unto him, Durvāsā Muni; *akṛta-āhāraḥ*—who refrained from taking food; *pratyāgamana*—returning; *kāṅkṣayā*—

desiring; *caraṇau*—the feet; *upasaṅgṛhya*—approaching; *prasādya*—pleasing in all respects; *samabhojayat*—fed sumptuously.

TRANSLATION

Expecting the return of Durvāsā Muni, the King had not taken his food. Therefore, when the sage returned, the King fell at his lotus feet, pleasing him in all respects, and fed him sumptuously.

TEXT 19

सोऽशित्वादृतमानीतमातिथ्यं सार्वकामिकम् ।
तृप्तात्मा नृपतिं प्राह भुज्यतामिति सादरम् ॥१९॥

so 'śitvādṛtam ānītam
ātithyaṁ sārva-kāmikam
tṛptātmā nṛpatiṁ prāha
bhujyatām iti sādaram

saḥ—he (Durvāsā); *aśitvā*—after eating sumptuously; *ādṛtam*—with great respect; *ānītam*—received; *ātithyam*—offered different varieties of food; *sārva-kāmikam*—fulfilling all kinds of tastes; *tṛpta-ātmā*—thus being fully satisfied; *nṛpatim*—unto the King; *prāha*—said; *bhujyatām*—my dear King, you eat also; *iti*—in this way; *sa-ādaram*—with great respect.

TRANSLATION

Thus the King respectfully received Durvāsā Muni, who after eating varieties of palatable food was so satisfied that with great affection he requested the King to eat also, saying, "Please take your meal."

TEXT 20

प्रीतोऽस्म्यनुगृहीतोऽस्मि तव भागवतस्य वै ।
दर्शनस्पर्शनालापैरातिथ्येनात्ममेधसा ॥२०॥

prīto 'smy anugṛhīto 'smi
tava bhāgavatasya vai

darśana-sparśanālāpair
ātithyenātma-medhasā

prītaḥ—very much satisfied; *asmi*—I am; *anugṛhītaḥ*—very much favored; *asmi*—I am; *tava*—your; *bhāgavatasya*—because of your being a pure devotee; *vai*—indeed; *darśana*—by seeing you; *sparśana*—and touching your feet; *ālāpaiḥ*—by talking with you; *ātithyena*—by your hospitality; *ātma-medhasā*—by my own intelligence.

TRANSLATION

Durvāsā Muni said: I am very pleased with you, my dear King. At first I thought of you as an ordinary human being and accepted your hospitality, but later I could understand, by my own intelligence, that you are the most exalted devotee of the Lord. Therefore, simply by seeing you, touching your feet and talking with you, I have been pleased and have become obliged to you.

PURPORT

It is said, *vaiṣṇavera kriyā mudrā vijñeha nā bujhaya:* even a very intelligent man cannot understand the activities of a pure Vaiṣṇava. Therefore, because Durvāsā Muni was a great mystic *yogī,* he first mistook Mahārāja Ambarīṣa for an ordinary human being and wanted to punish him. Such is the mistaken observation of a Vaiṣṇava. When Durvāsā Muni was persecuted by the Sudarśana *cakra,* however, his intelligence developed. Therefore the word *ātma-medhasā* is used to indicate that by his personal experience he would understand how great a Vaiṣṇava the King was. When Durvāsā Muni was chased by the Sudarśana *cakra,* he wanted to take shelter of Lord Brahmā and Lord Śiva, and he was even able to go to the spiritual world, meet the Personality of Godhead and talk with Him face to face, yet he was unable to be rescued from the attack of the Sudarśana *cakra.* Thus he could understand the influence of a Vaiṣṇava by personal experience. Durvāsā Muni was certainly a great *yogī* and a very learned *brāhmaṇa,* but despite his being a real *yogī* he was unable to understand the influence of a Vaiṣṇava. Therefore it is said, *vaiṣṇavera kriyā mudrā vijñeha nā bujhaya:* even the most learned person cannot understand the value of a

Vaiṣṇava. There is always a possibility for so-called *jñānīs* and *yogīs* to be mistaken when studying the character of a Vaiṣṇava. A Vaiṣṇava can be understood by how much he is favored by the Supreme Personality of Godhead in terms of his inconceivable activities.

TEXT 21

कर्मावदातमेतत् ते गायन्ति स्वःस्त्रियो मुहुः ।
कीर्तिं परमपुण्यां च कीर्तयिष्यति भूरियम् ॥२१॥

karmāvadātam etat te
gāyanti svaḥ-striyo muhuḥ
kīrtiṁ parama-puṇyāṁ ca
kīrtayiṣyati bhūr iyam

karma—activity; *avadātam*—without any tinge; *etat*—all this; *te*—your; *gāyanti*—will sing; *svaḥ-striyaḥ*—women from the heavenly planets; *muhuḥ*—always; *kīrtim*—glories; *parama-puṇyām*—highly glorified and pious; *ca*—also; *kīrtayiṣyati*—will continuously chant; *bhūḥ*—the whole world; *iyam*—this.

TRANSLATION

All the blessed women in the heavenly planets will continuously chant about your spotless character at every moment, and the people of this world will also chant your glories continuously.

TEXT 22

श्रीशुक उवाच
एवं संकीर्त्य राजानं दुर्वासाः परितोषितः ।
ययौ विहायसामन्त्र्य ब्रह्मलोकमहैतुकम् ॥२२॥

śrī-śuka uvāca
evaṁ saṅkīrtya rājānaṁ
durvāsāḥ paritoṣitaḥ
yayau vihāyasāmantrya
brahmalokam ahaitukam

śrī-śukaḥ uvāca—Śrī Śukadeva Gosvāmī said; *evam*—thus; *saṅkīrtya*—glorifying; *rājānam*—the King; *durvāsāḥ*—the great mystic *yogī* Durvāsā Muni; *paritoṣitaḥ*—being satisfied in all respects; *yayau*—left that place; *vihāyasā*—by the spaceways; *āmantrya*—taking permission; *brahmalokam*—to the topmost planet of this universe; *ahaitukam*—where there is no dry philosophical speculation.

TRANSLATION

Śrī Śukadeva Gosvāmī continued: Thus being satisfied in all respects, the great mystic yogī Durvāsā took permission and left, continuously glorifying the King. Through the skyways, he went to Brahmaloka, which is devoid of agnostics and dry philosophical speculators.

PURPORT

Although Durvāsā Muni went back to Brahmaloka through the spaceways, he did not need an airplane, for great mystic *yogīs* can transport themselves from any planet to any other without any machine. There is a planet named Siddhaloka whose inhabitants can go to any other planet because they naturally have all the perfection of *yoga* practice. Thus Durvāsā Muni, the great mystic *yogī*, could go through the skyways to any planet, even to Brahmaloka. In Brahmaloka, everyone is self-realized, and thus there is no need of philosophical speculation to come to the conclusion of the Absolute Truth. Durvāsā Muni's purpose in going to Brahmaloka was apparently to speak to the residents of Brahmaloka about how powerful a devotee is and how a devotee can surpass every living entity within this material world. The so-called *jñānīs* and *yogīs* cannot compare to a devotee.

TEXT 23

संवत्सरोऽत्यगात् तावद् यावता नागतो गतः ।
मुनिस्तद्दर्शनाकाङ्क्षो राजाब्भक्षो बभूव ह ॥२३॥

saṁvatsaro 'tyagāt tāvad
yāvatā nāgato gataḥ
munis tad-darśanākāṅkṣo
rājāb-bhakṣo babhūva ha

saṁvatsaraḥ—one complete year; *atyagāt*—passed; *tāvat*—as long as; *yāvatā*—so long; *na*—not; *āgataḥ*—returned; *gataḥ*—Durvāsā Muni, who had left that place; *muniḥ*—the great sage; *tat-darśana-ākāṅkṣaḥ*—desiring to see him again; *rājā*—the King; *ap-bhakṣaḥ*—taking only water; *babhūva*—remained; *ha*—indeed.

TRANSLATION

Durvāsā Muni had left the place of Mahārāja Ambarīṣa, and as long as he had not returned—for one complete year—the King had fasted, maintaining himself simply by drinking water.

TEXT 24

गतेऽथ दुर्वाससि सोऽम्बरीषो
द्विजोपयोगातिपवित्रमाहरत् ।
ऋषेर्विमोक्षं व्यसनं च वीक्ष्य
मेने स्ववीर्यं च परानुभावम् ॥२४॥

gate 'tha durvāsasi so 'mbarīṣo
dvijopayogātipavitram āharat
ṛṣer vimokṣaṁ vyasanaṁ ca vīkṣya
mene sva-vīryaṁ ca parānubhāvam

gate—on his return; *atha*—then; *durvāsasi*—the great mystic *yogī* Durvāsā; *saḥ*—he, the King; *ambarīṣaḥ*—Mahārāja Ambarīṣa; *dvija-upayoga*—most suitable for a pure *brāhmaṇa; ati-pavitram*—very pure food; *āharat*—gave him to eat and he also ate; *ṛṣeḥ*—of the great sage; *vimokṣam*—release; *vyasanam*—from the great danger of being burned by the Sudarśana *cakra; ca*—and; *vīkṣya*—seeing; *mene*—considered; *sva-vīryam*—about his own power; *ca*—also; *para-anubhāvam*—because of his pure devotion to the Supreme Lord.

TRANSLATION

After one year, when Durvāsā Muni had returned, King Ambarīṣa sumptuously fed him all varieties of pure food, and then he himself also ate. When the King saw that the brāhmaṇa Durvāsā

had been released from the great danger of being burned, he could understand that by the grace of the Lord he himself was also powerful, but he did not take any credit, for everything had been done by the Lord.

PURPORT

A devotee like Mahārāja Ambarīṣa is certainly always busy in many activities. Of course, this material world is full of dangers that one has to meet, but a devotee, because of his full dependence on the Supreme Personality of Godhead, is never disturbed. The vivid example is Mahārāja Ambarīṣa. He was the emperor of the entire world and had many duties to perform, and in the course of these duties there were many disturbances created by persons like Durvāsā Muni, but the King tolerated everything, patiently depending fully on the mercy of the Lord. The Lord, however, is situated in everyone's heart (*sarvasya cāhaṁ hṛdi sanniviṣṭaḥ*), and He manages things as He desires. Thus although Mahārāja Ambarīṣa was faced with many disturbances, the Lord, being merciful to him, managed things so nicely that in the end Durvāsā Muni and Mahārāja Ambarīṣa became great friends and parted cordially on the basis of *bhakti-yoga.* After all, Durvāsā Muni was convinced of the power of *bhakti-yoga,* although he himself was a great mystic *yogī.* Therefore, as stated by Lord Kṛṣṇa in *Bhagavad-gītā* (6.47):

yoginām api sarveṣāṁ
mad-gatenāntarātmanā
śraddhāvān bhajate yo māṁ
sa me yuktatamo mataḥ

"Of all *yogīs,* he who always abides in Me with great faith, worshiping Me in transcendental loving service, is most intimately united with Me in *yoga* and is the highest of all." Thus it is a fact that a devotee is the topmost *yogī,* as proved in the dealings of Mahārāja Ambarīṣa with Durvāsā Muni.

TEXT 25

एवं विधानेकगुणः स राजा
परात्मनि ब्रह्मणि वासुदेवे ।

क्रियाकलापैः समुवाह भक्तिं
ययाविरिञ्च्यान् निरयांश्चकार ॥२५॥

evaṁ vidhāneka-guṇaḥ sa rājā
parātmani brahmaṇi vāsudeve
kriyā-kalāpaiḥ samuvāha bhaktiṁ
yayāviriñcyān nirayāṁś cakāra

evam—in this way; *vidhā-aneka-guṇaḥ*—endowed with varieties of good qualities; *saḥ*—he, Mahārāja Ambarīṣa; *rājā*—the King; *para-ātmani*—unto the Supersoul; *brahmaṇi*—unto Brahman; *vāsudeve*—unto the Supreme Personality of Godhead, Kṛṣṇa, Vāsudeva; *kriyā-kalāpaiḥ*—by practical activities; *samuvāha*—executed; *bhaktim*—devotional service; *yayā*—by such activities; *āviriñcyān*—beginning from the topmost planet; *nirayān*—down to the hellish planets; *cakāra*—he experienced that there is danger everywhere.

TRANSLATION

In this way, because of devotional service, Mahārāja Ambarīṣa, who was endowed with varieties of transcendental qualities, was completely aware of Brahman, Paramātmā and the Supreme Personality of Godhead, and thus he executed devotional service perfectly. Because of his devotion, he thought even the topmost planet of this material world no better than the hellish planets.

PURPORT

An exalted and pure devotee like Mahārāja Ambarīṣa is in full awareness of Brahman, Paramātmā and Bhagavān; in other words, a devotee of Vāsudeva, Kṛṣṇa, is in full knowledge of the other features of the Absolute Truth. The Absolute Truth is realized in three features—Brahman, Paramātmā and Bhagavān (*brahmeti paramātmeti bhagavān iti śabdyate*). A devotee of the Supreme Personality of Godhead, Vāsudeva, knows everything (*vāsudevaḥ sarvam iti*) because Vāsudeva, Kṛṣṇa, includes both Paramātmā and Brahman. One does not have to realize Paramātmā by the *yoga* system, for the devotee always thinking of Vāsudeva is the topmost *yogī* (*yoginām api sarveṣām*). And as far as *jñāna* is concerned, if one is a perfect devotee of Vāsudeva, he is the greatest *mahātmā* (*vāsudevaḥ sarvam iti sa mahātmā sudurlabhaḥ*). A *mahātmā* is one who has full knowledge of the Absolute Truth. Thus Mahārāja Ambarīṣa, being a devotee of the Personality of Godhead, was in full awareness of Paramātmā, Brahman, *māyā*, the material world, the spiritual world, and how things are going on everywhere. Everything was known to him. *Yasmin vijñāte sarvam evaṁ vijñātaṁ bhavati.* Because the devotee knows Vāsudeva, he knows everything within the creation of Vāsudeva (*vāsudevaḥ sarvam iti sa mahātmā sudurlabhaḥ*). Such a devotee does not give much value to the highest standard of happiness within this material world.

nārāyaṇa-parāḥ sarve
na kutaścana bibhyati
svargāpavarga-narakeṣv
api tulyārtha-darśinaḥ
(*Bhāg.* 6.17.28)

Because he is fixed in devotional service, a devotee does not regard any position in the material world as important. Śrīla Prabodhānanda Sarasvatī has therefore written (*Caitanya-candrāmṛta* 5):

kaivalyaṁ narakāyate tridaśa-pūr ākāśa-puṣpāyate
durdāntendriya-kāla-sarpa-paṭalī protkhāta-daṁṣṭrāyate
viśvaṁ pūrṇa-sukhāyate vidhi-mahendrādiś ca kīṭāyate
yat-kāruṇya-kaṭākṣa-vaibhava-vatāṁ taṁ gauram eva stumaḥ

For one who becomes a pure devotee through devotional service to great personalities like Caitanya Mahāprabhu, *kaivalya*, or merging into Brahman, appears no better than hell. As far as the heavenly planets are concerned, to a devotee they are like a phantasmagoria or will-o'-the-wisp, and as far as yogic perfection is concerned, a devotee does not care a fig for such perfection, since the purpose of yogic perfection is achieved automatically by the devotee. This is all possible when one becomes a devotee of the Lord through the medium of Caitanya Mahāprabhu's instructions.

TEXT 26

श्रीशुक उवाच

अथाम्बरीषस्तनयेषु राज्यं
समानशीलेषु विसृज्य धीरः ।
वनं विवेशात्मनि वासुदेवे
मनो दधद् ध्वस्तगुणप्रवाहः ॥२६॥

śrī-śuka uvāca
athāmbarīṣas tanayeṣu rājyaṁ
samāna-śīleṣu visṛjya dhīraḥ
vanaṁ viveśātmani vāsudeve
mano dadhad dhvasta-guṇa-pravāhaḥ

śrī-śukaḥ uvāca—Śrī Śukadeva Gosvāmī said; *atha*—in this way; *ambarīṣaḥ*—King Ambarīṣa; *tanayeṣu*—unto his sons; *rājyam*—the kingdom; *samāna-śīleṣu*—who were equally as qualified as their father; *visṛjya*—dividing; *dhīraḥ*—the most learned person, Mahārāja Ambarīṣa; *vanam*—into the forest; *viveśa*—entered; *ātmani*—unto the Supreme Lord; *vāsudeve*—Lord Kṛṣṇa, who is known as Vāsudeva; *manaḥ*—mind; *dadhat*—concentrating; *dhvasta*—vanquished; *guṇa-pravāhaḥ*—the waves of the material modes of nature.

TRANSLATION

Śrīla Śukadeva Gosvāmī continued: Thereafter, because of his advanced position in devotional life, Mahārāja Ambarīṣa, who no longer desired to live with material things, retired from active family life. He divided his property among his sons, who were equally as qualified, and he himself took the order of vānaprastha and went to the forest to concentrate his mind fully upon Lord Vāsudeva.

PURPORT

As a pure devotee, Mahārāja Ambarīṣa was liberated in any condition of life because, as enunciated by Śrīla Rūpa Gosvāmī, a devotee is always liberated.

īhā yasya harer dāsye
karmaṇā manasā girā
nikhilāsv apy avasthāsu
jīvan-muktaḥ sa ucyate

In *Bhakti-rasāmṛta-sindhu*, Śrīla Rūpa Gosvāmī thus instructs that if one's only desire is service to the Lord, he is liberated in any condition of life. Mahārāja Ambarīṣa was undoubtedly liberated in any condition, but as an ideal king he accepted the *vānaprastha* order of retirement from family life. It is essential for one to renounce family responsibilities and fully concentrate on the lotus feet of Vāsudeva. Therefore Mahārāja Ambarīṣa divided the kingdom among his sons and retired from family life.

TEXT 27

इत्येतत् पुण्यमाख्यानमम्बरीषस्य भूपतेः ।
संकीर्तयन्ननुध्यायन् भक्तो भगवतो भवेत् ॥२७॥

ity etat puṇyam ākhyānam
ambarīṣasya bhūpate
saṅkīrtayann anudhyāyan
bhakto bhagavato bhavet

iti—thus; *etat*—this; *puṇyam ākhyānam*—most pious activity in history; *ambarīṣasya*—of Mahārāja Ambarīṣa; *bhūpate*—O King (Mahārāja Parīkṣit); *saṅkīrtayan*—by chanting, repeating; *anudhyāyan*—or by meditating upon; *bhaktaḥ*—a devotee; *bhagavataḥ*—of the Supreme Personality of Godhead; *bhavet*—one can become.

TRANSLATION

Anyone who chants this narration or even thinks of this narration about the activities of Mahārāja Ambarīṣa certainly becomes a pure devotee of the Lord.

PURPORT

Śrīla Viśvanātha Cakravartī Ṭhākura herein gives a very good example. When one is very eager for more and more money, he is not satisfied even when he is a millionaire or a multimillionaire, but wants to earn more and more money by any means. The same mentality is present in a devotee. The devotee is never satisfied, thinking, "This is the limit of my devotional service." The more he engages in the service of the Lord, the more service he wants to give. This is the position of a devotee. Mahārāja Ambarīṣa, in his family life, was certainly a pure devotee, complete in every respect, because his mind and all his senses were engaged in devotional service (*sa vai manaḥ kṛṣṇa-padāravindayor vacāṁsi vaikuṇṭha-guṇānuvarṇane*). Mahārāja Ambarīṣa was self-satisfied because all of his senses were engaged in devotional service (*sarvopādhi-vinirmuktaṁ tat-paratvena nirmalam/ hṛṣīkeṇa hṛṣīkeśa-sevanaṁ bhaktir ucyate*). Nonetheless, although Mahārāja Ambarīṣa had engaged all his senses in devotional service, he left his home and went to the forest to concentrate his mind fully at the lotus feet of Kṛṣṇa, exactly as a mercantile man, even though complete in wealth, tries to earn more and more. This mentality of getting more and more engaged in devotional service puts one in the most exalted position. Whereas on the *karma* platform the mercantile man who wants more and more money becomes increasingly bound and entangled, the devotee becomes increasingly liberated.

TEXT 28

अम्बरीषस्यचरितं येशृण्वन्तिमहात्मनः ।
मुक्तिं प्रयान्तितेसर्वेभक्त्याविष्णोः प्रसादतः ॥२८॥

ambarīṣasya caritaṁ
ye śṛṇvanti mahātmanaḥ
muktiṁ prayānti te sarve
bhaktyā viṣṇoḥ prasādataḥ

ambarīṣasya—of Mahārāja Ambarīṣa; *caritam*—character; *ye*—persons who; *śṛṇvanti*—hear; *mahā-ātmanaḥ*—of the great personality, the great devotee; *muktim*—liberation; *prayānti*—certainly they attain; *te*—such persons; *sarve*—all of them; *bhaktyā*—simply by devotional service; *viṣṇoḥ*—of Lord Viṣṇu; *prasādataḥ*—by the mercy.

TRANSLATION

By the grace of the Lord, those who hear about the activities of Mahārāja Ambarīṣa, the great devotee, certainly become liberated or become devotees without delay.

Thus end the Bhaktivedanta purports of the Ninth Canto, Fifth Chapter, of the Śrīmad-Bhāgavatam, *entitled "Durvāsā Muni's Life Spared."*

CHAPTER SIX

The Downfall of Saubhari Muni

After describing the descendants of Mahārāja Ambarīṣa, Śukadeva Gosvāmī described all the kings from Śaśāda to Māndhātā, and in this connection he also described how the great sage Saubhari married the daughters of Māndhātā.

Mahārāja Ambarīṣa had three sons, named Virūpa, Ketumān and Śambhu. The son of Virūpa was Pṛṣadaśva, and his son was Rathītara. Rathītara had no sons, but when he requested the favor of the great sage Aṅgirā, the sage begot several sons in the womb of Rathītara's wife. When the sons were born, they became the dynasty of Aṅgirā Ṛṣi and of Rathītara.

The son of Manu was Ikṣvāku, who had one hundred sons, of whom Vikukṣi, Nimi and Daṇḍakā were the eldest. The sons of Mahārāja Ikṣvāku became kings of different parts of the world. Because of violating sacrificial rules and regulations, one of these sons, Vikukṣi, was banished from the kingdom. By the mercy of Vasiṣṭha and the power of mystic *yoga*, Mahārāja Ikṣvāku attained liberation after giving up his material body. When Mahārāja Ikṣvāku expired, his son Vikukṣi returned and took charge of the kingdom. He performed various types of sacrifices, and thus he pleased the Supreme Personality of Godhead. This Vikukṣi later became celebrated as Śaśāda.

Vikukṣi's son fought with the demons for the sake of the demigods, and because of his valuable service he became famous as Purañjaya, Indravāha and Kakutstha. The son of Purañjaya was Anenā, the son of Anenā was Pṛthu, and the son of Pṛthu was Viśvagandhi. The son of Viśvagandhi was Candra, the son of Candra was Yuvanāśva, and his son was Śrāvasta, who constructed Śrāvastī Purī. The son of Śrāvasta was Bṛhadaśva. Bṛhadaśva's son Kuvalayāśva killed a demon named Dhundhu, and thus he became celebrated as Dhundhumāra, "the killer of Dhundhu." The sons of the killer of Dhundhu were Dṛḍhāśva, Kapilāśva and Bhadrāśva. He also had thousands of other sons, but they burned to ashes in the fire emanating from Dhundhu. The son of

Dṛḍhāśva was Haryaśva, the son of Haryaśva was Nikumbha, the son of Nikumbha was Bahulāśva, and the son of Bahulāśva was Kṛśāśva. The son of Kṛśāśva was Senajit, and his son was Yuvanāśva.

Yuvanāśva married one hundred wives, but he had no sons, and therefore he entered the forest. In the forest, the sages performed a sacrifice known as Indra-yajña on his behalf. Once, however, the King became so thirsty in the forest that he drank the water kept for performing *yajña.* Consequently, after some time, a son came forth from the right side of his abdomen. The son, who was very beautiful, was crying to drink breast milk, and Indra gave the child his index finger to suck. Thus the son became known as Māndhātā. In due course of time, Yuvanāśva achieved perfection by performing austerities.

Thereafter, Māndhātā became the emperor and ruled the earth, which consists of seven islands. Thieves and rogues were very much afraid of this powerful king, and therefore the king was known as Trasaddasyu, meaning "one who is very fearful to rogues and thieves." Māndhātā begot sons in the womb of his wife, Bindumatī. These sons were Purukutsa, Ambarīṣa and Mucukunda. These three sons had fifty sisters, all of whom became wives of the great sage known as Saubhari.

In this connection, Śukadeva Gosvāmī described the history of Saubhari Muni, who, because of sensual agitation caused by fish, fell from his *yoga* and wanted to marry all the daughters of Māndhātā for sexual pleasure. Later, Saubhari Muni became very regretful. Thus he accepted the order of *vānaprastha,* performed very severe austerities, and thus attained perfection. In this regard, Śukadeva Gosvāmī described how Saubhari Muni's wives also became perfect.

TEXT 1

श्रीशुक उवाच

विरूपः केतुमाञ्छम्भुरम्बरीषसुतास्त्रयः ।
विरूपात् पृषदश्वोऽभूत् तत्पुत्रस्तु रथीतरः ॥ १ ॥

śrī-śuka uvāca
virūpaḥ ketumāñ chambhur
ambarīṣa-sutās trayaḥ

virūpāt pṛṣadaśvo 'bhūt
tat-putras tu rathītaraḥ

śrī-śukaḥ uvāca—Śrī Śukadeva Gosvāmī said; *virūpaḥ*—by the name Virūpa; *ketumān*—by the name Ketumān; *śambhuḥ*—by the name Śambhu; *ambarīṣa*—of Ambarīṣa Mahārāja; *sutāḥ trayaḥ*—the three sons; *virūpāt*—from Virūpa; *pṛṣadaśvaḥ*—of the name Pṛṣadaśva; *abhūt*—there was; *tat-putraḥ*—his son; *tu*—and; *rathītaraḥ*—of the name Rathītara.

TRANSLATION

Śukadeva Gosvāmī said: O Mahārāja Parīkṣit, Ambarīṣa had three sons, named Virūpa, Ketumān and Śambhu. From Virūpa came a son named Pṛṣadaśva, and from Pṛṣadaśva came a son named Rathītara.

TEXT 2

रथीतरस्याप्रजस्य भार्यायां तन्तवेऽर्थितः ।
अङ्गिरा जनयामास ब्रह्मवर्चस्विनः सुतान् ॥ २ ॥

rathītarasyāprajasya
bhāryāyāṁ tantave 'rthitaḥ
aṅgirā janayām āsa
brahma-varcasvinaḥ sutān

rathītarasya—of Rathītara; *aprajasya*—who had no sons; *bhāryāyām*—unto his wife; *tantave*—for increasing offspring; *arthitaḥ*—being requested; *aṅgirāḥ*—the great sage Aṅgirā; *janayām āsa*—caused to take birth; *brahma-varcasvinaḥ*—who had brahminical qualities; *sutān*—sons.

TRANSLATION

Rathītara had no sons, and therefore he requested the great sage Aṅgirā to beget sons for him. Because of this request, Aṅgirā begot sons in the womb of Rathītara's wife. All these sons were born with brahminical prowess.

PURPORT

In the Vedic age a man was sometimes called upon to beget sons in the womb of a lesser man's wife for the sake of better progeny. In such an instance, the woman is compared to an agricultural field. A person possessing an agricultural field may employ another person to produce food grains from it, but because the grains are produced from the land, they are considered the property of the owner of the land. Similarly, a woman was sometimes allowed to be impregnated by someone other than her husband, but the sons born of her would then become her husband's sons. Such sons were called *kṣetra-jāta.* Because Rathītara had no sons, he took advantage of this method.

TEXT 3

एते क्षेत्रप्रसूता वै पुनस्त्वाङ्गिरसाः स्मृताः ।
रथीतराणां प्रवराः क्षेत्रोपेता द्विजातयः ॥ ३ ॥

ete kṣetra-prasūtā vai
punas tv āṅgirasāḥ smṛtāḥ
rathītarāṇāṁ pravarāḥ
kṣetropetā dvi-jātayaḥ

ete—the sons begotten by Aṅgirā; *kṣetra-prasūtāḥ*—became the children of Rathītara and belonged to his family (because they were born from the womb of his wife); *vai*—indeed; *punaḥ*—again; *tu*—but; *āṅgirasāḥ*—of the dynasty of Aṅgirā; *smṛtāḥ*—they were called; *rathītarāṇām*—of all the sons of Rathītara; *pravarāḥ*—the chief; *kṣetra-upetāḥ*—because of being born of the *kṣetra* (field); *dvi-jātayaḥ*—called *brāhmaṇa* (being a mixture of *brāhmaṇa* and *kṣatriya*).

TRANSLATION

Having been born from the womb of Rathītara's wife, all these sons were known as the dynasty of Rathītara, but because they were born from the semen of Aṅgirā, they were also known as the dynasty of Aṅgirā. Among all the progeny of Rathītara, these sons were the most prominent because, owing to their birth, they were considered brāhmaṇas.

PURPORT

Śrīla Viśvanātha Cakravartī Ṭhākura gives the meaning of *dvi-jātayaḥ* as "mixed caste," indicating a mixture of *brāhmaṇa* and *kṣatriya.*

TEXT 4

क्षुवतस्तु मनोर्जज्ञे इक्ष्वाकुर्घ्राणतः सुतः ।
तस्य पुत्रशतज्येष्ठा विकुक्षिनिमिदण्डकाः ॥ ४ ॥

kṣuvatas tu manor jajñe
ikṣvākur ghrāṇataḥ sutaḥ
tasya putra-śata-jyeṣṭhā
vikukṣi-nimi-daṇḍakāḥ

kṣuvataḥ—while sneezing; *tu*—but; *manoḥ*—of Manu; *jajñe*—was born; *ikṣvākuḥ*—by the name Ikṣvāku; *ghrāṇataḥ*—from the nostrils; *sutaḥ*—the son; *tasya*—of Ikṣvāku; *putra-śata*—one hundred sons; *jyeṣṭhāḥ*—prominent; *vikukṣi*—of the name Vikukṣi; *nimi*—by the name Nimi; *daṇḍakāḥ*—by the name Daṇḍakā.

TRANSLATION

The son of Manu was Ikṣvāku. When Manu was sneezing, Ikṣvāku was born from Manu's nostrils. King Ikṣvāku had one hundred sons, of whom Vikukṣi, Nimi and Daṇḍakā were the most prominent.

PURPORT

According to Śrīdhara Svāmī, although the *Bhāgavatam* (9.1.11–12) has previously included Ikṣvāku among the ten sons begotten by Manu in his wife Śraddhā, this was a generalization. It is here specifically explained that Ikṣvāku was born simply from the sneezing of Manu.

TEXT 5

तेषां पुरस्ताद्भवन्नार्यावर्ते नृपा नृप ।
पञ्चविंशतिः पश्चाच्च त्रयो मध्येऽपरेऽन्यतः ॥ ५ ॥

teṣāṁ purastād abhavann
āryāvarte nṛpā nṛpa
pañca-viṁśatiḥ paścāc ca
trayo madhye 'pare 'nyataḥ

teṣām—among all of those sons; *purastāt*—on the eastern side; *abhavan*—they became; *āryāvarte*—in the place within the Himalaya and Vindhya mountains known as Āryāvarta; *nṛpāḥ*—kings; *nṛpa*—O King (Mahārāja Parīkṣit); *pañca-viṁśatiḥ*—twenty-five; *paścāt*—on the western side; *ca*—also; *trayaḥ*—three of them; *madhye*—in the middle (between east and west); *apare*—others; *anyataḥ*—in other places.

TRANSLATION

Of the one hundred sons, twenty-five became kings in the western side of Āryāvarta, a place between the Himalaya and Vindhya mountains. Another twenty-five sons became kings in the east of Āryāvarta, and the three principal sons became kings in the middle. The other sons became kings in various other places.

TEXT 6

स एकदाष्टकाश्राद्धे इक्ष्वाकुः सुतमादिशत् ।
मांसमानीयतां मेध्यं विकुक्षे गच्छ मा चिरम् ॥ ६ ॥

sa ekadāṣṭakā-śrāddhe
ikṣvākuḥ sutam ādiśat
māṁsam ānīyatāṁ medhyaṁ
vikukṣe gaccha mā ciram

saḥ—that king (Mahārāja Ikṣvāku); *ekadā*—once upon a time; *aṣṭakā-śrāddhe*—during January, February and March, when offerings are made to the forefathers; *ikṣvākuḥ*—King Ikṣvāku; *sutam*—to his son; *ādiśat*—ordered; *māṁsam*—flesh; *ānīyatām*—bring here; *medhyam*—pure (obtained by hunting); *vikukṣe*—O Vikukṣi; *gaccha*—immediately go; *mā ciram*—without delay.

TRANSLATION

During the months of January, February and March, oblations offered to the forefathers are called aṣṭakā-śrāddha. The śrāddha ceremony is held during the dark fortnight of the month. When Mahārāja Ikṣvāku was performing his oblations in this ceremony, he ordered his son Vikukṣi to go immediately to the forest to bring some pure flesh.

TEXT 7

तथेति स वनं गत्वा मृगान् हत्वा क्रियार्हणान् ।
श्रान्तो बुभुक्षितो वीरः शशं चाददपस्मृतिः ॥ ७ ॥

tatheti sa vanaṁ gatvā
mṛgān hatvā kriyārhaṇān
śrānto bubhukṣito vīraḥ
śaśaṁ cādad apasmṛtiḥ

tathā—according to the direction; *iti*—thus; *saḥ*—Vikukṣi; *vanam*—to the forest; *gatvā*—going; *mṛgān*—animals; *hatvā*—killing; *kriyā-arhaṇān*—suitable for offering to the *yajña* in the *śrāddha* ceremony; *śrāntaḥ*—when he was fatigued; *bubhukṣitaḥ*—and hungry; *vīraḥ*—the hero; *śaśam*—a rabbit; *ca*—also; *ādat*—he ate; *apasmṛtiḥ*—forgetting (that the flesh was meant for offering in the *śrāddha*).

TRANSLATION

Thereafter, Ikṣvāku's son Vikukṣi went to the forest and killed many animals suitable for being offered as oblations. But when fatigued and hungry he became forgetful and ate a rabbit he had killed.

PURPORT

It is evident that *kṣatriyas* killed animals in the forest because the flesh of the animals was suitable to be offered at a particular type of *yajña.* Offering oblations to the forefathers in the ceremony known as *śrāddha* is also a kind of *yajña.* In this *yajña,* flesh obtained from the forest by hunting could be offered. However, in the present age, Kali-yuga, this kind of offering is forbidden. Quoting from the *Brahma-vaivarta Purāṇa*, Śrī Caitanya Mahāprabhu said:

aśvamedhaṁ gavālambhaṁ
sannyāsaṁ pala-paitṛkam
devareṇa sutotpattiṁ
kalau pañca vivarjayet

"In this age of Kali, five acts are forbidden: the offering of a horse in sacrifice, the offering of a cow in sacrifice, the acceptance of the order of *sannyāsa*, the offering of oblations of flesh to the forefathers, and a man's begetting children in his brother's wife." The word *pala-paitṛkam* refers to an offering of flesh in oblations to forefathers. Formerly, such an offering was allowed, but in this age it is forbidden. In this age, Kali-yuga, everyone is expert in hunting animals, but most of the people are *śūdras*, not *kṣatriyas*. According to Vedic injunctions, however, only *kṣatriyas* are allowed to hunt, whereas *śūdras* are allowed to eat flesh after offering goats or other insignificant animals before the deity of goddess Kālī or similar demigods. On the whole, meat-eating is not completely forbidden; a particular class of men is allowed to eat meat according to various circumstances and injunctions. As far as eating beef is concerned, however, it is strictly prohibited to everyone. Thus in *Bhagavad-gītā* Kṛṣṇa personally speaks of *go-rakṣyam*, cow protection. Meat-eaters, according to their different positions and the directions of the *śāstra*, are allowed to eat flesh, but never the flesh of cows. Cows must be given all protection.

TEXT 8

शेषं निवेदयामास पित्रे तेन च तद्गुरुः ।
चोदितः प्रोक्षणायाह दुष्टमेतदकर्मकम् ॥ ८ ॥

śeṣaṁ nivedayām āsa
pitre tena ca tad-guruḥ
coditaḥ prokṣaṇāyāha
duṣṭam etad akarmakam

śeṣam—the remnants; *nivedayām āsa*—he offered; *pitre*—to his father; *tena*—by him; *ca*—also; *tat-guruḥ*—their priest or spiritual master; *coditaḥ*—being requested; *prokṣaṇāya*—for purifying; *āha*—said; *duṣṭam*—polluted; *etat*—all this flesh; *akarmakam*—not fit to be used for offering in *śrāddha.*

TRANSLATION

Vikukṣi offered the remnants of the flesh to King Ikṣvāku, who gave it to Vasiṣṭha for purification. But Vasiṣṭha could immediately understand that part of the flesh had already been taken by Vikukṣi, and therefore he said that it was unfit to be used in the śrāddha ceremony.

PURPORT

That which is meant to be offered in *yajña* cannot be tasted by anyone before being offered to the Deity. In our temples, this regulation is in effect. One cannot eat food from the kitchen unless it is offered to the Deity. If something is taken before being offered to the Deity, the entire preparation is polluted and can no longer be offered. Those engaged in Deity worship must know this very well so that they may be saved from committing offenses in Deity worship.

TEXT 9

ज्ञात्वा पुत्रस्य तत् कर्म गुरुणाभिहितं नृपः ।
देशान्निःसारयामास सुतं त्यक्तविधिं रुषा ॥ ९ ॥

jñātvā putrasya tat karma
guruṇābhihitaṁ nṛpaḥ
deśān niḥsārayām āsa
sutaṁ tyakta-vidhiṁ ruṣā

jñātvā—knowing; *putrasya*—of his son; *tat*—that; *karma*—action; *guruṇā*—by the spiritual master (Vasiṣṭha); *abhihitam*—informed; *nṛpaḥ*—the King (Ikṣvāku); *deśāt*—from the country; *niḥsārayām āsa*—drove away; *sutam*—his son; *tyakta-vidhim*—because he violated the regulative principles; *ruṣā*—out of anger.

TRANSLATION

When King Ikṣvāku, thus informed by Vasiṣṭha, understood what his son Vikukṣi had done, he was extremely angry. Thus he ordered Vikukṣi to leave the country because Vikukṣi had violated the regulative principles.

TEXT 10

स तु विप्रेण संवादं ज्ञापकेन समाचरन् ।
त्यक्त्वा कलेवरं योगी स तेनावाप यत् परम् ॥१०॥

sa tu vipreṇa saṁvādaṁ
jñāpakena samācaran
tyaktvā kalevaraṁ yogī
sa tenāvāpa yat param

saḥ—Mahārāja Ikṣvāku; *tu*—indeed; *vipreṇa*—with the *brāhmaṇa* (Vasiṣṭha); *saṁvādam*—discussion; *jñāpakena*—with the informer; *samācaran*—doing accordingly; *tyaktvā*—giving up; *kalevaram*—this body; *yogī*—being a *bhakti-yogī* in the order of renunciation; *saḥ*—the King; *tena*—by such instruction; *avāpa*—achieved; *yat*—that position which; *param*—supreme.

TRANSLATION

Having been instructed by the great and learned brāhmaṇa Vasiṣṭha, who discoursed about the Absolute Truth, Mahārāja Ikṣvāku became renounced. By following the principles for a yogī, he certainly achieved the supreme perfection after giving up his material body.

TEXT 11

पितर्युपरतेऽभ्येत्य विकुक्षिः पृथिवीमिमाम् ।
शासदीजे हरिं यज्ञैः शशाद इति विश्रुतः ॥११॥

pitary uparate 'bhyetya
vikukṣiḥ pṛthivīm imām

śāsad īje hariṁ yajñaiḥ
śaśāda iti viśrutaḥ

pitari—when his father; *uparate*—upon being relieved of the kingdom; *abhyetya*—having come back; *vikukṣiḥ*—the son named Vikukṣi; *pṛthivīm*—the planet earth; *imām*—this; *śāsat*—ruling; *īje*—worshiped; *harim*—the Supreme Personality of Godhead; *yajñaiḥ*—by performing various sacrifices; *śaśa-adaḥ*—Śaśāda ("the eater of a rabbit"); *iti*—thus; *viśrutaḥ*—celebrated.

TRANSLATION

After his father's disappearance, Vikukṣi returned to the country and thus became the king, ruling the planet earth and performing various sacrifices to satisfy the Supreme Personality of Godhead. Vikukṣi later became celebrated as Śaśāda.

TEXT 12

पुरञ्जयस्तस्य सुत इन्द्रवाह इतीरितः ।
ककुत्स्थ इति चाप्युक्तः शृणु नामानि कर्मभिः ॥१२॥

purañjayas tasya suta
indravāha itīritaḥ
kakutstha iti cāpy uktaḥ
śṛṇu nāmāni karmabhiḥ

puram-jayaḥ—Purañjaya ("the conqueror of the residence"); *tasya*—his (Vikukṣi's); *sutaḥ*—son; *indra-vāhaḥ*—Indravāha ("he whose carrier is Indra"); *iti*—thus; *īritaḥ*—known as such; *kakutsthaḥ*—Kakutstha ("situated on the hump of a bull"); *iti*—thus; *ca*—also; *api*—indeed; *uktaḥ*—known as such; *śṛṇu*—just hear; *nāmāni*—all the names; *karmabhiḥ*—according to one's work.

TRANSLATION

The son of Śaśāda was Purañjaya, who is also known as Indravāha and sometimes as Kakutstha. Please hear from me how he received different names for different activities.

TEXT 13

कृतान्त आसीत् समरो देवानां सह दानवैः ।
पार्ष्णिग्राहो वृतो वीरो देवैर्दैत्यपराजितैः ॥१३॥

kṛtānta āsīt samaro
devānāṁ saha dānavaiḥ
pārṣṇigrāho vṛto vīro
devair daitya-parājitaiḥ

kṛta-antaḥ—a devastating war; *āsīt*—there was; *samaraḥ*—a fight; *devānām*—of the demigods; *saha*—with; *dānavaiḥ*—the demons; *pārṣṇigrāhaḥ*—a very good assistant; *vṛtaḥ*—accepted; *vīraḥ*—a hero; *devaiḥ*—by the demigods; *daitya*—by the demons; *parājitaiḥ*—who had been conquered.

TRANSLATION

Formerly, there was a devastating war between the demigods and the demons. The demigods, having been defeated, accepted Purañjaya as their assistant and then conquered the demons. Therefore this hero is known as Purañjaya, "he who conquered the residence of the demons."

TEXT 14

वचनाद् देवदेवस्य विष्णोर्विश्वात्मनः प्रभोः ।
वाहनत्वे वृतस्तस्य बभूवेन्द्रो महावृषः ॥१४॥

vacanād deva-devasya
viṣṇor viśvātmanaḥ prabhoḥ
vāhanatve vṛtas tasya
babhūvendro mahā-vṛṣaḥ

vacanāt—by the order or the words; *deva-devasya*—of the Supreme Lord of all demigods; *viṣṇoḥ*—Lord Viṣṇu; *viśva-ātmanaḥ*—the Supersoul of the entire creation; *prabhoḥ*—the Lord, the controller; *vāhanatve*—because of becoming the carrier; *vṛtaḥ*—engaged; *tasya*—

in the service of Purañjaya; *babhūva*—he became; *indraḥ*—the King of heaven; *mahā-vṛṣaḥ*—a great bull.

TRANSLATION

Purañjaya agreed to kill all the demons, on the condition that Indra would be his carrier. Because of pride, Indra could not accept this proposal, but later, by the order of the Supreme Lord, Viṣṇu, Indra did accept it and became a great bull carrier for Purañjaya.

TEXTS 15–16

स संनद्धो धनुर्दिव्यमादाय विशिखाञ्छितान् ।
स्तूयमानस्तमारुह्य युयुत्सुः ककुदि स्थितः ॥१५॥
तेजसाप्यायितो विष्णोः पुरुषस्य महात्मनः ।
प्रतीच्यां दिशि दैत्यानां न्यरुणत् त्रिदशैः पुरम् ॥१६॥

sa sannaddho dhanur divyam
ādāya viśikhāñ chitān
stūyamānas tam āruhya
yuyutsuḥ kakudi sthitaḥ

tejasāpyāyito viṣṇoḥ
puruṣasya mahātmanaḥ
pratīcyāṁ diśi daityānāṁ
nyaruṇat tridaśaiḥ puram

saḥ—he, Purañjaya; *sannaddhaḥ*—being well equipped; *dhanuḥ divyam*—a first-class or transcendental bow; *ādāya*—taking; *viśikhān*—arrows; *śitān*—very sharp; *stūyamānaḥ*—being praised very much; *tam*—him (the bull); *āruhya*—getting on; *yuyutsuḥ*—prepared to fight; *kakudi*—on the hump of the bull; *sthitaḥ*—being situated; *tejasā*—by the power; *āpyāyitaḥ*—being favored; *viṣṇoḥ*—of Lord Viṣṇu; *puruṣasya*—the Supreme Person; *mahā-ātmanaḥ*—the Supersoul; *pratīcyām*—on the western; *diśi*—direction; *daityānām*—of the demons; *nyaruṇat*—captured; *tridaśaiḥ*—surrounded by the demigods; *puram*—the residence.

TRANSLATION

Well protected by armor and desiring to fight, Purañjaya took up a transcendental bow and very sharp arrows, and, while being highly praised by the demigods, he got up on the back of the bull [Indra] and sat on its hump. Thus he is known as Kakutstha. Being empowered by Lord Viṣṇu, who is the Supersoul and the Supreme Person, Purañjaya sat on the great bull and is therefore known as Indravāha. Surrounded by the demigods, he attacked the residence of the demons in the west.

TEXT 17

तैस्तस्य चाभूत् प्रधनं तुमुलं लोमहर्षणम् ।
यमाय भल्लैरनयद् दैत्यान् अभिययुर्मृधे ॥१७॥

tais tasya cābhūt pradhanaṁ
tumulaṁ loma-harṣaṇam
yamāya bhallair anayad
daityān abhiyayur mṛdhe

taiḥ—with the demons; *tasya*—of him, Purañjaya; *ca*—also; *abhūt*—there was; *pradhanam*—a fight; *tumulam*—very fierce; *loma-harṣaṇam*—the hearing of which makes one's hairs stand on end; *yamāya*—to the residence of Yamarāja; *bhallaiḥ*—by arrows; *anayat*—sent; *daityān*—the demons; *abhiyayuḥ*—who came toward him; *mṛdhe*—in that fight.

TRANSLATION

There was a fierce battle between the demons and Purañjaya. Indeed, it was so fierce that when one hears about it one's hairs stand on end. All the demons bold enough to come before Purañjaya were immediately sent to the residence of Yamarāja by his arrows.

TEXT 18

तस्येषुपाताभिमुखं युगान्ताग्निमिवोल्बणम् ।
विसृज्य दुद्रुवुर्दैत्या हन्यमानाः स्वमालयम् ॥१८॥

tasyeṣu-pātābhimukhaṁ
yugāntāgnim ivolbaṇam
visṛjya dudruvur daityā
hanyamānāḥ svam ālayam

tasya—his (Purañjaya's); *iṣu-pāta*—the throwing of the arrows; *abhimukham*—in front of; *yuga-anta*—at the end of the millennium; *agnim*—the flames; *iva*—exactly like; *ulbaṇam*—fierce; *visṛjya*—giving up the attack; *dudruvuḥ*—ran away; *daityāḥ*—all the demons; *hanyamānāḥ*—being killed (by Purañjaya); *svam*—own; *ālayam*—to the residence.

TRANSLATION

To save themselves from the blazing arrows of Indravāha, which resembled the flames of devastation at the end of the millennium, the demons who remained when the rest of their army was killed fled very quickly to their respective homes.

TEXT 19

जित्वा परं धनं सर्वं सस्त्रीकं वज्रपाणये ।
प्रत्ययच्छत् स राजर्षिरिति नामभिराहृतः ॥१९॥

jitvā paraṁ dhanaṁ sarvaṁ
sastrīkaṁ vajra-pāṇaye
pratyayacchat sa rājarṣir
iti nāmabhir āhṛtaḥ

jitvā—conquering; *param*—enemies; *dhanam*—wealth; *sarvam*—everything; *sa-strīkam*—with their wives; *vajra-pāṇaye*—unto Indra, who carries the thunderbolt; *pratyayacchat*—returned and delivered; *saḥ*—that; *rāja-ṛṣiḥ*—saintly king (Purañjaya); *iti*—thus; *nāmabhiḥ*—by names; *āhṛtaḥ*—was called.

TRANSLATION

After conquering the enemy, the saintly king Purañjaya gave everything, including the enemy's riches and wives, to Indra, who

carries a thunderbolt. For this he is celebrated as Purañjaya. Thus Purañjaya is known by different names because of his different activities.

TEXT 20

पुरञ्जयस्य पुत्रोऽभूदनेनास्तत्सुतः पृथुः ।
विश्वगन्धिस्ततश्चन्द्रो युवनाश्वस्तु तत्सुतः ॥२०॥

purañjayasya putro 'bhūd
anenās tat-sutaḥ pṛthuḥ
viśvagandhis tataś candro
yuvanāśvas tu tat-sutaḥ

purañjayasya—of Purañjaya; *putraḥ*—son; *abhūt*—was born; *anenāḥ*—by the name Anenā; *tat-sutaḥ*—his son; *pṛthuḥ*—of the name Pṛthu; *viśvagandhiḥ*—of the name Viśvagandhi; *tataḥ*—his son; *candraḥ*—by the name Candra; *yuvanāśvaḥ*—of the name Yuvanāśva; *tu*—indeed; *tat-sutaḥ*—his son.

TRANSLATION

The son of Purañjaya was known as Anenā, Anenā's son was Pṛthu, and Pṛthu's son was Viśvagandhi. Viśvagandhi's son was Candra, and Candra's son was Yuvanāśva.

TEXT 21

श्रावस्तस्तत्सुतो येन श्रावस्ती निर्ममे पुरी ।
बृहदश्वस्तु श्रावस्तिस्ततः कुवलयाश्वकः ॥२१॥

śrāvastas tat-suto yena
śrāvastī nirmame purī
bṛhadaśvas tu śrāvastis
tataḥ kuvalayāśvakaḥ

śrāvastaḥ—by the name Śrāvasta; *tat-sutaḥ*—the son of Yuvanāśva; *yena*—by whom; *śrāvastī*—of the name Śrāvastī; *nirmame*—was constructed; *purī*—the great township; *bṛhadaśvaḥ*—Bṛhadaśva; *tu*—however; *śrāvastiḥ*—begotten by Śrāvasta; *tataḥ*—from him; *kuvalayāśvakaḥ*—of the name Kuvalayāśva.

TRANSLATION

The son of Yuvanāśva was Śrāvasta, who constructed a township known as Śrāvastī Purī. The son of Śrāvasta was Bṛhadaśva, and his son was Kuvalayāśva. In this way the dynasty increased.

TEXT 22

यः प्रियार्थमुतङ्कस्य धुन्धुनामासुरं बली ।
सुतानामेकविंशत्या सहस्रैरहनद् वृतः ॥२२॥

yaḥ priyārtham utaṅkasya
dhundhu-nāmāsuraṁ balī
sutānām eka-viṁśatyā
sahasrair ahanad vṛtaḥ

yaḥ—he who; *priya-artham*—for the satisfaction; *utaṅkasya*—of the great sage Utaṅka; *dhundhu-nāma*—of the name Dhundhu; *asuram*—a demon; *balī*—very powerful (Kuvalayāśva); *sutānām*—of sons; *eka-viṁśatyā*—by twenty-one; *sahasraiḥ*—thousands; *ahanat*—killed; *vṛtaḥ*—surrounded.

TRANSLATION

To satisfy the sage Utaṅka, the greatly powerful Kuvalayāśva killed a demon named Dhundhu. He did this with the assistance of his twenty-one thousand sons.

TEXTS 23–24

धुन्धुमार इति ख्यातस्तत्सुतास्ते च जज्वलुः ।
धुन्धोर्मुखाग्निना सर्वे त्रय एवावशेषिताः ॥२३॥
दृढाश्वः कपिलाश्वश्च भद्राश्व इति भारत ।
दृढाश्वपुत्रो हर्यश्वो निकुम्भस्तत्सुतः स्मृतः ॥२४॥

dhundhumāra iti khyātas
tat-sutās te ca jajvaluḥ
dhundhor mukhāgninā sarve
traya evāvaśeṣitāḥ

dṛḍhāśvaḥ kapilāśvaś ca
bhadrāśva iti bhārata
dṛḍhāśva-putro haryaśvo
nikumbhas tat-sutaḥ smṛtaḥ

dhundhu-māraḥ—the killer of Dhundhu; *iti*—thus; *khyātaḥ*—celebrated; *tat-sutāḥ*—his sons; *te*—all of them; *ca*—also; *jajvaluḥ*—burned; *dhundhoḥ*—of Dhundhu; *mukha-agninā*—by the fire emanating from the mouth; *sarve*—all of them; *trayaḥ*—three; *eva*—only; *avaśeṣitāḥ*—remained alive; *dṛḍhāśvaḥ*—Dṛḍhāśva; *kapilāśvaḥ*—Kapilāśva; *ca*—and; *bhadrāśvaḥ*—Bhadrāśva; *iti*—thus; *bhārata*—O Mahārāja Parīkṣit; *dṛḍhāśva-putraḥ*—the son of Dṛḍhāśva; *haryaśvaḥ*—named Haryaśva; *nikumbhaḥ*—Nikumbha; *tat-sutaḥ*—his son; *smṛtaḥ*—well known.

TRANSLATION

O Mahārāja Parīkṣit, for this reason Kuvalayāśva is celebrated as Dhundhumāra ["the killer of Dhundhu"]. All but three of his sons, however, were burned to ashes by the fire emanating from Dhundhu's mouth. The remaining sons were Dṛḍhāśva, Kapilāśva and Bhadrāśva. From Dṛḍhāśva came a son named Haryaśva, whose son is celebrated as Nikumbha.

TEXT 25

बहुलाश्वो निकुम्भस्य कृशाश्वोऽथास्य सेनजित् ।
युवनाश्वोऽभवत् तस्य सोऽनपत्यो वनं गतः ॥२५॥

bahulāśvo nikumbhasya
kṛśāśvo 'thāsya senajit
yuvanāśvo 'bhavat tasya
so 'napatyo vanaṁ gataḥ

bahulāśvaḥ—of the name Bahulāśva; *nikumbhasya*—of Nikumbha; *kṛśāśvaḥ*—of the name Kṛśāśva; *atha*—thereafter; *asya*—of Kṛśāśva; *senajit*—Senajit; *yuvanāśvaḥ*—of the name Yuvanāśva; *abhavat*—was born; *tasya*—of Senajit; *saḥ*—he; *anapatyaḥ*—without any sons; *vanam gataḥ*—retired to the forest as a *vānaprastha.*

TRANSLATION

The son of Nikumbha was Bahulāśva, the son of Bahulāśva was Kṛśāśva, the son of Kṛśāśva was Senajit, and the son of Senajit was Yuvanāśva. Yuvanāśva had no sons, and thus he retired from family life and went to the forest.

TEXT 26

भार्याशतेन निर्विण्ण ऋषयोऽस्य कृपालवः ।
इष्टिं स्म वर्तयाञ्चक्रुरैन्द्रीं ते सुसमाहिताः ॥२६॥

bhāryā-śatena nirviṇṇa
ṛṣayo 'sya kṛpālavaḥ
iṣṭiṁ sma vartayāṁ cakrur
aindrīṁ te susamāhitāḥ

bhāryā-śatena—with one hundred wives; *nirviṇṇaḥ*—very morose; *ṛṣayaḥ*—the sages (in the forest); *asya*—upon him; *kṛpālavaḥ*—very merciful; *iṣṭim*—a ritualistic ceremony; *sma*—in the past; *vartayām cakruḥ*—began to execute; *aindrīm*—known as an Indra-yajña; *te*—all of them; *su-samāhitāḥ*—being very careful and attentive.

TRANSLATION

Although Yuvanāśva went into the forest with his one hundred wives, all of them were very morose. The sages in the forest, however, being very kind to the King, began very carefully and attentively performing an Indra-yajña so that the King might have a son.

PURPORT

One may enter the *vānaprastha* order of life with his wife, but the *vānaprastha* order means complete retirement from household life.

Although King Yuvanāśva retired from family life, he and his wives were always morose because he had no son.

TEXT 27

राजा तद्यज्ञसदनं प्रविष्टो निशि तर्षितः ।
दृष्ट्वा शयानान् विप्रांस्तान् पपौ मन्त्रजलं स्वयम् ॥२७॥

rājā tad-yajña-sadanaṁ
praviṣṭo niśi tarṣitaḥ
dṛṣṭvā śayānān viprāṁs tān
papau mantra-jalaṁ svayam

rājā—the King (Yuvanāśva); *tat-yajña-sadanam*—the arena of sacrifice; *praviṣṭaḥ*—entered; *niśi*—at night; *tarṣitaḥ*—being thirsty; *dṛṣṭvā*—seeing; *śayānān*—lying down; *viprān*—all the *brāhmaṇas; tān*—all of them; *papau*—drank; *mantra-jalam*—water sanctified by *mantras; svayam*—personally.

TRANSLATION

Being thirsty one night, the King entered the arena of sacrifice, and when he saw all the brāhmaṇas lying down, he personally drank the sanctified water meant to be drunk by his wife.

PURPORT

Yajñas performed by *brāhmaṇas* according to Vedic ritualistic ceremonies are so potent that the sanctifying of water by Vedic *mantras* can bring about the desired result. In this instance, the *brāhmaṇas* sanctified the water so that the King's wife might drink it in the *yajña*, but by providence the King himself went there at night and, being thirsty, drank the water.

TEXT 28

उत्थितास्ते निशम्याथ व्युदकं कलशं प्रभो ।
पप्रच्छुः कस्य कर्मेदं पीतं पुंसवनं जलम् ॥२८॥

utthitās te niśamyātha
vyudakaṁ kalaśaṁ prabho
papracchuḥ kasya karmedaṁ
pītaṁ puṁsavanaṁ jalam

utthitāḥ—after awakening; *te*—all of them; *niśamya*—seeing; *atha*—thereafter; *vyudakam*—empty; *kalaśam*—the waterpot; *prabho*—O King Parīkṣit; *papracchuḥ*—inquired; *kasya*—whose; *karma*—act; *idam*—this; *pītam*—drunk; *puṁsavanam*—which was to cause the birth of a child; *jalam*—water.

TRANSLATION

When the brāhmaṇas got up from bed and saw the waterpot empty, they inquired who had done this work of drinking the water meant for begetting a child.

TEXT 29

राज्ञा पीतं विदित्वा वै ईश्वरप्रहितेन ते ।
ईश्वराय नमश्चक्रुरहो दैवबलं बलम् ॥२९॥

rājñā pītaṁ viditvā vai
īśvara-prahitena te
īśvarāya namaś cakrur
aho daiva-balaṁ balam

rājñā—by the King; *pītam*—drunk; *viditvā*—understanding this; *vai*—indeed; *īśvara-prahitena*—inspired by providence; *te*—all of them; *īśvarāya*—unto the Supreme Personality of Godhead, the supreme controller; *namaḥ cakruḥ*—offered respectful obeisances; *aho*—alas; *daiva-balam*—providential power; *balam*—is actual power.

TRANSLATION

When the brāhmaṇas came to understand that the King, inspired by the supreme controller, had drunk the water, they all exclaimed "Alas! The power of providence is real power. No one can

counteract the power of the Supreme." In this way they offered their respectful obeisances unto the Lord.

TEXT 30

ततः काल उपावृत्ते कुक्षिं निर्भिद्य दक्षिणम् ।
युवनाश्वस्य तनयश्चक्रवर्ती जजान ह ॥३०॥

tataḥ kāla upāvṛtte
kukṣiṁ nirbhidya dakṣiṇam
yuvanāśvasya tanayaś
cakravartī jajāna ha

tataḥ—thereafter; *kāle*—time; *upāvṛtte*—being mature; *kukṣim*—the lower part of the abdomen; *nirbhidya*—piercing; *dakṣiṇam*—the right side; *yuvanāśvasya*—of King Yuvanāśva; *tanayaḥ*—a son; *cakravartī*—with all the good symptoms of a king; *jajāna*—generated; *ha*—in the past.

TRANSLATION

Thereafter, in due course of time, a son with all the good symptoms of a powerful king came forth from the lower right side of King Yuvanāśva's abdomen.

TEXT 31

कं धास्यति कुमारोऽयं स्तन्ये रोरूयते भृशम् ।
मां धाता वत्स मा रोदीरितीन्द्रो देशिनीमदात् ॥३१॥

kaṁ dhāsyati kumāro 'yaṁ
stanye rorūyate bhṛśam
māṁ dhātā vatsa mā rodīr
itīndro deśinīm adāt

kam—by whom; *dhāsyati*—will he be cared for by being supplied breast milk; *kumāraḥ*—child; *ayam*—this; *stanye*—for drinking breast milk; *rorūyate*—is crying; *bhṛśam*—so much; *mām dhātā*—just drink me; *vatsa*—my dear child; *mā rodīḥ*—do not cry; *iti*—thus; *indraḥ*—King Indra; *deśinīm*—the index finger; *adāt*—gave him to suck.

TRANSLATION

The baby cried so much for breast milk that all the brāhmaṇas were very unhappy. "Who will take care of this baby?" they said. Then Indra, who was worshiped in that yajña, came and solaced the baby. "Do not cry," Indra said. Then Indra put his index finger in the baby's mouth and said, "You may drink me."

TEXT 32

न ममार पिता तस्य विप्रदेवप्रसादतः ।
युवनाश्वोऽथ तत्रैव तपसा सिद्धिमन्वगात् ॥३२॥

na mamāra pitā tasya
vipra-deva-prasādataḥ
yuvanāśvo 'tha tatraiva
tapasā siddhim anvagāt

na—not; *mamāra*—died; *pitā*—the father; *tasya*—of the baby; *vipra-deva-prasādataḥ*—because of the mercy and blessings of the *brāhmaṇas; yuvanāśvaḥ*—King Yuvanāśva; *atha*—thereafter; *tatra eva*—in that very place; *tapasā*—by executing austerity; *siddhim*—perfection; *anvagāt*—achieved.

TRANSLATION

Because Yuvanāśva, the father of the baby, was blessed by the brāhmaṇas, he did not fall a victim to death. After this incident, he performed severe austerities and achieved perfection in that very spot.

TEXTS 33–34

त्रसद्दस्युरितीन्द्रोऽङ्ग विदधे नाम यस्य वै ।
यस्मात् त्रसन्ति ह्युद्विग्ना दस्यवो रावणादयः ॥३३॥

यौवनाश्वोऽथ मान्धाता चक्रवर्त्यवनीं प्रभुः ।
सप्तद्वीपवतीमेकः शशासाच्युततेजसा ॥३४॥

trasaddasyur itīndro 'ṅga
vidadhe nāma yasya vai
yasmāt trasanti hy udvignā
dasyavo rāvaṇādayaḥ

yauvanāśvo 'tha māndhātā
cakravarty avanīṁ prabhuḥ
sapta-dvīpavatīm ekaḥ
śaśāsācyuta-tejasā

trasat-dasyuḥ—of the name Trasaddasyu ("one who threatens thieves and rogues"); *iti*—thus; *indraḥ*—the King of heaven; *aṅga*—my dear King; *vidadhe*—gave; *nāma*—the name; *yasya*—whom; *vai*—indeed; *yasmāt*—from whom; *trasanti*—are afraid; *hi*—indeed; *udvignāḥ*—the cause of anxiety; *dasyavaḥ*—thieves and rogues; *rāvaṇa-ādayaḥ*—headed by great Rākṣasas like Rāvaṇa; *yauvanāśvaḥ*—the son of Yuvanāśva; *atha*—thus; *māndhātā*—known as Māndhātā; *cakravartī*—the emperor of the world; *avanīm*—this surface of the world; *prabhuḥ*—the master; *sapta-dvīpa-vatīm*—consisting of seven islands; *ekaḥ*—one alone; *śaśāsa*—ruled; *acyuta-tejasā*—being powerful by the favor of the Supreme Personality of Godhead.

TRANSLATION

Māndhātā, the son of Yuvanāśva, was the cause of fear for Rāvaṇa and other thieves and rogues who caused anxiety. O King Parīkṣit, because they feared him, the son of Yuvanāśva was known as Trasaddasyu. This name was given by King Indra. By the mercy of the Supreme Personality of Godhead, the son of Yuvanāśva was so powerful that when he became emperor he ruled the entire world, consisting of seven islands, without any second ruler.

TEXTS 35–36

ईजे च यज्ञं क्रतुभिरात्मविद् भूरिदक्षिणैः ।
सर्वदेवमयं देवं सर्वात्मकमतीन्द्रियम् ॥३५॥
द्रव्यं मन्त्रो विधिर्यज्ञो यजमानस्तथर्त्विजः ।
धर्मो देशश्च कालश्च सर्वमेतद् यदात्मकम् ॥३६॥

īje ca yajñaṁ kratubhir
ātma-vid bhūri-dakṣiṇaiḥ
sarva-devamayaṁ devaṁ
sarvātmakam atīndriyam

dravyaṁ mantro vidhir yajño
yajamānas tathartvijaḥ
dharmo deśaś ca kālaś ca
sarvam etad yad ātmakam

īje—he worshiped; *ca*—also; *yajñam*—the Lord of sacrifices; *kratubhiḥ*—by great ritualistic performances; *ātma-vit*—fully conscious by self-realization; *bhūri-dakṣiṇaiḥ*—by giving large contributions to the *brāhmaṇas; sarva-deva-mayam*—consisting of all the demigods; *devam*—the Lord; *sarva-ātmakam*—the Supersoul of everyone; *ati-indriyam*—transcendentally situated; *dravyam*—ingredients; *mantraḥ*—chanting of the Vedic hymns; *vidhiḥ*—regulative principles; *yajñaḥ*—worshiping; *yajamānaḥ*—the performer; *tathā*—with; *ṛtvijaḥ*—the priests; *dharmaḥ*—religious principles; *deśaḥ*—the country; *ca*—and; *kālaḥ*—the time; *ca*—also; *sarvam*—everything; *etat*—all these; *yat*—that which is; *ātmakam*—favorable for self-realization.

TRANSLATION

The Supreme Personality of Godhead is not different from the auspicious aspects of great sacrifices, such as the ingredients of the sacrifice, the chanting of Vedic hymns, the regulative principles, the performer, the priests, the result of the sacrifice, the arena of sacrifice, and the time of sacrifice. Knowing the principles of

self-realization, Māndhātā worshiped that transcendentally situated Supreme Soul, the Supreme Personality of Godhead, Lord Viṣṇu, who comprises all the demigods. He also gave immense charity to the brāhmaṇas, and thus he performed yajña to worship the Lord.

TEXT 37

यावत् सूर्य उदेति स्म यावच्च प्रतितिष्ठति ।
तत् सर्वं यौवनाश्वस्य मान्धातुः क्षेत्रमुच्यते ॥३७॥

yāvat sūrya udeti sma
yāvac ca pratitiṣṭhati
tat sarvaṁ yauvanāśvasya
māndhātuḥ kṣetram ucyate

yāvat—as long as; *sūryaḥ*—the sun; *udeti*—has risen on the horizon; *sma*—in the past; *yāvat*—as long as; *ca*—also; *pratitiṣṭhati*—continues to stay; *tat*—all those things mentioned above; *sarvam*—everything; *yauvanāśvasya*—of the son of Yuvanāśva; *māndhātuḥ*—called Māndhātā; *kṣetram*—location; *ucyate*—is said to be.

TRANSLATION

All places, from where the sun rises on the horizon, shining brilliantly, to where the sun sets, are known as the possession of the celebrated Māndhātā, the son of Yuvanāśva.

TEXT 38

शशबिन्दोर्दुहितरि बिन्दुमत्यामधान्नृपः ।
पुरुकुत्समम्बरीषं मुचुकुन्दं च योगिनम् ।
तेषां स्वसारः पञ्चाशत् सौभरिं वव्रिरे पतिम् ॥३८॥

śaśabindor duhitari
bindumatyām adhān nṛpaḥ
purukutsam ambarīṣaṁ
mucukundaṁ ca yoginam

teṣāṁ svasāraḥ pañcāśat
saubhariṁ vavrire patim

śaśabindoḥ—of a king known as Śaśabindu; *duhitari*—unto the daughter; *bindumatyām*—whose name was Bindumatī; *adhāt*—begot; *nṛpaḥ*—the King (Māndhātā); *purukutsam*—Purukutsa; *ambarīṣam*—Ambarīṣa; *mucukundam*—Mucukunda; *ca*—and; *yoginam*—a highly elevated mystic; *teṣām*—of them; *svasāraḥ*—the sisters; *pañcāśat*—fifty; *saubharim*—unto the great sage Saubhari; *vavrire*—accepted; *patim*—as husband.

TRANSLATION

Māndhātā begot three sons in the womb of Bindumatī, the daughter of Śaśabindu. These sons were Purukutsa, Ambarīṣa, and Mucukunda, a great mystic yogī. These three brothers had fifty sisters, who all accepted the great sage Saubhari as their husband.

TEXTS 39–40

यमुनान्तर्जले मग्नस्तप्यमानः परं तपः ।
निर्वृतिं मीनराजस्य दृष्ट्वा मैथुनधर्मिणः ॥३९॥
जातस्पृहो नृपं विप्रः कन्यामेकामयाचत ।
सोऽप्याह गृह्यतां ब्रह्मन् कामं कन्या स्वयंवरे ॥४०॥

yamunāntar-jale magnas
tapyamānaḥ paraṁ tapaḥ
nirvṛtiṁ mīna-rājasya
dṛṣṭvā maithuna-dharmiṇaḥ

jāta-spṛho nṛpaṁ vipraḥ
kanyām ekām ayācata
so 'py āha gṛhyatāṁ brahman
kāmaṁ kanyā svayaṁvare

yamunā-antaḥ-jale—in the deep water of the River Yamunā; *magnaḥ*—merged completely; *tapyamānaḥ*—executing austerities;

param—uncommon; *tapaḥ*—austerity; *nirvṛtim*—pleasure; *mīna-rājasya*—of a big fish; *dṛṣṭvā*—seeing; *maithuna-dharmiṇaḥ*—engaged in sexual affairs; *jāta-spṛhaḥ*—became sexually inclined; *nṛpam*—unto the King (Māndhātā); *vipraḥ*—the *brāhmaṇa* (Saubhari Ṛṣi); *kanyām ekām*—one daughter; *ayācata*—begged for; *saḥ*—he, the King; *api*—also; *āha*—said; *gṛhyatām*—you can take; *brahman*—O *brāhmaṇa;* *kāmam*—as she desires; *kanyā*—daughter; *svayaṁvare*—a personal selection.

TRANSLATION

Saubhari Ṛṣi was engaged in austerity, deep in the water of the River Yamunā, when he saw a pair of fish engaged in sexual affairs. Thus he perceived the pleasure of sex life, and induced by this desire he went to King Māndhātā and begged for one of the King's daughters. In response to this request, the King said, "O brāhmaṇa, any of my daughters may accept any husband according to her personal selection."

PURPORT

This is the beginning of the story of Saubhari Ṛṣi. According to Viśvanātha Cakravartī Ṭhākura, Māndhātā was the king of Mathurā, and Saubhari Ṛṣi was engaged in austerity while submerged deep within the River Yamunā. When the *ṛṣi* felt sexual desire, he emerged from the water and went to King Māndhātā to ask that one of the King's daughters become his wife.

TEXTS 41–42

स विचिन्त्याप्रियं स्त्रीणां जरठोऽहमसंमतः ।
वलीपलित एजत्क इत्यहं प्रत्युदाहृतः ॥४१॥
साधयिष्ये तथात्मानं सुरस्त्रीणामभीप्सितम् ।
किं पुनर्मनुजेन्द्राणामिति व्यवसितः प्रभुः ॥४२॥

sa vicintyāpriyaṁ strīṇāṁ
jaraṭho 'ham asan-mataḥ
valī-palita ejat-ka
ity ahaṁ pratyudāhṛtaḥ

sādhayiṣye tathātmānaṁ
sura-strīṇām abhīpsitam
kiṁ punar manujendrāṇām
iti vyavasitaḥ prabhuḥ

saḥ—he, Saubhari Muni; *vicintya*—thinking to himself; *apriyam*—not liked; *strīṇām*—by the women; *jaraṭhaḥ*—being infirm because of old age; *aham*—I; *asat-mataḥ*—not desired by them; *valī*—wrinkled; *palitaḥ*—grey-haired; *ejat-kaḥ*—with the head always trembling; *iti*—in this way; *aham*—I; *pratyudāhṛtaḥ*—rejected (by them); *sādhayiṣye*—I shall act in such a way; *tathā*—as; *ātmānam*—my body; *sura-strīṇām*—to the celestial women of the heavenly planets; *abhīpsitam*—desirable; *kim*—what to speak of; *punaḥ*—yet; *manuja-indrāṇām*—of the daughters of worldly kings; *iti*—in this way; *vyavasitaḥ*—determined; *prabhuḥ*—Saubhari, the greatly powerful mystic.

TRANSLATION

Saubhari Muni thought: I am now feeble because of old age. My hair has become grey, my skin is slack, and my head always trembles. Besides, I am a yogī. Therefore women do not like me. Since the King has thus rejected me, I shall reform my body in such a way as to be desirable even to celestial women, what to speak of the daughters of worldly kings.

TEXT 43

मुनिः प्रवेशितः क्षत्रा कन्यान्तःपुरमृद्धिमत् ।
वृतः स राजकन्याभिरेकं पञ्चाशता वरः ॥४३॥

muniḥ praveśitaḥ kṣatrā
kanyāntaḥpuram ṛddhimat
vṛtaḥ sa rāja-kanyābhir
ekaṁ pañcāśatā varaḥ

muniḥ—Saubhari Muni; *praveśitaḥ*—admitted; *kṣatrā*—by the palace messenger; *kanyā-antaḥpuram*—into the residential quarters of the princesses; *ṛddhi-mat*—extremely opulent in all respects; *vṛtaḥ*—accepted; *saḥ*—he; *rāja-kanyābhiḥ*—by all the princesses; *ekam*—he alone; *pañcāśatā*—by all fifty; *varaḥ*—the husband.

TRANSLATION

Thereafter, when Saubhari Muni became quite a young and beautiful person, the messenger of the palace took him inside the residential quarters of the princesses, which were extremely opulent. All fifty princesses then accepted him as their husband, although he was only one man.

TEXT 44

तासां कलिरभूद् भूयांस्तदर्थेऽपोह्य सौहृदम् ।
ममानुरूपो नायं व इति तद्गतचेतसाम् ॥४४॥

tāsāṁ kalir abhūd bhūyāṁs
tad-arthe 'pohya sauhṛdam
mamānurūpo nāyaṁ va
iti tad-gata-cetasām

tāsām—of all the princesses; *kaliḥ*—disagreement and quarrel; *abhūt*—there was; *bhūyān*—very much; *tat-arthe*—for the sake of Saubhari Muni; *apohya*—giving up; *sauhṛdam*—a good relationship; *mama*—mine; *anurūpaḥ*—the fit person; *na*—not; *ayam*—this; *vaḥ*—yours; *iti*—in this way; *tat-gata-cetasām*—being attracted by him.

TRANSLATION

Thereafter, the princesses, being attracted by Saubhari Muni, gave up their sisterly relationship and quarreled among themselves, each one of them contending, "This man is just suitable for me, and not for you." In this way there ensued a great disagreement.

TEXTS 45–46

स बह्वृचस्ताभिरपारणीय-
तपःश्रियानर्घ्यपरिच्छदेषु ।

गृहेषु नानोपवनामलाम्भः-
सरःसु सौगन्धिककाननेषु ॥४५॥
महार्हशय्यासनवस्त्रभूषण-
स्नानानुलेपाभ्यवहारमाल्यकैः ।
स्वलङ्कृतस्त्रीपुरुषेषु नित्यदा
रेमेऽनुगायद्द्विजभृङ्गवन्दिषु ॥४६॥

sa bahv-ṛcas tābhir apāraṇīya-
tapaḥ-śriyānarghya-paricchadeṣu
gṛheṣu nānopavanāmalāmbhaḥ-
sarahsu saugandhika-kānaneṣu

mahārha-śayyāsana-vastra-bhūṣaṇa-
snānānulepābhyavahāra-mālyakaiḥ
svalaṅkṛta-strī-puruṣeṣu nityadā
reme 'nugāyad-dvija-bhṛṅga-vandiṣu

saḥ—he, Saubhari Ṛṣi; *bahu-ṛcaḥ*—quite expert in utilizing Vedic *mantras; tābhiḥ*—with his wives; *apāraṇīya*—unlimited; *tapaḥ*—the result of austerity; *śriyā*—by opulences; *anarghya*—paraphernalia for enjoyment; *paricchadeṣu*—equipped with different garments and dresses; *gṛheṣu*—in the house and rooms; *nānā*—varieties of; *upavana*—parks; *amala*—clean; *ambhaḥ*—water; *sarahsu*—in lakes; *saugandhika*—very fragrant; *kānaneṣu*—in gardens; *mahā-arha*—very costly; *śayyā*—bedding; *āsana*—sitting places; *vastra*—clothing; *bhūṣaṇa*—ornaments; *snāna*—bathing places; *anulepa*—sandalwood; *abhyavahāra*—palatable dishes; *mālyakaiḥ*—and with garlands; *su-alaṅkṛta*—properly dressed and decorated; *strī*—women; *puruṣeṣu*—with men also; *nityadā*—constantly; *reme*—enjoyed; *anugāyat*—followed by the singing of; *dvija*—birds; *bhṛṅga*—bumblebees; *vandiṣu*—and professional singers.

TRANSLATION

Because Saubhari Muni was expert in chanting mantras perfectly, his severe austerities resulted in an opulent home, with

garments, ornaments, properly dressed and decorated maidservants and manservants, and varieties of parks with clear-water lakes and gardens. In the gardens, fragrant with varieties of flowers, birds chirped and bees hummed, surrounded by professional singers. Saubhari Muni's home was amply provided with valuable beds, seats, ornaments, and arrangements for bathing, and there were varieties of sandalwood creams, flower garlands, and palatable dishes. Thus surrounded by opulent paraphernalia, the muni engaged in family affairs with his numerous wives.

PURPORT

Saubhari Ṛṣi was a great *yogī.* Yogic perfection makes available eight material opulences—*aṇimā, laghimā, mahimā, prāpti, prākāmya, īśitva, vaśitva* and *kāmāvasāyitā.* Saubhari Muni exhibited superexcellence in material enjoyment by dint of his yogic perfection. The word *bahv-ṛca* means "expert in chanting *mantras.*" As material opulence can be achieved by ordinary material means, it can also be achieved by subtle means through *mantras.* By chanting *mantras,* Saubhari Muni arranged for material opulence, but this was not perfection in life. As will be seen, Saubhari Muni became very dissatisfied with material opulence and thus left everything and reentered the forest in the *vānaprastha* order and achieved final success. Those who are not *ātma-tattva-vit,* who do not know the spiritual value of life, can be satisfied with external material opulences, but those who are *ātma-tattva-vit* are not inspired by material opulence. This is the instruction we can derive from the life and activities of Saubhari Muni.

TEXT 47

यद्गार्हस्थ्यं तु संवीक्ष्य सप्तद्वीपवतीपतिः ।
विस्मितः स्तम्भमजहात् सार्वभौमश्रियान्वितम् ॥ ४७॥

yad-gārhasthyaṁ tu saṁvīkṣya
sapta-dvīpavatī-patiḥ
vismitaḥ stambham ajahāt
sārvabhauma-śriyānvitam

yat—he whose; *gārhasthyam*—family life, householder life; *tu*—but; *saṁvīkṣya*—observing; *sapta-dvīpa-vatī-patiḥ*—Māndhātā, who was the King of the entire world, consisting of seven islands; *vismitaḥ*—was struck with wonder; *stambham*—pride due to a prestigious position; *ajahāt*—he gave up; *sārva-bhauma*—the emperor of the entire world; *śriyā-anvitam*—blessed with all kinds of opulence.

TRANSLATION

Māndhātā, the King of the entire world, consisting of seven islands, was struck with wonder when he saw the household opulence of Saubhari Muni. Thus he gave up his false prestige in his position as emperor of the world.

PURPORT

Everyone is proud of his own position, but here was an astounding experience, in which the emperor of the entire world felt himself defeated in all details of material happiness by the opulence of Saubhari Muni.

TEXT 48

एवं गृहेष्वभिरतो विषयान् विविधैः सुखैः ।
सेवमानो न चातुष्यदाज्यस्तोकैरिवानलः ॥४८॥

evaṁ gṛheṣv abhirato
viṣayān vividhaiḥ sukhaiḥ
sevamāno na cātuṣyad
ājya-stokair ivānalaḥ

evam—in this way; *gṛheṣu*—in household affairs; *abhirataḥ*—being always engaged; *viṣayān*—material paraphernalia; *vividhaiḥ*—with varieties of; *sukhaiḥ*—happiness; *sevamānaḥ*—enjoying; *na*—not; *ca*—also; *atuṣyat*—satisfied him; *ājya-stokaiḥ*—by drops of fat; *iva*—like; *analaḥ*—a fire.

TRANSLATION

In this way, Saubhari Muni enjoyed sense gratification in the material world, but he was not at all satisfied, just as a fire never ceases blazing if constantly supplied with drops of fat.

PURPORT

Material desire is just like a blazing fire. If a fire is continually supplied with drops of fat, the fire will increase more and more and never be extinguished. Therefore the policy of trying to satisfy material desires by catering to one's material demands will never be successful. In modern civilization, everyone is engaged in economic development, which is another way of constantly dropping fat into the material fire. The Western countries have reached the summit of material civilization, but people are still dissatisfied. Real satisfaction is Kṛṣṇa consciousness. This is confirmed in *Bhagavad-gītā* (5.29), where Kṛṣṇa says:

bhoktāraṁ yajña-tapasāṁ
sarva-loka-maheśvaram
suhṛdaṁ sarva-bhūtānāṁ
jñātvā māṁ śāntim ṛcchati

"The sages, knowing Me as the ultimate purpose of all sacrifices and austerities, the Supreme Lord of all planets and demigods and the benefactor and well-wisher of all living entities, attain peace from the pangs of material miseries." One must therefore take to Kṛṣṇa consciousness and advance in Kṛṣṇa consciousness by properly following the regulative principles. Then one can attain an eternal, blissful life in peace and knowledge.

TEXT 49

स कदाचिदुपासीन आत्मापह्नवमात्मनः ।
ददर्श बह्वृचाचार्यो मीनसङ्गसमुत्थितम् ॥४९॥

sa kadācid upāsīna
ātmāpahnavam ātmanaḥ

dadarśa bahv-ṛcācāryo
mīna-saṅga-samutthitam

saḥ—he, Saubhari Muni; *kadācit*—one day; *upāsīnaḥ*—sitting down; *ātma-apahnavam*—degrading oneself from the platform of *tapasya; ātmanaḥ*—self-caused; *dadarśa*—observed; *bahu-ṛca-ācāryaḥ*—Saubhari Muni, who was expert in chanting *mantras; mīna-saṅga*—the sexual affairs of fish; *samutthitam*—caused by this incident.

TRANSLATION

Thereafter, one day while Saubhari Muni, who was expert in chanting mantras, was sitting in a secluded place, he thought to himself about the cause of his falldown, which was simply that he had associated himself with the sexual affairs of the fish.

PURPORT

Viśvanātha Cakravartī Ṭhākura remarks that Saubhari Muni had fallen from his austerity because of a *vaiṣṇava-aparādha.* The history is that when Garuḍa wanted to eat fish, Saubhari Muni unnecessarily gave the fish shelter under his care. Because Garuḍa's plans for eating were disappointed, Saubhari Muni certainly committed a great offense to a Vaiṣṇava. Because of this *vaiṣṇava-aparādha,* an offense at the lotus feet of a Vaiṣṇava, Saubhari Muni fell from his exalted position of mystic *tapasya.* One should not, therefore, impede the activities of a Vaiṣṇava. This is the lesson we must learn from this incident concerning Saubhari Muni.

TEXT 50

अहो इमं पश्यत मे विनाशं
तपस्विनः सच्चरितव्रतस्य ।
अन्तर्जले वारिचरप्रसङ्गात्
प्रच्यावितं ब्रह्म चिरं धृतं यत् ॥५०॥

aho imaṁ paśyata me vināśaṁ
tapasvinaḥ sac-carita-vratasya

antarjale vāri-cara-prasaṅgāt
pracyāvitaṁ brahma ciraṁ dhṛtaṁ yat

aho—alas; *imam*—this; *paśyata*—just see; *me*—of me; *vināśam*—falldown; *tapasvinaḥ*—who was such a great mystic performing austerity; *sat-carita*—of very good character, observing all necessary rules and regulations; *vratasya*—of one who has taken a vow strictly; *antaḥ-jale*—in the depths of the water; *vāri-cara-prasaṅgāt*—because of the affairs of the aquatics; *pracyāvitam*—fallen; *brahma*—from the activities of Brahman realization or austerity; *ciram*—for a long time; *dhṛtam*—executed; *yat*—which.

TRANSLATION

Alas! While practicing austerity, even within the depths of the water, and while observing all the rules and regulations practiced by saintly persons, I lost the results of my long austerities simply by association with the sexual affairs of fish. Everyone should observe this falldown and learn from it.

TEXT 51

सङ्गं त्यजेत मिथुनव्रतीनां मुमुक्षुः
सर्वात्मना न विसृजेद् बहिरिन्द्रियाणि ।
एकश्चरन् रहसि चित्तमनन्त ईशे
युञ्जीत तद्व्रतिषु साधुषु चेत् प्रसङ्गः ॥५१॥

saṅgaṁ tyajeta mithuna-vratīnāṁ mumukṣuḥ
sarvātmanā na visṛjed bahir-indriyāṇi
ekaś caran rahasi cittam ananta īśe
yuñjīta tad-vratiṣu sādhuṣu cet prasaṅgaḥ

saṅgam—association; *tyajeta*—must give up; *mithuna-vratīnām*—of a person engaged in sexual affairs, legal or illegal; *mumukṣuḥ*—persons who desire liberation; *sarva-ātmanā*—in all respects; *na*—do not; *visṛjet*—employ; *bahiḥ-indriyāṇi*—external senses; *ekaḥ*—alone; *caran*—moving; *rahasi*—in a secluded place; *cittam*—the heart; *anante īśe*—

fixed at the lotus feet of the unlimited Supreme Personality of Godhead; *yuñjīta*—one can engage himself; *tat-vratiṣu*—with persons of the same category (desiring liberation from material bondage); *sādhuṣu*—such saintly persons; *cet*—if; *prasaṅgaḥ*—one wants association.

TRANSLATION

A person desiring liberation from material bondage must give up the association of persons interested in sex life and should not employ his senses externally [in seeing, hearing, talking, walking and so on]. One should always stay in a secluded place, completely fixing his mind at the lotus feet of the unlimited Personality of Godhead, and if one wants any association at all, he should associate with persons similarly engaged.

PURPORT

Saubhari Muni, giving conclusions derived from his practical experience, instructs us that persons interested in crossing to the other side of the material ocean must give up the association of persons interested in sex life and accumulating money. This is also advised by Śrī Caitanya Mahāprabhu:

niṣkiñcanasya bhagavad-bhajanonmukasya
pāraṁ paraṁ jigamiṣor bhava-sāgarasya
sandarśanaṁ viṣayiṇām atha yoṣitāṁ ca
hā hanta hanta viṣa-bhakṣaṇato 'py asādhu
(*Caitanya-candrodaya-nāṭaka* 8.27)

"Alas, for a person seriously desiring to cross the material ocean and engage in the transcendental loving service of the Lord without material motives, seeing a materialist engaged in sense gratification and seeing a woman who is similarly interested is more abominable than drinking poison willingly."

One who desires complete freedom from material bondage can engage himself in the transcendental loving service of the Lord. He must not associate with *viṣayī*—materialistic persons or those interested in sex life. Every materialist is interested in sex. Thus in plain language it is advised that an exalted saintly person avoid the association of those who are materially inclined. Śrīla Narottama dāsa Ṭhākura also recommends that one engage in the service of the *ācāryas*, and if one wants to live in association, he must live in the association of devotees (*tāṅdera caraṇa sevi bhakta-sane vāsa*). The Kṛṣṇa consciousness movement is creating many centers just to create devotees so that by associating with the members of such a center people will automatically become uninterested in material affairs. Although this is an ambitious proposal, this association is proving effective by the mercy of Śrī Caitanya Mahāprabhu. By gradually associating with the members of the Kṛṣṇa consciousness movement, simply by taking *prasāda* and taking part in chanting of the Hare Kṛṣṇa *mantra*, ordinary persons are being considerably elevated. Saubhari Muni regrets that he had bad association even in the deepest part of the water. Because of the bad association of the sexually engaged fish, he fell down. A secluded place is also not secure unless there is good association.

TEXT 52

एकस्तपस्व्यहमथाम्भसि मत्स्यसङ्गात्
पञ्चाशदासमुत पञ्चसहस्रसर्गः ।
नान्तं व्रजाम्युभयकृत्यमनोरथानां
मायागुणैर्हृतमतिर्विषयेऽर्थभावः ॥५२॥

ekas tapasvy aham athāmbhasi matsya-saṅgāt
pañcāśad āsam uta pañca-sahasra-sargaḥ
nāntaṁ vrajāmy ubhaya-kṛtya-manorathānāṁ
māyā-guṇair hṛta-matir viṣaye 'rtha-bhāvaḥ

ekaḥ—one only; *tapasvī*—great sage; *aham*—I; *atha*—thus; *ambhasi*—in the deep water; *matsya-saṅgāt*—by associating with the fish; *pañcāśat*—fifty; *āsam*—got wives; *uta*—and what to speak of begetting one hundred sons in each of them; *pañca-sahasra-sargaḥ*—procreation of five thousand; *na antam*—no end; *vrajāmi*—I can find; *ubhaya-kṛtya*—duties of this life and the next; *manorathānām*—mental concoctions; *māyā-guṇaiḥ*—influenced by the modes of material nature; *hṛta*—lost; *matiḥ viṣaye*—great attraction for material things; *artha-bhāvaḥ*—matters of self-interest.

TRANSLATION

In the beginning I was alone and engaged in performing the austerities of mystic yoga, but later, because of the association of fish engaged in sex, I desired to marry. Then I became the husband of fifty wives, and in each of them I begot one hundred sons, and thus my family increased to five thousand members. By the influence of the modes of material nature, I became fallen and thought that I would be happy in material life. Thus there is no end to my material desires for enjoyment, in this life and the next.

TEXT 53

एवं वसन् गृहे कालं विरक्तो न्यासमास्थितः ।
वनं जगामानुययुस्तत्पत्न्यः पतिदेवताः ॥५३॥

evaṁ vasan gṛhe kālaṁ
virakto nyāsam āsthitaḥ
vanaṁ jagāmānuyayus
tat-patnyaḥ pati-devatāḥ

evam—in this way; *vasan*—living; *gṛhe*—at home; *kālam*—passing away time; *viraktaḥ*—became detached; *nyāsam*—in the renounced order of life; *āsthitaḥ*—became situated; *vanam*—in the forest; *jagāma*—he went; *anuyayuḥ*—was followed by; *tat-patnyaḥ*—all his wives; *pati-devatāḥ*—because their only worshipable object was their husband.

TRANSLATION

In this way he passed his life in household affairs for some time, but then he became detached from material enjoyment. To renounce material association, he accepted the vānaprastha order and went to the forest. His devoted wives followed him, for they had no shelter other than their husband.

TEXT 54

तत्र तप्त्वा तपस्तीक्ष्णमात्मदर्शनमात्मवान् ।
सहैवाग्निभिरात्मानं युयोज परमात्मनि ॥५४॥

tatra taptvā tapas tīkṣṇam
ātma-darśanam ātmavān
sahaivāgnibhir ātmānaṁ
yuyoja paramātmani

tatra—in the forest; *taptvā*—executing austerity; *tapaḥ*—the regulative principles of austerity; *tīkṣṇam*—very severely; *ātma-darśanam*—which helps self-realization; *ātmavān*—conversant with the self; *saha*—with; *eva*—certainly; *agnibhiḥ*—fires; *ātmānam*—the personal self; *yuyoja*—he engaged; *parama-ātmani*—dealing with the Supreme Soul.

TRANSLATION

When Saubhari Muni, who was quite conversant with the self, went to the forest, he performed severe penances. In this way, in the fire at the time of death, he ultimately engaged himself in the service of the Supreme Personality of Godhead.

PURPORT

At the time of death, fire burns the gross body, and if there is no more desire for material enjoyment the subtle body is also ended, and in this way a pure soul remains. This is confirmed in *Bhagavad-gītā* (*tyaktvā dehaṁ punar janma naiti*). If one is free from the bondage of both the gross and subtle material bodies and remains a pure soul, he returns home, back to Godhead, to be engaged in the service of the Lord. *Tyaktvā dehaṁ punar janma naiti mām eti:* he goes back home, back to Godhead. Thus it appears that Saubhari Muni attained that perfect stage.

TEXT 55

ताः स्वपत्युर्महाराज निरीक्ष्याध्यात्मिकीं गतिम् ।
अन्वीयुस्तत्प्रभावेण अग्निं शान्तमिवार्चिषः ॥५५॥

tāḥ sva-patyur mahārāja
nirīkṣyādhyātmikīṁ gatim
anvīyus tat-prabhāveṇa
agniṁ śāntam ivārciṣaḥ

tāḥ—all the wives of Saubhari; *sva-patyuḥ*—with their own husband; *mahārāja*—O King Parīkṣit; *nirīkṣya*—observing; *adhyātmikīm*—spiritual; *gatim*—progress; *anvīyuḥ*—followed; *tat-prabhāveṇa*—by the influence of their husband (although they were unfit, by the influence of their husband they also could go to the spiritual world); *agnim*—the fire; *śāntam*—completely merged; *iva*—like; *arciṣaḥ*—the flames.

TRANSLATION

O Mahārāja Parīkṣit, by observing their husband progressing in spiritual existence, Saubhari Muni's wives were also able to enter the spiritual world by his spiritual power, just as the flames of a fire cease when the fire is extinguished.

PURPORT

As stated in *Bhagavad-gītā* (9.32), *striyo vaiśyās tathā śūdrās te 'pi yānti paraṁ gatim.* Women are not considered very powerful in following spiritual principles, but if a woman is fortunate enough to get a suitable husband who is spiritually advanced and if she always engages in his service, she also gets the same benefit as her husband. Here it is clearly said that the wives of Saubhari Muni also entered the spiritual world by the influence of their husband. They were unfit, but because they were faithful followers of their husband, they also entered the spiritual world with him. Thus a woman should be a faithful servant of her husband, and if the husband is spiritually advanced, the woman will automatically get the opportunity to enter the spiritual world.

Thus end the Bhaktivedanta purports of the Ninth Canto, Sixth Chapter, of the Śrīmad-Bhāgavatam, *entitled "The Downfall of Saubhari Muni."*

CHAPTER SEVEN

The Descendants of King Māndhātā

In this chapter the descendants of King Māndhātā are described, and in this connection the histories of Purukutsa and Hariścandra are also given.

The most prominent son of Māndhātā was Ambarīṣa, his son was Yauvanāśva, and Yauvanāśva's son was Hārīta. These three personalities were the best in the dynasty of Māndhātā. Purukutsa, another son of Māndhātā, married the sister of the snakes (*sarpa-gaṇa*) named Narmadā. The son of Purukutsa was Trasaddasyu, whose son was Anaraṇya. Anaraṇya's son was Haryaśva, Haryaśva's son was Prāruṇa, Prāruṇa's son was Tribandhana, and Tribandhana's son was Satyavrata, also known as Triśaṅku. When Triśaṅku kidnapped the daughter of a *brāhmaṇa*, his father cursed him for this sinful act, and Triśaṅku became a *caṇḍāla*, worse than a *śūdra*. Later, by the influence of Viśvāmitra, he was brought to the heavenly planets, but by the influence of the demigods he fell back downward. He was stopped in his fall, however, by the influence of Viśvāmitra. The son of Triśaṅku was Hariścandra. Hariścandra once performed a Rājasūya-yajña, but Viśvāmitra cunningly took all of Hariścandra's possessions as a *dakṣiṇā* contribution and chastised Hariścandra in various ways. Because of this, a quarrel arose between Viśvāmitra and Vasiṣṭha. Hariścandra had no sons, but on the advice of Nārada he worshiped Varuṇa and in this way got a son named Rohita. Hariścandra promised that Rohita would be used to perform a Varuṇa-yajña. Varuṇa reminded Hariścandra repeatedly about this *yajña*, but the King, because of affection for his son, gave various arguments to avoid sacrificing him. Thus time passed, and gradually the son grew up. To safeguard his life, the boy then took bow and arrows in hand and went to the forest. Meanwhile, at home, Hariścandra suffered from dropsy because of an attack from Varuṇa. When Rohita received the news that his father was suffering, he wanted to return to the capital, but King Indra prevented him from doing so. Following the instructions of Indra, Rohita lived in the forest for six years and then returned home. Rohita purchased Śunaḥśepha, the second son of Ajīgarta, and gave him to his father, Hariścandra, as the sacrificial animal. In this way, the sacrifice was performed, Varuṇa and the other demigods were pacified, and Hariścandra was freed from disease. In this sacrifice, Viśvāmitra was the *hotā* priest, Jamadagni was the *adhvaryu*, Vasiṣṭha was the *brahmā*, and Ayāsya was the *udgātā*. King Indra, being very satisfied by the sacrifice, gave Hariścandra a golden chariot, and Viśvāmitra gave him transcendental knowledge. Thus Śukadeva Gosvāmī describes how Hariścandra achieved perfection.

TEXT 1

श्रीशुक उवाच
मान्धातुः पुत्रप्रवरो योऽम्बरीषः प्रकीर्तितः ।
पितामहेन प्रवृतो यौवनाश्वस्तु तत्सुतः ।
हारीतस्तस्य पुत्रोऽभून्मान्धातृप्रवरा इमे ॥ १ ॥

śrī-śuka uvāca
māndhātuḥ putra-pravaro
yo 'mbarīṣaḥ prakīrtitaḥ
pitāmahena pravṛto
yauvanāśvas tu tat-sutaḥ
hārītas tasya putro 'bhūn
māndhātṛ-pravarā ime

śrī-śukaḥ uvāca—Śrī Śukadeva Gosvāmī said; *māndhātuḥ*—of Māndhātā; *putra-pravaraḥ*—the prominent son; *yaḥ*—the one who; *ambarīṣaḥ*—by the name Ambarīṣa; *prakīrtitaḥ*—celebrated; *pitāmahena*—by his grandfather Yuvanāśva; *pravṛtaḥ*—accepted; *yauvanāśvaḥ*—named Yauvanāśva; *tu*—and; *tat-sutaḥ*—the son of Ambarīṣa; *hārītaḥ*—by the name Hārīta; *tasya*—of Yauvanāśva; *putraḥ*—the son; *abhūt*—became; *māndhātṛ*—in the dynasty of Māndhātā; *pravarāḥ*—most prominent; *ime*—all of them.

TRANSLATION

Śukadeva Gosvāmī said: The most prominent among the sons of Māndhātā was he who is celebrated as Ambarīṣa. Ambarīṣa was ac-

cepted as son by his grandfather Yuvanāśva. Ambarīṣa's son was Yauvanāśva, and Yauvanāśva's son was Hārīta. In Māndhātā's dynasty, Ambarīṣa, Hārīta and Yauvanāśva were very prominent.

TEXT 2

नर्मदा भ्रातृभिर्दत्ता पुरुकुत्साय योरगैः ।
तया रसातलं नीतो भुजगेन्द्रप्रयुक्तया ॥ २ ॥

narmadā bhrātṛbhir dattā
purukutsāya yoragaiḥ
tayā rasātalaṁ nīto
bhujagendra-prayuktayā

narmadā—by the name Narmadā; *bhrātṛbhiḥ*—by her brothers; *dattā*—was given in charity; *purukutsāya*—unto Purukutsa; *yā*—she who; *uragaiḥ*—by the serpents (*sarpa-gaṇa*); *tayā*—by her; *rasātalam*—to the lower region of the universe; *nītaḥ*—was brought; *bhujaga-indra-prayuktayā*—engaged by Vāsuki, the King of the serpents.

TRANSLATION

The serpent brothers of Narmadā gave Narmadā to Purukutsa. Being sent by Vāsuki, she took Purukutsa to the lower region of the universe.

PURPORT

Before describing the descendants of Purukutsa, the son of Māndhātā, Śukadeva Gosvāmī first describes how Purukutsa was married to Narmadā, who was induced to take him to the lower region of the universe.

TEXT 3

गन्धर्वानवधीत् तत्र वध्यान् वै विष्णुशक्तिधृक् ।
नागाल्लब्धवरः सर्पादभयं स्मरतामिदम् ॥ ३ ॥

gandharvān avadhīt tatra
vadhyān vai viṣṇu-śakti-dhṛk
nāgāl labdha-varaḥ sarpād
abhayaṁ smaratām idam

gandharvān—the inhabitants of Gandharvaloka; *avadhīt*—he killed; *tatra*—there (in the lower region of the universe); *vadhyān*—who deserved to be killed; *vai*—indeed; *viṣṇu-śakti-dhṛk*—being empowered by Lord Viṣṇu; *nāgāt*—from the Nāgas; *labdha-varaḥ*—having received a benediction; *sarpāt*—from the snakes; *abhayam*—assurances; *smaratām*—of those who remember; *idam*—this incident.

TRANSLATION

There in Rasātala, the lower region of the universe, Purukutsa, being empowered by Lord Viṣṇu, was able to kill all the Gandharvas who deserved to be killed. Purukutsa received the benediction from the serpents that anyone who remembers this history of his being brought by Narmadā to the lower region of the universe will be assured of safety from the attack of snakes.

TEXT 4

त्रसद्दस्युः पौरुकुत्सो योऽनरण्यस्य देहकृत् ।
हर्यश्वस्तत्सुतस्तस्मात्प्रारुणोऽथ त्रिबन्धनः ॥ ४ ॥

trasaddasyuḥ paurukutso
yo 'naraṇyasya deha-kṛt
haryaśvas tat-sutas tasmāt
prāruṇo 'tha tribandhanaḥ

trasaddasyuḥ—by the name Trasaddasyu; *paurukutsaḥ*—the son of Purukutsa; *yaḥ*—who; *anaraṇyasya*—of Anaraṇya; *deha-kṛt*—the father; *haryaśvaḥ*—by the name Haryaśva; *tat-sutaḥ*—the son of Anaraṇya; *tasmāt*—from him (Haryaśva); *prāruṇaḥ*—by the name Prāruṇa; *atha*—then, from Prāruṇa; *tribandhanaḥ*—his son, Tribandhana.

TRANSLATION

The son of Purukutsa was Trasaddasyu, who was the father of Anaraṇya. Anaraṇya's son was Haryaśva, the father of Prāruṇa. Prāruṇa was the father of Tribandhana.

TEXTS 5–6

तस्य सत्यव्रतः पुत्रस्त्रिशङ्कुरिति विश्रुतः ।
प्राप्तश्चाण्डालतां शापाद् गुरोः कौशिकतेजसा ॥ ५ ॥
सशरीरो गतः स्वर्गमद्यापि दिवि दृश्यते ।
पातितोऽवाक्शिरा देवैस्तेनैव स्तम्भितो बलात् ॥ ६ ॥

tasya satyavrataḥ putras
triśaṅkur iti viśrutaḥ
prāptaś cāṇḍālatāṁ śāpād
guroḥ kauśika-tejasā

saśarīro gataḥ svargam
adyāpi divi dṛśyate
pātito 'vāk-śirā devais
tenaiva stambhito balāt

tasya—of Tribandhana; *satyavrataḥ*—by the name Satyavrata; *putraḥ*—the son; *triśaṅkuḥ*—by the name Triśaṅku; *iti*—thus; *viśrutaḥ*—celebrated; *prāptaḥ*—had obtained; *cāṇḍālatām*—the quality of a *caṇḍāla*, lower than a *śūdra; śāpāt*—from the curse; *guroḥ*—of his father; *kauśika-tejasā*—by the prowess of Kauśika (Viśvāmitra); *sa-śarīraḥ*—while in this body; *gataḥ*—went; *svargam*—to the heavenly planet; *adya api*—until today; *divi*—in the sky; *dṛśyate*—can be seen; *pātitaḥ*—having fallen down; *avāk-śirāḥ*—with his head hanging downward; *devaiḥ*—by the prowess of the demigods; *tena*—by Viśvāmitra; *eva*—indeed; *stambhitaḥ*—fixed; *balāt*—by superior power.

TRANSLATION

The son of Tribandhana was Satyavrata, who is celebrated by the name Triśaṅku. Because he kidnapped the daughter of a brāhmaṇa

when she was being married, his father cursed him to become a caṇḍāla, lower than a śūdra. Thereafter, by the influence of Viśvāmitra, he went to the higher planetary system, the heavenly planets, in his material body, but because of the prowess of the demigods he fell back downward. Nonetheless, by the power of Viśvāmitra, he did not fall all the way down; even today he can still be seen hanging in the sky, head downward.

TEXT 7

त्रैशङ्कवो हरिश्चन्द्रो विश्वामित्रवसिष्ठयोः ।
यन्निमित्तमभूद् युद्धं पक्षिणोर्बहुवार्षिकम् ॥ ७ ॥

traiśaṅkavo hariścandro
viśvāmitra-vasiṣṭhayoḥ
yan-nimittam abhūd yuddhaṁ
pakṣiṇor bahu-vārṣikam

traiśaṅkavaḥ—the son of Triśaṅku; *hariścandraḥ*—by the name Hariścandra; *viśvāmitra-vasiṣṭhayoḥ*—between Viśvāmitra and Vasiṣṭha; *yat-nimittam*—because of Hariścandra; *abhūt*—there was; *yuddham*—a great fight; *pakṣiṇoḥ*—both of whom had been converted into birds; *bahu-vārṣikam*—for many years.

TRANSLATION

The son of Triśaṅku was Hariścandra. Because of Hariścandra there was a quarrel between Viśvāmitra and Vasiṣṭha, who for many years fought one another, having been transformed into birds.

PURPORT

Viśvāmitra and Vasiṣṭha were always inimical. Formerly, Viśvāmitra was a *kṣatriya*, and by undergoing severe austerities he wanted to become a *brāhmaṇa*, but Vasiṣṭha would not agree to accept him. In this way there was always disagreement between the two. Later, however, Vasiṣṭha accepted him because of Viśvāmitra's quality of forgiveness. Once Hariścandra performed a *yajña* for which Viśvāmitra was the priest, but Viśvāmitra, being angry at Hariścandra, took away all his possessions, claiming them as a contribution of *dakṣiṇā.* Vasiṣṭha, however, did not like this, and therefore a fight arose between Vasiṣṭha and Viśvāmitra. The fighting became so severe that each of them cursed the other. One of them said, "May you become a bird," and the other said, "May you become a duck." Thus both of them became birds and continued fighting for many years because of Hariścandra. We can see that such a great mystic *yogī* as Saubhari became a victim of sense gratification, and such great sages as Vasiṣṭha and Viśvāmitra became birds. This is the material world. *Ābrahma-bhuvanāl lokāḥ punar āvartino 'rjuna.* Within this material world, or within this universe, however elevated one may be in material qualities, one must suffer the conditions of birth, death, old age and disease (*janma-mṛtyu-jarā-vyādhi*). Therefore Kṛṣṇa says that this material world is simply miserable (*duḥkhālayam aśāśvatam*). The *Bhāgavatam* says, *padaṁ padaṁ yad vipadām:* at every step here there is danger. Therefore, because the Kṛṣṇa consciousness movement provides the opportunity for the human being to get out of this material world simply by chanting the Hare Kṛṣṇa *mantra*, this movement is the greatest benediction in human society.

TEXT 8

सोऽनपत्यो विषण्णात्मा नारदस्योपदेशतः ।
वरुणं शरणं यातः पुत्रो मे जायतां प्रभो ॥ ८ ॥

so 'napatyo viṣaṇṇātmā
nāradasyopadeśataḥ
varuṇaṁ śaraṇaṁ yātaḥ
putro me jāyatāṁ prabho

saḥ—that Hariścandra; *anapatyaḥ*—being without a son; *viṣaṇṇa-ātmā*—therefore very morose; *nāradasya*—of Nārada; *upadeśataḥ*—by the advice; *varuṇam*—unto Varuṇa; *śaraṇam yātaḥ*—took shelter; *putraḥ*—a son; *me*—of me; *jāyatām*—let there be born; *prabho*—O my lord.

TRANSLATION

Hariścandra had no son and was therefore extremely morose. Once, therefore, following the advice of Nārada, he took shelter of

Varuṇa and said to him, "My lord, I have no son. Would you kindly give me one?"

TEXT 9

यदि वीरो महाराज तेनैव त्वां यजे इति ।
तथेति वरुणेनास्य पुत्रो जातस्तु रोहितः ॥ ९ ॥

yadi vīro mahārāja
tenaiva tvāṁ yaje iti
tatheti varuṇenāsya
putro jātas tu rohitaḥ

yadi—if; *vīraḥ*—there is a son; *mahārāja*—O Mahārāja Parīkṣit; *tena eva*—even by that son; *tvām*—unto you; *yaje*—I shall offer sacrifice; *iti*—thus; *tathā*—as you desire; *iti*—thus accepted; *varuṇena*—by Varuṇa; *asya*—of Mahārāja Hariścandra; *putraḥ*—a son; *jātaḥ*—was born; *tu*—indeed; *rohitaḥ*—by the name Rohita.

TRANSLATION

O King Parīkṣit, Hariścandra begged Varuṇa, "My lord, if a son is born to me, with that son I shall perform a sacrifice for your satisfaction." When Hariścandra said this, Varuṇa replied, "Let it be so." Because of Varuṇa's benediction, Hariścandra begot a son named Rohita.

TEXT 10

जातः सुतो ह्यनेनाङ्ग मां यजस्वेति सोऽब्रवीत्।
यदा पशुर्निर्दशः स्यादथ मेध्यो भवेदिति ॥१०॥

jātaḥ suto hy anenāṅga
māṁ yajasveti so 'bravīt
yadā paśur nirdaśaḥ syād
atha medhyo bhaved iti

jātaḥ—has been born; *sutaḥ*—a son; *hi*—indeed; *anena*—by this son; *aṅga*—O Hariścandra; *mām*—unto me; *yajasva*—offer sacrifice;

iti—thus; *saḥ*—he, Varuṇa; *abravīt*—said; *yadā*—when; *paśuḥ*—an animal; *nirdaśaḥ*—has passed ten days; *syāt*—should become; *atha*—then; *medhyaḥ*—suitable for offering in sacrifice; *bhavet*—becomes; *iti*—thus (Hariścandra said).

TRANSLATION

Thereafter, when the child was born, Varuṇa approached Hariścandra and said, "Now you have a son. With this son you can offer me a sacrifice." In answer to this, Hariścandra said, "After ten days have passed since an animal's birth, the animal becomes fit to be sacrificed."

TEXT 11

निर्दशे च स आगत्य यजस्वेत्याह सोऽब्रवीत् ।
दन्ताः पशोर्यज्जायेरन्नथ मेध्यो भवेदिति ॥११॥

nirdaśe ca sa āgatya
yajasvety āha so 'bravīt
dantāḥ paśor yaj jāyerann
atha medhyo bhaved iti

nirdaśe—after ten days; *ca*—also; *saḥ*—he, Varuṇa; *āgatya*—coming there; *yajasva*—now sacrifice; *iti*—thus; *āha*—said; *saḥ*—he, Hariścandra; *abravīt*—replied; *dantāḥ*—the teeth; *paśoḥ*—of the animal; *yat*—when; *jāyeran*—have appeared; *atha*—then; *medhyaḥ*—fit for being sacrificed; *bhavet*—will become; *iti*—thus.

TRANSLATION

After ten days, Varuṇa came again and said to Hariścandra, "Now you can perform the sacrifice." Hariścandra replied, "When an animal grows teeth, then it becomes pure enough to be sacrificed."

TEXT 12

दन्ता जाता यजस्वेति स प्रत्याहाथ सोऽब्रवीत् ।
यदा पतन्त्यस्य दन्ता अथ मेध्यो भवेदिति ॥१२॥

dantā jātā yajasveti
sa pratyāhātha so 'bravīt
yadā patanty asya dantā
atha medhyo bhaved iti

dantāḥ—the teeth; *jātāḥ*—have grown; *yajasva*—now sacrifice; *iti*—thus; *saḥ*—he, Varuṇa; *pratyāha*—said; *atha*—thereupon; *saḥ*—he, Hariścandra; *abravīt*—replied; *yadā*—when; *patanti*—fall out; *asya*—his; *dantāḥ*—teeth; *atha*—then; *medhyaḥ*—fit for sacrifice; *bhavet*—will become; *iti*—thus.

TRANSLATION

When the teeth grew, Varuṇa came and said to Hariścandra, "Now the animal has grown teeth, and you can perform the sacrifice." Hariścandra replied, "When all its teeth have fallen out, then it will be fit for sacrifice."

TEXT 13

पशोर्निपतिता दन्ता यजस्वेत्याह सोऽब्रवीत् ।
यदा पशोः पुनर्दन्ता जायन्तेऽथ पशुः शुचिः ॥१३॥

paśor nipatitā dantā
yajasvety āha so 'bravīt
yadā paśoḥ punar dantā
jāyante 'tha paśuḥ śuciḥ

paśoḥ—of the animal; *nipatitāḥ*—have fallen out; *dantāḥ*—the teeth; *yajasva*—now sacrifice him; *iti*—thus; *āha*—said (Varuṇa); *saḥ*—he, Hariścandra; *abravīt*—replied; *yadā*—when; *paśoḥ*—of the animal; *punaḥ*—again; *dantāḥ*—the teeth; *jāyante*—grow; *atha*—then; *paśuḥ*—the animal; *śuciḥ*—is purified for being sacrificed.

TRANSLATION

When the teeth had fallen out, Varuṇa returned and said to Hariścandra, "Now the animal's teeth have fallen out, and you can perform the sacrifice." But Hariścandra replied, "When the

animal's teeth grow in again, then he will be pure enough to be sacrificed."

TEXT 14

पुनर्जाता यजस्वेति स प्रत्याहाथ सोऽब्रवीत् ।
सान्नाहिको यदा राजन् राजन्योऽथ पशुः शुचिः ॥१४॥

punar jātā yajasveti
sa pratyāhātha so 'bravīt
sānnāhiko yadā rājan
rājanyo 'tha paśuḥ śuciḥ

punaḥ—again; *jātāḥ*—have grown; *yajasva*—now you offer the sacrifice; *iti*—thus; *saḥ*—he, Varuṇa; *pratyāha*—replied; *atha*—thereafter; *saḥ*—he, Hariścandra; *abravīt*—said; *sānnāhikaḥ*—able to equip himself with a shield; *yadā*—when; *rājan*—O King Varuṇa; *rājanyaḥ*—the *kṣatriya;* *atha*—then; *paśuḥ*—the sacrificial animal; *śuciḥ*—becomes purified.

TRANSLATION

When the teeth grew in again, Varuṇa came and said to Hariścandra, "Now you can perform the sacrifice." But Hariścandra then said, "O King, when the sacrificial animal becomes a kṣatriya and is able to shield himself to fight with the enemy, then he will be purified."

TEXT 15

इति पुत्रानुरागेण स्नेहयन्त्रितचेतसा ।
कालं वञ्चयता तं तमुक्तो देवस्तमैक्षत ॥१५॥

iti putrānurāgeṇa
sneha-yantrita-cetasā
kālaṁ vañcayatā taṁ tam
ukto devas tam aikṣata

iti—in this way; *putra-anurāgeṇa*—because of affection for the son; *sneha-yantrita-cetasā*—his mind being controlled by such affection;

kālam—time; *vañcayatā*—cheating; *tam*—unto him; *tam*—that; *uktaḥ*—said; *devaḥ*—the demigod Varuṇa; *tam*—unto him, Hariścandra; *aikṣata*—waited for the fulfillment of his promise.

TRANSLATION

Hariścandra was certainly very much attached to his son. Because of this affection, he asked the demigod Varuṇa to wait. Thus Varuṇa waited and waited for the time to come.

TEXT 16

रोहितस्तदभिज्ञाय पितुः कर्म चिकीर्षितम् ।
प्राणप्रेप्सुर्धनुष्पाणिररण्यं प्रत्यपद्यत ॥१६॥

rohitas tad abhijñāya
pituḥ karma cikīrṣitam
prāṇa-prepsur dhanuṣ-pāṇir
araṇyaṁ pratyapadyata

rohitaḥ—the son of Hariścandra; *tat*—this fact; *abhijñāya*—having thoroughly understood; *pituḥ*—of his father; *karma*—action; *cikīrṣitam*—which he was practically doing; *prāṇa-prepsuḥ*—wishing to save his life; *dhanuḥ-pāṇiḥ*—taking his bow and arrows; *araṇyam*—to the forest; *pratyapadyata*—left.

TRANSLATION

Rohita could understand that his father intended to offer him as the animal for sacrifice. Therefore, just to save himself from death, he equipped himself with bow and arrows and went to the forest.

TEXT 17

पितरं वरुणग्रस्तं श्रुत्वा जातमहोदरम् ।
रोहितो ग्राममेयाय तमिन्द्रः प्रत्यषेधत ॥१७॥

pitaraṁ varuṇa-grastaṁ
śrutvā jāta-mahodaram

rohito grāmam eyāya
tam indraḥ pratyaṣedhata

pitaram—about his father; *varuṇa-grastam*—having been attacked with dropsy by Varuṇa; *śrutvā*—after hearing; *jāta*—had grown; *mahā-udaram*—inflated abdomen; *rohitaḥ*—his son Rohita; *grāmam eyāya*—wanted to come back to the capital; *tam*—unto him (Rohita); *indraḥ*—King Indra; *pratyaṣedhata*—forbade to go there.

TRANSLATION

When Rohita heard that his father had been attacked by dropsy due to Varuṇa and that his abdomen had grown very large, he wanted to return to the capital, but King Indra forbade him to do so.

TEXT 18

भूमेः पर्यटनं पुण्यं तीर्थक्षेत्रनिषेवणैः ।
रोहितायादिशच्छक्रः सोऽप्यरण्येऽवसत् समाम् ॥१८॥

bhūmeḥ paryaṭanaṁ puṇyaṁ
tīrtha-kṣetra-niṣevaṇaiḥ
rohitāyādiśac chakraḥ
so 'py araṇye 'vasat samām

bhūmeḥ—of the surface of the world; *paryaṭanam*—traveling; *puṇyam*—holy places; *tīrtha-kṣetra*—places of pilgrimage; *niṣevaṇaiḥ*—by serving or going to and coming from such places; *rohitāya*—unto Rohita; *ādiśat*—ordered; *śakraḥ*—King Indra; *saḥ*—he, Rohita; *api*—also; *araṇye*—in the forest; *avasat*—lived; *samām*—for one year.

TRANSLATION

King Indra advised Rohita to travel to different pilgrimage sites and holy places, for such activities are pious indeed. Following this instruction, Rohita went to the forest for one year.

TEXT 19

एवं द्वितीये तृतीये चतुर्थे पञ्चमे तथा ।
अभ्येत्याभ्येत्य स्थविरो विप्रो भूत्वाह वृत्रहा ॥१९॥

evaṁ dvitīye tṛtīye
caturthe pañcame tathā
abhyetyābhyetya sthaviro
vipro bhūtvāha vṛtra-hā

evam—in this way; *dvitīye*—on the second year; *tṛtīye*—on the third year; *caturthe*—on the fourth year; *pañcame*—on the fifth year; *tathā*—as well as; *abhyetya*—coming before him; *abhyetya*—again coming before him; *sthaviraḥ*—a very old man; *vipraḥ*—a *brāhmaṇa; bhūtvā*—becoming so; *āha*—said; *vṛtra-hā*—Indra.

TRANSLATION

In this way, at the end of the second, third, fourth and fifth years, when Rohita wanted to return to his capital, the King of heaven, Indra, approached him as an old brāhmaṇa and forbade him to return, repeating the same words as in the previous year.

TEXT 20

षष्ठं संवत्सरं तत्र चरित्वा रोहितः पुरीम् ।
उपव्रजन्नजीगर्तादक्रीणान्मध्यमं सुतम् ।
शुनःशेफं पशुं पित्रे प्रदाय समवन्दत ॥२०॥

ṣaṣṭhaṁ saṁvatsaraṁ tatra
caritvā rohitaḥ purīm
upavrajann ajīgartād
akrīṇān madhyamaṁ sutam
śunaḥśephaṁ paśuṁ pitre
pradāya samavandata

ṣaṣṭham—the sixth; *saṁvatsaram*—year; *tatra*—in the forest; *caritvā*—wandering; *rohitaḥ*—the son of Hariścandra; *purīm*—in his capital; *upavrajan*—went there; *ajīgartāt*—from Ajīgarta; *akrīṇāt*—purchased; *madhyamam*—the second; *sutam*—son; *śunaḥśepham*—whose name was Śunaḥśepha; *paśum*—to use as the sacrificial animal; *pitre*—unto his father; *pradāya*—offering; *samavandata*—respectfully offered his obeisances.

TRANSLATION

Thereafter, in the sixth year, after wandering in the forest, Rohita returned to the capital of his father. He purchased from Ajīgarta his second son, named Śunaḥśepha. Then he offered Śunaḥśepha to his father, Hariścandra, to be used as the sacrificial animal and offered Hariścandra his respectful obeisances.

PURPORT

It appears that in those days a man could be purchased for any purpose. Hariścandra was in need of a person to sacrifice as the animal in a *yajña* and thus fulfill his promise to Varuṇa, and a man was purchased from another man for this purpose. Millions of years ago, animal sacrifice and slave trade both existed. Indeed, they have existed since time immemorial.

TEXT 21

ततः पुरुषमेधेन हरिश्चन्द्रो महायशाः ।
मुक्तोदरोऽयजद् देवान् वरुणादीन् महत्कथः ॥२१॥

tataḥ puruṣa-medhena
hariścandro mahā-yaśāḥ
muktodaro 'yajad devān
varuṇādīn mahat-kathaḥ

tataḥ—thereafter; *puruṣa-medhena*—by sacrificing a man in the *yajña; hariścandraḥ*—King Hariścandra; *mahā-yaśāḥ*—very famous; *mukta-udaraḥ*—became free from dropsy; *ayajat*—offered sacrifices; *devān*—unto the demigods; *varuṇa-ādīn*—headed by Varuṇa and others; *mahat-kathaḥ*—famous in history with other exalted personalities.

TRANSLATION

Thereafter, the famous King Hariścandra, one of the exalted persons in history, performed grand sacrifices by sacrificing a man and pleased all the demigods. In this way his dropsy created by Varuṇa was cured.

TEXT 22

विश्वामित्रोऽभवत् तस्मिन् होता चाध्वर्युरात्मवान् ।
जमदग्निरभूद् ब्रह्मा वसिष्ठोऽयास्यः सामगः ॥२२॥

viśvāmitro 'bhavat tasmin
hotā cādhvaryur ātmavān
jamadagnir abhūd brahmā
vasiṣṭho 'yāsyaḥ sāma-gaḥ

viśvāmitraḥ—the great sage and mystic Viśvāmitra; *abhavat*—became; *tasmin*—in that great sacrifice; *hotā*—the chief priest to offer oblations; *ca*—also; *adhvaryuḥ*—a person who recites hymns from the *Yajur Veda* and performs ritualistic ceremonies; *ātmavān*—fully self-realized; *jamadagniḥ*—Jamadagni; *abhūt*—became; *brahmā*—acting as the chief *brāhmaṇa; vasiṣṭhaḥ*—the great sage; *ayāsyaḥ*—another great sage; *sāma-gaḥ*—engaged as the reciter of the *Sāma Veda mantras.*

TRANSLATION

In that great human sacrifice, Viśvāmitra was the chief priest to offer oblations, the perfectly self-realized Jamadagni had the responsibility for chanting the mantras from the Yajur Veda, Vasiṣṭha was the chief brahminical priest, and the sage Ayāsya was the reciter of the hymns of the Sāma Veda.

TEXT 23

तस्मै तुष्टो ददाविन्द्रः शातकौम्भमयं रथम् ।
शुनःशेफस्य माहात्म्यमुपरिष्टात् प्रचक्ष्यते ॥२३॥

tasmai tuṣṭo dadāv indraḥ
śātakaumbhamayaṁ ratham
śunaḥśephasya māhātmyam
upariṣṭāt pracakṣyate

tasmai—unto him, King Hariścandra; *tuṣṭaḥ*—being very pleased; *dadau*—delivered; *indraḥ*—the King of heaven; *śātakaumbhamayam*—made of gold; *ratham*—a chariot; *śunaḥśephasya*—about Śunaḥśepha; *māhātmyam*—glories; *upariṣṭāt*—in the course of describing the sons of Viśvāmitra; *pracakṣyate*—will be narrated.

TRANSLATION

King Indra, being very pleased with Hariścandra, offered him a gift of a golden chariot. Śunaḥśepha's glories will be presented along with the description of the son of Viśvāmitra.

TEXT 24

सत्यं सारं धृतिं दृष्ट्वा सभार्यस्य च भूपतेः ।
विश्वामित्रो भृशं प्रीतो ददावविहतां गतिम् ॥२४॥

satyaṁ sāraṁ dhṛtiṁ dṛṣṭvā
sabhāryasya ca bhūpateḥ
viśvāmitro bhṛśaṁ prīto
dadāv avihatāṁ gatim

satyam—truthfulness; *sāram*—firmness; *dhṛtim*—forbearance; *dṛṣṭvā*—by seeing; *sa-bhāryasya*—with his wife; *ca*—and; *bhūpateḥ*—of Mahārāja Hariścandra; *viśvāmitraḥ*—the great sage Viśvāmitra; *bhṛśam*—very much; *prītaḥ*—being pleased; *dadau*—gave him; *avihatām gatim*—imperishable knowledge.

TRANSLATION

The great sage Viśvāmitra saw that Mahārāja Hariścandra, along with his wife, was truthful, forbearing and concerned with the

essence. Thus he gave them imperishable knowledge for fulfillment of the human mission.

TEXTS 25–26

मनः पृथिव्यां तामद्भिस्तेजसापोऽनिलेन तत् ।
खे वायुं धारयंस्तच्च भूतादौ तं महात्मनि ॥२५॥
तस्मिञ्ज्ञानकलां ध्यात्वा तयाज्ञानं विनिर्दहन् ।
हित्वा तां स्वेन भावेन निर्वाणसुखसंविदा ।
अनिर्देश्याप्रतर्क्येण तस्थौ विध्वस्तबन्धनः ॥२६॥

manaḥ pṛthivyāṁ tām adbhis
tejasāpo 'nilena tat
khe vāyuṁ dhārayaṁs tac ca
bhūtādau taṁ mahātmani

tasmiñ jñāna-kalāṁ dhyātvā
tayājñānaṁ vinirdahan
hitvā tāṁ svena bhāvena
nirvāṇa-sukha-saṁvidā
anirdeśyāpratarkyeṇa
tasthau vidhvasta-bandhanaḥ

manaḥ—the mind (full of material desires for eating, sleeping, mating and defending); *pṛthivyām*—in the earth; *tām*—that; *adbhiḥ*—with water; *tejasā*—and with fire; *apaḥ*—the water; *anilena*—in the fire; *tat*—that; *khe*—in the sky; *vāyum*—the air; *dhārayan*—amalgamating; *tat*—that; *ca*—also; *bhūta-ādau*—in the false ego, the origin of material existence; *tam*—that (false ego); *mahā-ātmani*—in the *mahat-tattva*, the total material energy; *tasmin*—in the total material energy; *jñāna-kalām*—spiritual knowledge and its different branches; *dhyātvā*—by meditating; *tayā*—by this process; *ajñānam*—ignorance; *vinirdahan*—specifically subdued; *hitvā*—giving up; *tām*—material ambition; *svena*—by self-realization; *bhāvena*—in devotional service; *nirvāṇa-sukha-saṁvidā*—by transcendental bliss, putting an end to material existence; *anirdeśya*—imperceptible; *apratarkyeṇa*—inconceivable;

tasthau—remained; *vidhvasta*—completely freed from; *bandhanaḥ*—material bondage.

TRANSLATION

Mahārāja Hariścandra first purified his mind, which was full of material enjoyment, by amalgamating it with the earth. Then he amalgamated the earth with water, the water with fire, the fire with the air, and the air with the sky. Thereafter, he amalgamated the sky with the total material energy, and the total material energy with spiritual knowledge. This spiritual knowledge is realization of one's self as part of the Supreme Lord. When the self-realized spiritual soul is engaged in service to the Lord, he is eternally imperceptible and inconceivable. Thus established in spiritual knowledge, he is completely freed from material bondage.

Thus end the Bhaktivedanta purports of the Ninth Canto, Seventh Chapter, of the Śrīmad-Bhāgavatam, *entitled "The Descendants of King Māndhātā."*

CHAPTER EIGHT

The Sons of Sagara Meet Lord Kapiladeva

In this Eighth Chapter the descendants of Rohita are described. In the dynasty of Rohita there was a king named Sagara, whose history is described in relation to Kapiladeva and the destruction of the sons of Sagara.

The son of Rohita was known as Harita, and the son of Harita was Campa, who constructed a township known as Campāpurī. The son of Campa was Sudeva, the son of Sudeva was Vijaya, the son of Vijaya was Bharuka, and the son of Bharuka was Vṛka. Bāhuka, the son of Vṛka, was greatly disturbed by his enemies, and therefore he left home with his wife and went to the forest. When he died there, his wife wanted to accept the principles of *satī*, dying with her husband, but when she was about to die a sage named Aurva found that she was pregnant and forbade her to do so. The co-wives of this wife of Bāhuka gave her poison with her food, but still her son was born with the poison. The son was therefore named Sagara (*sa* means "with," and *gara* means "poison"). Following the instructions of the great sage Aurva, King Sagara reformed many clans, including the Yavanas, Śakas, Haihayas and Barbaras. The king did not kill them, but reformed them. Then, again following the instructions of Aurva, King Sagara performed *aśvamedha* sacrifices, but the horse needed for such a sacrifice was stolen by Indra, the King of heaven. King Sagara had two wives, named Sumati and Keśinī. While searching for the horse, the sons of Sumati extensively dug up the surface of the earth and in this way dug a trench, which later became known as the Sāgara Ocean. In the course of this search, they came upon the great personality Kapiladeva and thought Him to have stolen the horse. With this offensive understanding, they attacked Him and were all burned to ashes. Keśinī, the second wife of King Sagara, had a son named Asamañjasa, whose son Aṁśumān later searched for the horse and delivered his uncles. Upon approaching Kapiladeva, Aṁśumān saw both the horse meant for sacrifice and a pile of ashes. Aṁśumān offered prayers to Kapiladeva, who was very pleased by his prayers and who returned the horse. After getting back the horse, however, Aṁśumān still stood before Kapiladeva, and Kapiladeva could understand that Aṁśumān was praying for the deliverance of his forefathers. Thus Kapiladeva offered the instruction that they could be delivered by water from the Ganges. Aṁśumān then offered respectful obeisances to Kapiladeva, circumambulated Him, and left that place with the horse for sacrifice. When King Sagara finished his *yajña,* he handed over the kingdom to Aṁśumān and, following the advice of Aurva, attained salvation.

TEXT 1

श्रीशुक उवाच
हरितो रोहितसुतश्चम्पस्तस्माद् विनिर्मिता ।
चम्पापुरी सुदेवोऽतो विजयो यस्य चात्मजः ॥ १ ॥

śrī-śuka uvāca
harito rohita-sutaś
campas tasmād vinirmitā
campāpurī sudevo 'to
vijayo yasya cātmajaḥ

śrī-śukaḥ uvāca—Śrī Śukadeva Gosvāmī said; *haritaḥ*—the king named Harita; *rohita-sutaḥ*—the son of King Rohita; *campaḥ*—by the name Campa; *tasmāt*—from Harita; *vinirmitā*—was constructed; *campā-purī*—the township known as Campāpurī; *sudevaḥ*—by the name Sudeva; *ataḥ*—thereafter (from Campa); *vijayaḥ*—by the name Vijaya; *yasya*—of whom (Sudeva); *ca*—also; *ātma-jaḥ*—the son.

TRANSLATION

Śukadeva Gosvāmī continued: The son of Rohita was Harita, and Harita's son was Campa, who constructed the town of Campāpurī. The son of Campa was Sudeva, and his son was Vijaya.

TEXT 2

भरुकस्तत्सुतस्तस्माद् वृकस्तस्यापि बाहुकः ।
सोऽरिभिर्हृतभू राजा सभार्यो वनमाविशत् ॥ २ ॥

bharukas tat-sutas tasmād
vṛkas tasyāpi bāhukaḥ
so 'ribhir hṛta-bhū rājā
sabhāryo vanam āviśat

bharukaḥ—by the name Bharuka; *tat-sutaḥ*—the son of Vijaya; *tasmāt*—from him (Bharuka); *vṛkaḥ*—by the name Vṛka; *tasya*—his; *api*—also; *bāhukaḥ*—by the name Bāhuka; *saḥ*—he, the King; *aribhiḥ*—by his enemies; *hṛta-bhūḥ*—his land having been taken away; *rājā*—the King (Bāhuka); *sa-bhāryaḥ*—with his wife; *vanam*—the forest; *āviśat*—entered.

TRANSLATION

The son of Vijaya was Bharuka, Bharuka's son was Vṛka, and Vṛka's son was Bāhuka. The enemies of King Bāhuka took away all his possessions, and therefore the King entered the order of vānaprastha and went to the forest with his wife.

TEXT 3

वृद्धं तं पञ्चतां प्राप्तं महिष्यनुमरिष्यती ।
और्वेण जानतात्मानं प्रजावन्तं निवारिता ॥ ३ ॥

vṛddhaṁ taṁ pañcatāṁ prāptaṁ
mahiṣy anumariṣyatī
aurveṇa jānatātmānaṁ
prajāvantaṁ nivāritā

vṛddham—when he was old; *tam*—him; *pañcatām*—death; *prāptam*—who had obtained; *mahiṣī*—the queen; *anumariṣyatī*—who wanted to die with him and become *satī; aurveṇa*—by the great sage

Aurva; *jānatā*—understanding that; *ātmānam*—the body of the queen; *prajā-vantam*—bore a son within the womb; *nivāritā*—was forbidden.

TRANSLATION

Bāhuka died when he was old, and one of his wives wanted to die with him, following the satī rite. At that time, however, Aurva Muni, knowing her to be pregnant, forbade her to die.

TEXT 4

आज्ञायास्यै सपत्नीभिर्गरो दत्तोऽन्धसा सह ।
सह तेनैव संजातः सगराख्यो महायशाः ।
सगरश्चक्रवर्त्यासीत् सागरो यत्सुतैः कृतः ॥ ४ ॥

ājñāyāsyai sapatnībhir
garo datto 'ndhasā saha
saha tenaiva sañjātaḥ
sagarākhyo mahā-yaśāḥ
sagaraś cakravarty āsīt
sāgaro yat-sutaiḥ kṛtaḥ

ājñāya—knowing (this); *asyai*—unto that pregnant queen; *sapatnībhiḥ*—by the co-wives of the wife of Bāhuka; *garaḥ*—poison; *dattaḥ*—was given; *andhasā saha*—with her food; *saha tena*—with that poison; *eva*—also; *sañjātaḥ*—was born; *sagara-ākhyaḥ*—by the name Sagara; *mahā-yaśāḥ*—having a great reputation; *sagaraḥ*—King Sagara; *cakravartī*—the emperor; *āsīt*—became; *sāgaraḥ*—the place known as Gaṅgāsāgara; *yat-sutaiḥ*—by the sons of whom; *kṛtaḥ*—was excavated.

TRANSLATION

Knowing that she was pregnant, the co-wives of the wife of Bāhuka conspired to give her poison with her food, but it did not act. Instead, the son was born along with the poison. Therefore he became famous as Sagara ["one who is born with poison"]. Sagara later became the emperor. The place known as Gaṅgāsāgara was excavated by his sons.

TEXTS 5–6

यस्तालजङ्घान् यवनाञ्छकान् हैहयबर्बरान् ।
नावधीद् गुरुवाक्येन चक्रे विकृतवेषिणः ॥ ५ ॥
मुण्डाञ्छ्मश्रुधरान् कांश्चिन्मुक्तकेशार्धमुण्डितान् ।
अनन्तर्वाससः कांश्चिदबहिर्वाससोऽपरान् ॥ ६ ॥

yas tālajaṅghān yavanāñ
chakān haihaya-barbarān
nāvadhīd guru-vākyena
cakre vikṛta-veṣiṇaḥ

muṇḍāñ chmaśru-dharān kāṁścin
mukta-keśārdha-muṇḍitān
anantar-vāsasaḥ kāṁścid
abahir-vāsaso 'parān

yaḥ—Mahārāja Sagara who; *tālajaṅghān*—the uncivilized clan named Tālajaṅgha; *yavanān*—persons averse to the Vedic literature; *śakān*—another class of atheist; *haihaya*—the uncivilized; *barbarān*—and the Barbaras; *na*—not; *avadhīt*—did kill; *guru-vākyena*—by the order of his spiritual master; *cakre*—made them; *vikṛta-veṣiṇaḥ*—dressed awkwardly; *muṇḍān*—shaved clean; *śmaśru-dharān*—wearing mustaches; *kāṁścit*—some of them; *mukta-keśa*—loose hair; *ardha-muṇḍitān*—half-shaven; *anantaḥ-vāsasaḥ*—without underwear; *kāṁścit*—some of them; *abahiḥ-vāsasaḥ*—without covering garments; *aparān*—others.

TRANSLATION

Sagara Mahārāja, following the order of his spiritual master, Aurva, did not kill the uncivilized men like the Tālajaṅghas, Yavanas, Śakas, Haihayas and Barbaras. Instead, some of them he made dress awkwardly, some of them he shaved clean but allowed to wear mustaches, some of them he left wearing loose hair, some he half shaved, some he left without underwear, and some without external garments. Thus these different clans were made to dress differently, but King Sagara did not kill them.

TEXT 7

सोऽश्वमेधैरयजत सर्ववेदसुरात्मकम् ।
और्वोपदिष्टयोगेन हरिमात्मानमीश्वरम् ।
तस्योत्सृष्टं पशुं यज्ञे जहाराश्वं पुरन्दरः ॥ ७ ॥

so 'śvamedhair ayajata
sarva-veda-surātmakam
aurvopadiṣṭa-yogena
harim ātmānam īśvaram
tasyotsṛṣṭaṁ paśuṁ yajñe
jahārāśvaṁ purandaraḥ

saḥ—he, Mahārāja Sagara; *aśvamedhaiḥ*—by performing *aśva-medha-yajñas; ayajata*—worshiped; *sarva-veda*—of all Vedic knowledge; *sura*—and of all learned sages; *ātmakam*—the Supersoul; *aurva-upadiṣṭa-yogena*—by the mystic *yoga* practice advised by Aurva; *harim*—unto the Supreme Personality of Godhead; *ātmānam*—unto the Supersoul; *īśvaram*—unto the supreme controller; *tasya*—of him (Sagara Mahārāja); *utsṛṣṭam*—which was meant for offering; *paśum*—the sacrificial animal; *yajñe*—in the sacrifice; *jahāra*—stole; *aśvam*—the horse; *purandaraḥ*—the King of heaven, Indra.

TRANSLATION

Following the instructions of the great sage Aurva, Sagara Mahārāja performed aśvamedha sacrifices and thus satisfied the Supreme Lord, who is the supreme controller, the Supersoul of all learned scholars, and the knower of all Vedic knowledge, the Supreme Personality of Godhead. But Indra, the King of heaven, stole the horse meant to be offered at the sacrifice.

TEXT 8

सुमत्यास्तनया दृप्ताः पितुरादेशकारिणः ।
हयमन्वेषमाणास्ते समन्तान्न्यखनन् महीम् ॥ ८ ॥

sumatyās tanayā dṛptāḥ
pitur ādeśa-kāriṇaḥ
hayam anveṣamāṇās te
samantān nyakhanan mahīm

sumatyāḥ tanayāḥ—the sons born of Queen Sumati; *dṛptāḥ*—very proud of their prowess and influence; *pituḥ*—of their father (Mahārāja Sagara); *ādeśa-kāriṇaḥ*—following the order; *hayam*—the horse (stolen by Indra); *anveṣamāṇāḥ*—while seeking; *te*—all of them; *samantāt*—everywhere; *nyakhanan*—dug; *mahīm*—the earth.

TRANSLATION

[King Sagara had two wives, Sumati and Keśinī.] The sons of Sumati, who were very proud of their prowess and influence, following the order of their father, searched for the lost horse. While doing so, they dug into the earth very extensively.

TEXTS 9–10

प्रागुदीच्यां दिशि हयं ददृशुः कपिलान्तिके ।
एष वाजिहरश्चौर आस्ते मीलितलोचनः ॥ ९ ॥
हन्यतां हन्यतां पाप इति षष्टिसहस्रिणः ।
उदायुधा अभिययुरुन्मिमेष तदा मुनिः ॥१०॥

prāg-udīcyāṁ diśi hayaṁ
dadṛśuḥ kapilāntike
eṣa vāji-haraś caura
āste mīlita-locanaḥ

hanyatāṁ hanyatāṁ pāpa
iti ṣaṣṭi-sahasriṇaḥ
udāyudhā abhiyayur
unmimeṣa tadā muniḥ

prāk-udīcyām—in the northeastern; *diśi*—direction; *hayam*—the horse; *dadṛśuḥ*—they saw; *kapila-antike*—near the *āśrama* of Kapila;

eṣaḥ—here is; *vāji-haraḥ*—the horse thief; *cauraḥ*—the thief; *āste*—existing; *mīlita-locanaḥ*—with closed eyes; *hanyatām hanyatām*—kill him, kill him; *pāpaḥ*—a most sinful person; *iti*—in this way; *ṣaṣṭi-sahasriṇaḥ*—the sixty thousand sons of Sagara; *udāyudhāḥ*—raising their respective weapons; *abhiyayuḥ*—they approached; *unmimeṣa*—opened His eyes; *tadā*—at that time; *muniḥ*—Kapila Muni.

TRANSLATION

Thereafter, in the northeastern direction, they saw the horse near the āśrama of Kapila Muni. "Here is the man who has stolen the horse," they said. "He is staying there with closed eyes. Certainly he is very sinful. Kill him! Kill him!" Shouting like this, the sons of Sagara, sixty thousand all together, raised their weapons. When they approached the sage, the sage opened His eyes.

TEXT 11

स्वशरीराग्निना तावन्महेन्द्रहृतचेतसः ।
महद्व्यतिक्रमहता भस्मसादभवन् क्षणात् ॥११॥

sva-śarīrāgninā tāvan
mahendra-hṛta-cetasaḥ
mahad-vyatikrama-hatā
bhasmasād abhavan kṣaṇāt

sva-śarīra-agninā—by the fire emanating from their own bodies; *tāvat*—immediately; *mahendra*—by the tricks of Indra, the King of heaven; *hṛta-cetasaḥ*—their consciousness having been taken away; *mahat*—a great personality; *vyatikrama-hatāḥ*—defeated by the fault of insulting; *bhasmasāt*—turned to ashes; *abhavan*—became; *kṣaṇāt*—immediately.

TRANSLATION

By the influence of Indra, the King of heaven, the sons of Sagara had lost their intelligence and disrespected a great personality. Consequently, fire emanated from their own bodies, and they were immediately burned to ashes.

PURPORT

The material body is a combination of earth, water, fire, air and ether. There is already fire within the body, and our practical experience is that the heat of this fire sometimes increases and sometimes decreases. The fire within the bodies of the sons of Sagara Mahārāja became so much hotter that all of them burned to ashes. The fire's increased heat was due to their misbehavior toward a great personality. Such misbehavior is called *mahad-vyatikrama.* They were killed by the fire of their own bodies because of insulting a great personality.

TEXT 12

न साधुवादो मुनिकोपभर्जिता
नृपेन्द्रपुत्रा इति सत्त्वधामनि ।
कथं तमो रोषमयं विभाव्यते
जगत्पवित्रात्मनि खे रजो भुवः ॥१२॥

na sādhu-vādo muni-kopa-bharjitā
nṛpendra-putrā iti sattva-dhāmani
kathaṁ tamo roṣamayaṁ vibhāvyate
jagat-pavitrātmani khe rajo bhuvaḥ

na—not; *sādhu-vādaḥ*—the opinion of learned persons; *muni-kopa*—by the anger of Kapila Muni; *bharjitāḥ*—were burned to ashes; *nṛpendra-putrāḥ*—all the sons of Sagara Mahārāja; *iti*—thus; *sattva-dhāmani*—in Kapila Muni, in whom the mode of goodness was predominant; *katham*—how; *tamaḥ*—the mode of ignorance; *roṣa-mayam*—manifested in the form of anger; *vibhāvyate*—can be manifested; *jagat-pavitra-ātmani*—in He whose body can purify the whole world; *khe*—in the sky; *rajaḥ*—dust; *bhuvaḥ*—earthly.

TRANSLATION

It is sometimes argued that the sons of King Sagara were burned to ashes by the fire emanating from the eyes of Kapila Muni. This statement, however, is not approved by great learned persons, for Kapila Muni's body is completely in the mode of goodness and

therefore cannot manifest the mode of ignorance in the form of anger, just as the pure sky cannot be polluted by the dust of the earth.

TEXT 13

यस्येरिता सांख्यमयी दृढेह नौ-
र्यया मुमुक्षुस्तरते दुरत्ययम् ।
भवार्णवं मृत्युपथं विपश्चितः
परात्मभूतस्य कथं पृथङ्मतिः ॥१३॥

yasyeritā sāṅkhyamayī dṛḍheha naur
yayā mumukṣus tarate duratyayam
bhavārṇavaṁ mṛtyu-pathaṁ vipaścitaḥ
parātma-bhūtasya kathaṁ pṛthaṅ-matiḥ

yasya—by whom; *īritā*—had been explained; *sāṅkhya-mayī*—having the form of the philosophy analyzing the material world (Sāṅkhya philosophy); *dṛḍhā*—very strong (to deliver people from this material world); *iha*—in this material world; *nauḥ*—a boat; *yayā*—by which; *mumukṣuḥ*—a person desiring to be liberated; *tarate*—can cross over; *duratyayam*—very difficult to cross; *bhava-arṇavam*—the ocean of nescience; *mṛtyu-patham*—a material life of repeated birth and death; *vipaścitaḥ*—of a learned person; *parātma-bhūtasya*—who has been elevated to the transcendental platform; *katham*—how; *pṛthak-matiḥ*—a sense of distinction (between enemy and friend).

TRANSLATION

Kapila Muni enunciated in this material world the Sāṅkhya philosophy, which is a strong boat with which to cross over the ocean of nescience. Indeed, a person eager to cross the ocean of the material world may take shelter of this philosophy. In such a greatly learned person, situated on the elevated platform of transcendence, how can there be any distinction between enemy and friend?

PURPORT

One who is promoted to the transcendental position (*brahma-bhūta*) is always jubilant (*prasannātmā*). He is unaffected by the false distinctions between good and bad in the material world. Therefore, such an exalted person is *samaḥ sarveṣu bhūteṣu;* that is to say, he is equal toward everyone, not distinguishing between friend and enemy. Because he is on the absolute platform, free from material contamination, he is called *parātma-bhūta* or *brahma-bhūta.* Kapila Muni, therefore, was not at all angry at the sons of Sagara Mahārāja; rather, they were burnt to ashes by the heat of their own bodies.

TEXT 14

योऽसमञ्जस इत्युक्तः स केशिन्या नृपात्मजः ।
तस्य पुत्रोंऽशुमान् नाम पितामहहिते रतः ॥१४॥

yo 'samañjasa ity uktaḥ
sa keśinyā nṛpātmajaḥ
tasya putro 'ṁśumān nāma
pitāmaha-hite rataḥ

yaḥ—one of the sons of Sagara Mahārāja; *asamañjasaḥ*—whose name was Asamañjasa; *iti*—as such; *uktaḥ*—known; *saḥ*—he; *keśinyāḥ*—in the womb of Keśinī, the other queen of Sagara Mahārāja; *nṛpa-ātmajaḥ*—the son of the King; *tasya*—of him (Asamañjasa); *putraḥ*—the son; *aṁśumān nāma*—was known as Aṁśumān; *pitāmaha-hite*—in doing good for his grandfather, Sagara Mahārāja; *rataḥ*—always engaged.

TRANSLATION

Among the sons of Sagara Mahārāja was one named Asamañjasa, who was born from the King's second wife, Keśinī. The son of Asamañjasa was known as Aṁśumān, and he was always engaged in working for the good of Sagara Mahārāja, his grandfather.

TEXTS 15–16

असमञ्जस आत्मानं दर्शयन्नसमञ्जसम् ।
जातिस्मरः पुरा सङ्गाद् योगी योगाद् विचालितः ॥१५॥
आचरन् गर्हितं लोके ज्ञातीनां कर्म विप्रियम् ।
सरय्वां क्रीडतो बालान् प्रास्यदुद्वेजयञ्जनम् ॥१६॥

asamañjasa ātmānaṁ
darśayann asamañjasam
jāti-smaraḥ purā saṅgād
yogī yogād vicālitaḥ

ācaran garhitaṁ loke
jñātīnāṁ karma vipriyam
sarayvāṁ krīḍato bālān
prāsyad udvejayañ janam

asamañjasaḥ—the son of Sagara Mahārāja; *ātmānam*—personally; *darśayan*—exhibiting; *asamañjasam*—very disturbing; *jāti-smaraḥ*—able to remember his past life; *purā*—formerly; *saṅgāt*—from bad association; *yogī*—although he was a great mystic *yogī; yogāt*—from the path of executing mystic *yoga; vicālitaḥ*—fell down; *ācaran*—behaving; *garhitam*—very badly; *loke*—in the society; *jñātīnām*—of his relatives; *karma*—activities; *vipriyam*—not very favorable; *sarayvām*—in the River Sarayū; *krīḍataḥ*—while engaged in sports; *bālān*—all the boys; *prāsyat*—would throw; *udvejayan*—giving trouble; *janam*—to people in general.

TRANSLATION

Formerly, in his previous birth, Asamañjasa had been a great mystic yogī, but by bad association he had fallen from his exalted position. Now, in this life, he was born in a royal family and was a jāti-smara; that is, he had the special advantage of being able to remember his past birth. Nonetheless, he wanted to display himself as a miscreant, and therefore he would do things that were abominable in the eyes of the public and unfavorable to his relatives. He would disturb the boys sporting in the River Sarayū by throwing them into the depths of the water.

TEXT 17

एवं वृत्तः परित्यक्तः पित्रा स्नेहमपोह्य वै ।
योगैश्वर्येण बालांस्तान् दर्शयित्वा ततो ययौ ॥१७॥

evaṁ vṛttaḥ parityaktaḥ
pitrā sneham apohya vai
yogaiśvaryeṇa bālāṁs tān
darśayitvā tato yayau

evam vṛttaḥ—thus engaged (in abominable activities); *parityaktaḥ*—condemned; *pitrā*—by his father; *sneham*—affection; *apohya*—giving up; *vai*—indeed; *yoga-aiśvaryeṇa*—by mystic power; *bālān tān*—all those boys (thrown in the water and killed); *darśayitvā*—after again showing them all to their parents; *tataḥ yayau*—he left that place.

TRANSLATION

Because Asamañjasa engaged in such abominable activities, his father gave up affection for him and had him exiled. Then Asamañjasa exhibited his mystic power by reviving the boys and showing them to the King and their parents. After this, Asamañjasa left Ayodhyā.

PURPORT

Asamañjasa was a *jāti-smara;* because of his mystic power, he did not forget his previous consciousness. Thus he could give life to the dead. By exhibiting wonderful activities in relation to the dead children, he certainly attracted the attention of the King and the people in general. Then he left that place immediately.

TEXT 18

अयोध्यावासिनः सर्वे बालकान् पुनरागतान् ।
दृष्ट्वा विसिस्मिरे राजन् राजा चाप्यन्वतप्यत ॥१८॥

ayodhyā-vāsinaḥ sarve
bālakān punar āgatān
dṛṣṭvā visismire rājan
rājā cāpy anvatapyata

ayodhyā-vāsinaḥ—the inhabitants of Ayodhyā; *sarve*—all of them; *bālakān*—their sons; *punaḥ*—again; *āgatān*—having come back to life;

dṛṣṭvā—after seeing this; *visismire*—became astounded; *rājan*—O King Parīkṣit; *rājā*—King Sagara; *ca*—also; *api*—indeed; *anvatapyata*—very much lamented (the absence of his son).

TRANSLATION

O King Parīkṣit, when all the inhabitants of Ayodhyā saw that their boys had come back to life, they were astounded, and King Sagara greatly lamented the absence of his son.

TEXT 19

अंशुमांश्चोदितो राज्ञा तुरगान्वेषणे ययौ ।
पितृव्यखातानुपथं भस्मान्ति ददृशे हयम् ॥१९॥

aṁśumāṁś codito rājñā
turagānveṣaṇe yayau
pitṛvya-khātānupathaṁ
bhasmānti dadṛśe hayam

aṁśumān—the son of Asamañjasa; *coditaḥ*—being ordered; *rajñā*—by the King; *turaga*—the horse; *anveṣaṇe*—to search for; *yayau*—went out; *pitṛvya-khāta*—as described by his father's brothers; *anupatham*—following that path; *bhasma-anti*—near the stack of ashes; *dadṛśe*—he saw; *hayam*—the horse.

TRANSLATION

Thereafter, Aṁśumān, the grandson of Mahārāja Sagara, was ordered by the King to search for the horse. Following the same path traversed by his uncles, Aṁśumān gradually reached the stack of ashes and found the horse nearby.

TEXT 20

तत्रासीनं मुनिं वीक्ष्य कपिलाख्यमधोक्षजम् ।
अस्तौत् समाहितमनाः प्राञ्जलिः प्रणतो महान् ॥२०॥

tatrāsīnaṁ muniṁ vīkṣya
kapilākhyam adhokṣajam

astaut samāhita-manāḥ
prāñjaliḥ praṇato mahān

tatra—there; *āsīnam*—seated; *munim*—the great sage; *vīkṣya*—seeing; *kapila-ākhyam*—known as Kapila Muni; *adhokṣajam*—the incarnation of Viṣṇu; *astaut*—offered prayers; *samāhita-manāḥ*—with great attention; *prāñjaliḥ*—with folded hands; *praṇataḥ*—falling down, offered obeisances; *mahān*—Aṁśumān, the great personality.

TRANSLATION

The great Aṁśumān saw the sage named Kapila, the saint who is an incarnation of Viṣṇu, sitting there by the horse. Aṁśumān offered Him respectful obeisances, folded his hands and offered Him prayers with great attention.

TEXT 21

अंशुमानुवाच
न पश्यति त्वां परमात्मनोऽजनो
न बुध्यतेऽद्यापि समाधियुक्तिभिः ।
कुतोऽपरे तस्य मनःशरीरधी-
विसर्गसृष्टा वयमप्रकाशाः ॥२१॥

aṁśumān uvāca
na paśyati tvāṁ param ātmano 'jano
na budhyate 'dyāpi samādhi-yuktibhiḥ
kuto 'pare tasya manaḥ-śarīra-dhī-
visarga-sṛṣṭā vayam aprakāśāḥ

aṁśumān uvāca—Aṁśumān said; *na*—not; *paśyati*—can see; *tvām*—Your Lordship; *param*—transcendental; *ātmanaḥ*—of us living beings; *ajanaḥ*—Lord Brahmā; *na*—not; *budhyate*—can understand; *adya api*—even today; *samādhi*—by meditation; *yuktibhiḥ*—or by mental speculation; *kutaḥ*—how; *apare*—others; *tasya*—his; *manaḥ-śarīra-dhī*—who consider the body or mind to be the self;

visarga-sṛṣṭāḥ—created beings within the material world; *vayam*—we; *aprakāśāḥ*—without transcendental knowledge.

TRANSLATION

Aṁśumān said: My Lord, even Lord Brahmā is to this very day unable to understand Your position, which is far beyond himself, either by meditation or by mental speculation. So what to speak of others like us, who have been created by Brahmā in various forms as demigods, animals, human beings, birds and beasts? We are completely in ignorance. Therefore, how can we know You, who are the Transcendence?

PURPORT

icchā-dveṣa-sammutthena
dvandva-mohena bhārata
sarva-bhūtāni sammohaṁ
sarge yānti parantapa

"O scion of Bharata [Arjuna], O conqueror of the foe, all living entities are born into delusion, overcome by the dualities of desire and hate." (Bg. 7.27) All living beings in the material world are influenced by the three modes of material nature. Even Lord Brahmā is in the mode of goodness. Similarly, the demigods are generally in the mode of passion, and living entities lower than the demigods, such as human beings and animals, are in the mode of ignorance, or in mixed goodness, passion and ignorance. Therefore Aṁśumān wanted to explain that because his uncles, who had burnt to ashes, were under the modes of material nature, they could not understand Lord Kapiladeva. "Because You are beyond even the direct and indirect intelligence of Lord Brahmā," he prayed, "unless we are enlightened by Your Lordship it will not be possible for us to understand You."

athāpi te deva padāmbuja-dvaya-
prasāda-leśānugṛhīta eva hi
jānāti tattvaṁ bhagavan-mahimno
na cānya eko 'pi ciraṁ vicinvan

"My Lord, if one is favored by even a slight trace of the mercy of Your lotus feet, he can understand the greatness of Your personality. But those who speculate to understand the Supreme Personality of Godhead are unable to know You, even though they continue to study the *Vedas* for many years." (*Bhāg.* 10.14.29) The Lord, the Supreme Personality of Godhead, can be understood by one who is favored by the Lord; the Lord cannot be understood by others.

TEXT 22

ये देहभाजस्त्रिगुणप्रधाना
गुणान् विपश्यन्त्युत वा तमश्च ।
यन्मायया मोहितचेतसस्त्वां
विदुः स्वसंस्थं न बहिःप्रकाशाः ॥२२॥

ye deha-bhājas tri-guṇa-pradhānā
guṇān vipaśyanty uta vā tamaś ca
yan-māyayā mohita-cetasas tvāṁ
viduḥ sva-saṁsthaṁ na bahiḥ-prakāśāḥ

ye—those persons who; *deha-bhājaḥ*—have accepted the material body; *tri-guṇa-pradhānāḥ*—influenced by the three modes of material nature; *guṇān*—the manifestation of the three modes of material nature; *vipaśyanti*—can see only; *uta*—it is so said; *vā*—either; *tamaḥ*—the mode of ignorance; *ca*—and; *yat-māyayā*—by the illusory energy of whom; *mohita*—has been bewildered; *cetasaḥ*—the core of whose heart; *tvām*—Your Lordship; *viduḥ*—know; *sva-saṁstham*—situated in one's own body; *na*—not; *bahiḥ-prakāśāḥ*—those who can see only the products of external energy.

TRANSLATION

My Lord, You are fully situated in everyone's heart, but the living entities, covered by the material body, cannot see You, for they are influenced by the external energy, conducted by the three modes of material nature. Their intelligence being covered by

sattva-guṇa, rajo-guṇa and tamo-guṇa, they can see only the actions and reactions of these three modes of material nature. Because of the actions and reactions of the mode of ignorance, whether the living entities are awake or sleeping, they can see only the workings of material nature; they cannot see Your Lordship.

PURPORT

Unless one is situated in the transcendental loving service of the Lord, one is unable to understand the Supreme Personality of Godhead. The Lord is situated in everyone's heart. However, because the conditioned souls are influenced by material nature, they can see only the actions and reactions of material nature, but not the Supreme Personality of Godhead. One therefore must purify himself internally and externally:

apavitraḥ pavitro vā
sarvāvasthāṁ gato 'pi vā
yaḥ smaret puṇḍarīkākṣaṁ
sa bāhyābhyantaraḥ śuciḥ

To keep ourselves externally clean we should bathe three times daily, and for internal cleanliness we must cleanse the heart by chanting the Hare Kṛṣṇa *mantra.* The members of the Kṛṣṇa consciousness movement must always follow this principle (*bāhyābhyantaraḥ śuciḥ*). Then it will one day be possible to see the Supreme Personality of Godhead face to face.

TEXT 23

तं त्वामहं ज्ञानघनं स्वभाव-
प्रध्वस्तमायागुणभेदमोहैः ।
सनन्दनाद्यैर्मुनिभिर्विभाव्यं
कथं विमूढः परिभावयामि ॥२३॥

taṁ tvāṁ ahaṁ jñāna-ghanaṁ svabhāva-
pradhvasta-māyā-guṇa-bheda-mohaiḥ
sanandanādyair munibhir vibhāvyaṁ
kathaṁ vimūḍhaḥ paribhāvayāmi

tam—that personality; *tvām*—unto You; *aham*—I; *jñāna-ghanam*—Your Lordship, who are concentrated knowledge; *svabhāva*—by spiritual nature; *pradhvasta*—free from contamination; *māyā-guṇa*—caused by the three modes of material nature; *bheda-mohaiḥ*—by exhibition of the bewilderment of differentiation; *sanandana-ādyaiḥ*—by such personalities as the four Kumāras (Sanat-kumāra, Sanaka, Sanandana and Sanātana); *munibhiḥ*—by such great sages; *vibhāvyam*—worshipable; *katham*—how; *vimūḍhaḥ*—being fooled by the material nature; *paribhāvayāmi*—can I think of You.

TRANSLATION

O my Lord, sages freed from the influence of the three modes of material nature—sages such as the four Kumāras [Sanat, Sanaka, Sanandana and Sanātana]—are able to think of You, who are concentrated knowledge. But how can an ignorant person like me think of You?

PURPORT

The word *svabhāva* refers to one's own spiritual nature or original constitutional position. When situated in this original position, the living entity is unaffected by the modes of material nature. *Sa guṇān samatītyaitān brahma-bhūyāya kalpate* (Bg. 14.26). As soon as one is freed from the influence of the three modes of material nature, he is situated on the Brahman platform. Vivid examples of personalities thus situated are the four Kumāras and Nārada. Such authorities can by nature understand the position of the Supreme Personality of Godhead, but a conditioned soul not freed from the influence of material nature is unable to realize the Supreme. In *Bhagavad-gītā* (2.45), therefore, Kṛṣṇa advises Arjuna, *traiguṇya-viṣayā vedā nistraiguṇyo bhavārjuna:* one must rise above the influence of the three modes of material nature. One who stays within the influence of the three material modes is unable to understand the Supreme Personality of Godhead.

TEXT 24

प्रशान्त मायागुणकर्मलिङ्ग-
मनामरूपं सदसद्विमुक्तम् ।

ज्ञानोपदेशाय गृहीतदेहं
नमामहे त्वां पुरुषं पुराणम् ॥२४॥

praśānta māyā-guṇa-karma-liṅgam
anāma-rūpaṁ sad-asad-vimuktam
jñānopadeśāya gṛhīta-dehaṁ
namāmahe tvāṁ puruṣaṁ purāṇam

praśānta—O completely peaceful one; *māyā-guṇa*—the modes of material nature; *karma-liṅgam*—symptomized by fruitive activities; *anāma-rūpam*—one who has no material name or form; *sat-asat-vimuktam*—transcendental to the manifested and nonmanifested modes of material nature; *jñāna-upadeśāya*—for distributing transcendental knowledge (as in *Bhagavad-gītā*); *gṛhīta-deham*—has assumed a form like a material body; *namāmahe*—I offer my respectful obeisances; *tvām*—unto You; *puruṣam*—the Supreme Person; *purāṇam*—the original.

TRANSLATION

O completely peaceful Lord, although material nature, fruitive activities and their consequent material names and forms are Your creation, You are unaffected by them. Therefore, Your transcendental name is different from material names, and Your form is different from material forms. You assume a form resembling a material body just to give us instructions like those of Bhagavad-gītā, but actually You are the supreme original person. I therefore offer my respectful obeisances unto You.

PURPORT

Śrīla Yāmunācārya has recited this verse in his *Stotra-ratna* (43):

bhavantam evānucaran nirantaraḥ
praśānta-niḥśeṣa-manorathāntaraḥ
kadāham aikāntika-nitya-kiṅkaraḥ
praharṣayiṣyāmi sanātha-jīvitam

"By serving You constantly, one is freed from all material desires and is completely pacified. When shall I engage as Your permanent eternal servant and always feel joyful to have such a fitting master?"

Manorathenāsati dhāvato bahiḥ: one who acts on the mental platform must descend to material activities. Material contamination, however, is completely absent from the Supreme Personality of Godhead and His pure devotee. Therefore the Lord is addressed as *praśānta*, completely peaceful, free from the disturbances of material existence. The Supreme Lord has no material name or form; only the foolish think that the Lord's name and form are material (*avajānanti māṁ mūḍhā mānuṣīṁ tanum āśritam*). The identity of the Supreme Lord is that He is the original person. Nonetheless, those who have but a poor fund of knowledge think that the Lord is formless. The Lord is formless in the material sense, but He has His transcendental form (*sac-cid-ānanda-vigraha*).

TEXT 25

त्वन्मायारचिते लोके वस्तुबुद्ध्या गृहादिषु ।
भ्रमन्ति कामलोभेर्ष्यामोहविभ्रान्तचेतसः ॥२५॥

tvan-māyā-racite loke
vastu-buddhyā gṛhādiṣu
bhramanti kāma-lobherṣyā-
moha-vibhrānta-cetasaḥ

tvat-māyā—through Your material energy; *racite*—which is manufactured; *loke*—in this world; *vastu-buddhyā*—accepting as factual; *gṛha-ādiṣu*—in hearth and home, etc.; *bhramanti*—wander; *kāma*—by lusty desires; *lobha*—by greed; *īrṣyā*—by envy; *moha*—and by illusion; *vibhrānta*—is bewildered; *cetasaḥ*—the cores of whose hearts.

TRANSLATION

O my Lord, those whose hearts are bewildered by the influence of lust, greed, envy and illusion are interested only in false hearth and home in this world created by Your māyā. Attached to home, wife and children, they wander in this material world perpetually.

TEXT 26

अद्य नः सर्वभूतात्मन् कामकर्मेन्द्रियाशयः ।
मोहपाशो दृढश्छिन्नो भगवंस्तव दर्शनात् ॥२६॥

adya naḥ sarva-bhūtātman
kāma-karmendriyāśayaḥ
moha-pāśo dṛḍhaś chinno
bhagavaṁs tava darśanāt

adya—today; *naḥ*—our; *sarva-bhūta-ātman*—O You, who are the Supersoul; *kāma-karma-indriya-āśayaḥ*—being under the influence of lusty desires and fruitive activities; *moha-pāśaḥ*—this hard knot of illusion; *dṛḍhaḥ*—very strong; *chinnaḥ*—broken; *bhagavan*—O my Lord; *tava darśanāt*—simply by seeing You.

TRANSLATION

O Supersoul of all living entities, O Personality of Godhead, simply by seeing You I have now been freed from all lusty desires, which are the root cause of insurmountable illusion and bondage in the material world.

TEXT 27

श्रीशुक उवाच
इत्थंगीतानुभावस्तं भगवान् कपिलो मुनिः ।
अंशुमन्तमुवाचेदमनुग्राह्य धिया नृप ॥२७॥

śrī-śuka uvāca
itthaṁ gītānubhāvas taṁ
bhagavān kapilo muniḥ
aṁśumantam uvācedam
anugrāhya dhiyā nṛpa

śrī-śukaḥ uvāca—Śrī Śukadeva Gosvāmī said; *ittham*—in this way; *gīta-anubhāvaḥ*—whose glories are described; *tam*—unto Him; *bhagavān*—the Personality of Godhead; *kapilaḥ*—named Kapila Muni; *muniḥ*—the great sage; *aṁśumantam*—unto Aṁśumān; *uvāca*—said;

idam—this; *anugrāhya*—being very merciful; *dhiyā*—with the path of knowledge; *nṛpa*—O King Parīkṣit.

TRANSLATION

O King Parīkṣit, when Aṁśumān had glorified the Lord in this way, the great sage Kapila, the powerful incarnation of Viṣṇu, being very merciful to him, explained to him the path of knowledge.

TEXT 28

श्रीभगवानुवाच
अश्वोऽयं नीयतां वत्स पितामहपशुस्तव ।
इमे च पितरो दग्धा गङ्गाम्भोऽर्हन्ति नेतरत् ॥२८॥

śrī-bhagavān uvāca
aśvo 'yaṁ nīyatāṁ vatsa
pitāmaha-paśus tava
ime ca pitaro dagdhā
gaṅgāmbho 'rhanti netarat

śrī-bhagavān uvāca—the great personality Kapila Muni said; *aśvaḥ*—horse; *ayam*—this; *nīyatām*—take; *vatsa*—O My son; *pitāmaha*—of your grandfather; *paśuḥ*—this animal; *tava*—your; *ime*—all these; *ca*—also; *pitaraḥ*—bodies of forefathers; *dagdhāḥ*—burnt to ashes; *gaṅgā-ambhaḥ*—the water of the Ganges; *arhanti*—can be saved; *na*—not; *itarat*—any other means.

TRANSLATION

The Personality of Godhead said: My dear Aṁśumān, here is the animal sought by your grandfather for sacrifice. Please take it. As for your forefathers, who have been burnt to ashes, they can be delivered only by Ganges water, and not by any other means.

TEXT 29

तं परिक्रम्य शिरसा प्रसाद्य हयमानयत् ।
सगरस्तेन पशुना यज्ञशेषं समापयत् ॥२९॥

taṁ parikramya śirasā
prasādya hayam ānayat
sagaras tena paśunā
yajña-śeṣaṁ samāpayat

tam—that great sage; *parikramya*—after circumambulating; *śirasā*—(by bowing down) with his head; *prasādya*—making Him fully satisfied; *hayam*—the horse; *ānayat*—brought back; *sagaraḥ*—King Sagara; *tena*—by that; *paśunā*—animal; *yajña-śeṣam*—the last ritualistic ceremony of the sacrifice; *samāpayat*—executed.

TRANSLATION

Thereafter, Aṁśumān circumambulated Kapila Muni and offered Him respectful obeisances, bowing his head. After fully satisfying Him in this way, Aṁśumān brought back the horse meant for sacrifice, and with this horse Mahārāja Sagara performed the remaining ritualistic ceremonies.

TEXT 30

राज्यमंशुमते न्यस्य निःस्पृहो मुक्तबन्धनः ।
और्वोपदिष्टमार्गेण लेभे गतिमनुत्तमाम् ॥३०॥

rājyam aṁśumate nyasya
niḥspṛho mukta-bandhanaḥ
aurvopadiṣṭa-mārgeṇa
lebhe gatim anuttamām

rājyam—his kingdom; *aṁśumate*—unto Aṁśumān; *nyasya*—after delivering; *niḥspṛhaḥ*—without further material desires; *mukta-bandhanaḥ*—completely freed from material bondage; *aurva-upadiṣṭa*—instructed by the great sage Aurva; *mārgeṇa*—by following that path; *lebhe*—achieved; *gatim*—destination; *anuttamām*—supreme.

TRANSLATION

After delivering charge of his kingdom to Aṁśumān and thus being freed from all material anxiety and bondage, Sagara

Mahārāja, following the means instructed by Aurva Muni, achieved the supreme destination.

Thus end the Bhaktivedanta purports of the Ninth Canto, Eighth Chapter, of the Śrīmad-Bhāgavatam, *entitled "The Sons of Sagara Meet Lord Kapiladeva."*

Appendixes

The Author

His Divine Grace A. C. Bhaktivedanta Swami Prabhupāda appeared in this world in 1896 in Calcutta, India. He first met his spiritual master, Śrīla Bhaktisiddhānta Sarasvatī Gosvāmī, in Calcutta in 1922. Bhaktisiddhānta Sarasvatī, a prominent devotional scholar and the founder of sixty-four Gauḍīya Maṭhas (Vedic institutes), liked this educated young man and convinced him to dedicate his life to teaching Vedic knowledge. Śrīla Prabhupāda became his student, and eleven years later (1933) at Allahabad he became his formally initiated disciple.

At their first meeting, in 1922, Śrīla Bhaktisiddhānta Sarasvatī Ṭhākura requested Śrīla Prabhupāda to broadcast Vedic knowledge through the English language. In the years that followed, Śrīla Prabhupāda wrote a commentary on the *Bhagavad-gītā*, assisted the Gauḍīya Maṭha in its work and, in 1944, without assistance, started an English fortnightly magazine, edited it, typed the manuscripts and checked the galley proofs. He even distributed the individual copies freely and struggled to maintain the publication. Once begun, the magazine never stopped; it is now being continued by his disciples in the West.

Recognizing Śrīla Prabhupāda's philosophical learning and devotion, the Gauḍīya Vaiṣṇava Society honored him in 1947 with the title "Bhaktivedanta." In 1950, at the age of fifty-four, Śrīla Prabhupāda retired from married life, and four years later he adopted the *vānaprastha* (retired) order to devote more time to his studies and writing. Śrīla Prabhupāda traveled to the holy city of Vṛndāvana, where he lived in very humble circumstances in the historic medieval temple of Rādhā-Dāmodara. There he engaged for several years in deep study and writing. He accepted the renounced order of life (*sannyāsa*) in 1959. At Rādhā-Dāmodara, Śrīla Prabhupāda began work on his life's masterpiece: a multivolume translation and commentary on the eighteen thousand verse *Śrīmad-Bhāgavatam* (*Bhāgavata Purāṇa*). He also wrote *Easy Journey to Other Planets.*

After publishing three volumes of *Bhāgavatam*, Śrīla Prabhupāda came to the United States, in 1965, to fulfill the mission of his spiritual master. Since that time, His Divine Grace has written over forty volumes of authoritative translations, commentaries and summary studies of the philosophical and religious classics of India.

In 1965, when he first arrived by freighter in New York City, Śrīla Prabhupāda was practically penniless. It was after almost a year of great difficulty that he established the International Society for Krishna Consciousness in July of 1966. Under his careful guidance, the Society has grown within a decade to a worldwide confederation of almost one hundred *āśramas*, schools, temples, institutes and farm communities.

In 1968, Śrīla Prabhupāda created New Vṛndāvana, an experimental Vedic community in the hills of West Virginia. Inspired by the success of New Vṛndāvana, now a thriving farm community of more than one thousand acres, his students have since founded several similar communities in the United States and abroad.

In 1972, His Divine Grace introduced the Vedic system of primary and secondary education in the West by founding the Gurukula school in Dallas, Texas. The school began with 3 children in 1972, and by the beginning of 1975 the enrollment had grown to 150.

Śrīla Prabhupāda has also inspired the construction of a large international center at Śrīdhāma Māyāpur in West Bengal, India, which is also the site for a planned Institute of Vedic Studies. A similar project is the magnificent Kṛṣṇa-Balarāma Temple and International Guest House in Vṛndāvana, India. These are centers where Westerners can live to gain firsthand experience of Vedic culture.

Śrīla Prabhupāda's most significant contribution, however, is his books. Highly respected by the academic community for their authoritativeness, depth and clarity, they are used as standard textbooks in numerous college courses. His writings have been translated into eleven languages. The Bhaktivedanta Book Trust, established in 1972 exclusively to publish the works of His Divine Grace, has thus become the world's largest publisher of books in the field of Indian religion and philosophy. Its latest project is the publishing of Śrīla Prabhupāda's most recent work: a seventeen-volume translation and commentary—completed by Śrīla Prabhupāda in only eighteen months—on the Bengali religious classic *Śrī Caitanya-caritāmṛta.*

In the past ten years, in spite of his advanced age, Śrīla Prabhupāda has circled the globe twelve times on lecture tours that have taken him to six continents. In spite of such a vigorous schedule, Śrīla Prabhupāda continues to write prolifically. His writings constitute a veritable library of Vedic philosophy, religion, literature and culture.

References

The purports of *Śrīmad-Bhāgavatam* are all confirmed by standard Vedic authorities. The following authentic scriptures are specifically cited in this volume:

Bhagavad-gītā, 22–23, 40–41, 48, 99, 100, 101, 108, 112, 125, 130, 141, 143–144, 168, 208, 214, 215, 252, 255

Bhakti-rasāmṛta-sindhu, 108, 172

Brahma-saṁhitā, 41

Brahma-vaivarta Purāṇa, 182

Caitanya-candrāmṛta, 107

Caitanya-candrodaya-nāṭaka, 211

Garuḍa Purāṇa, 147

Śikṣāṣṭaka, 12–13

Śrīmad-Bhāgavatam, 13, 43–44, 48, 66, 102, 106, 110, 111, 123, 124, 141, 170, 179, 223, 252–253

Stotra-ratna, 256–257

GENEALOGICAL TABLE
The Descendants of Vaivasvata Manu

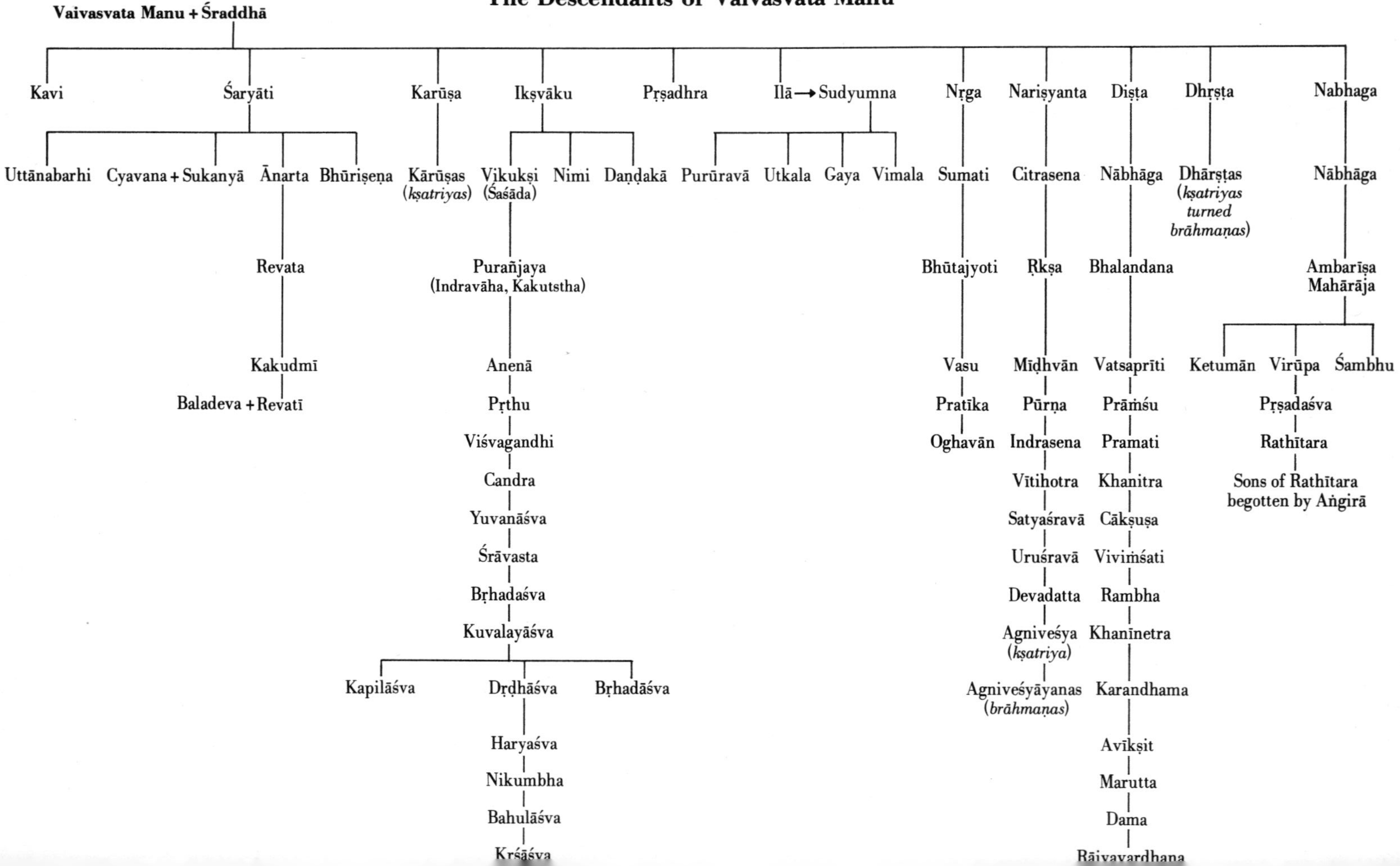
Vaivasvata Manu + Śraddhā
Kavi
Śaryāti
Karūṣa
Ikṣvāku
Pṛṣadhra
Ilā → Sudyumna
Nṛga
Nariṣyanta
Diṣṭa
Dhṛṣṭa
Nabhaga
Uttānabarhi
Cyavana + Sukanyā
Ānarta
Bhūriṣeṇa
Kārūṣas (kṣatriyas)
Vikukṣi (Śaśāda)
Nimi
Daṇḍakā
Purūravā
Utkala
Gaya
Vimala
Sumati
Citrasena
Nābhāga
Dhārṣṭas (kṣatriyas turned brāhmaṇas)
Nābhāga
Revata
Purañjaya (Indravāha, Kakutstha)
Bhūtajyoti
Ṛkṣa
Bhalandana
Ambarīṣa Mahārāja
Kakudmī
Baladeva + Revatī
Anenā
Pṛthu
Viśvagandhi
Candra
Yuvanāśva
Śrāvasta
Bṛhadaśva
Kuvalayāśva
Kapilāśva
Dṛḍhāśva
Bṛhadāśva
Haryaśva
Nikumbha
Bahulāśva
Kṛśāśva
Vasu
Pratīka
Oghavān
Mīḍhvān
Pūrṇa
Indrasena
Vītihotra
Satyaśravā
Uruśravā
Devadatta
Agniveśya (kṣatriya)
Agniveśyāyanas (brāhmaṇas)
Vatsaprīti
Prāṁśu
Pramati
Khanitra
Cākṣuṣa
Viviṁśati
Rambha
Khanīnetra
Karandhama
Avīkṣit
Marutta
Dama
Rājyavardhana
Ketumān
Virūpa
Śambhu
Pṛṣadaśva
Rathītara
Sons of Rathītara begotten by Aṅgirā

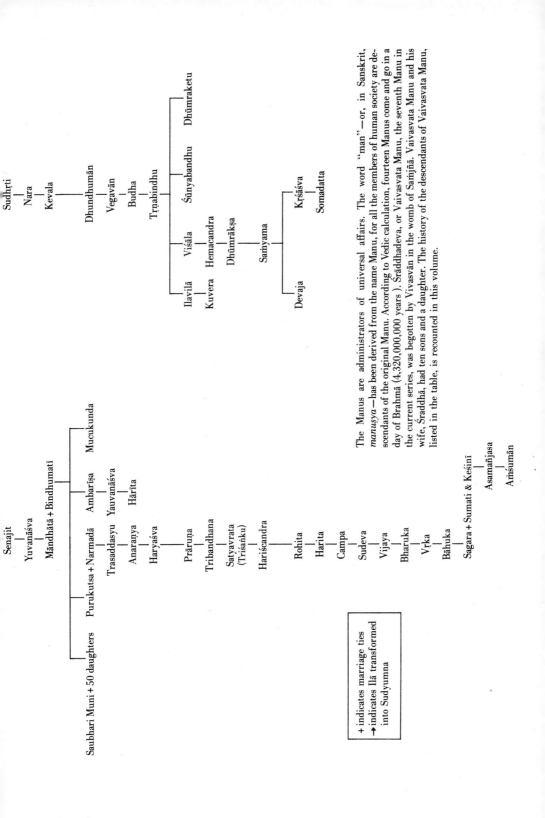

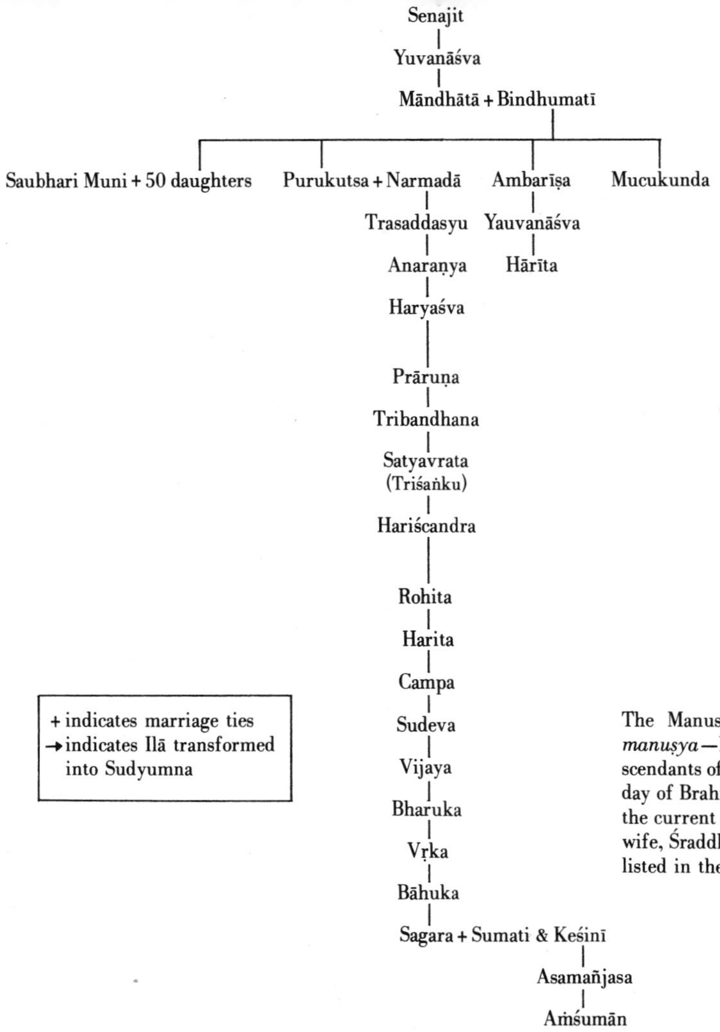

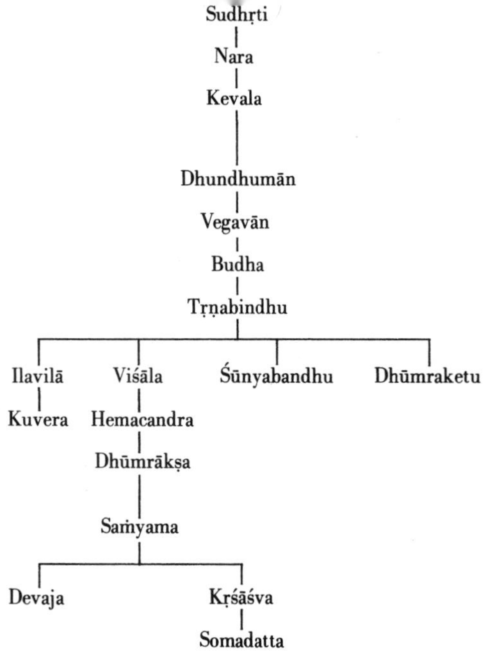

+ indicates marriage ties
→ indicates Ilā transformed into Sudyumna

The Manus are administrators of universal affairs. The word "man"—or, in Sanskrit, *manuṣya*—has been derived from the name Manu, for all the members of human society are descendants of the original Manu. According to Vedic calculation, fourteen Manus come and go in a day of Brahmā (4,320,000,000 years). Śrāddhadeva, or Vaivasvata Manu, the seventh Manu in the current series, was begotten by Vivasvān in the womb of Saṁjñā. Vaivasvata Manu and his wife, Śraddhā, had ten sons and a daughter. The history of the descendants of Vaivasvata Manu, listed in the table, is recounted in this volume.

Glossary

A

Ācārya—a spiritual master who teaches by example.

Ārati—a ceremony for greeting the Lord with offerings of food, lamps, fans, flowers and incense.

Arcanā—the devotional process of Deity worship.

Āśrama—(1) the four spiritual orders of life: celibate student, householder, retired life and renounced life. (2) the residence of a saintly person.

Asuras—atheistic demons.

Avatāra—a descent of the Supreme Lord.

B

Bhagavad-gītā—the basic directions for spiritual life spoken by the Lord Himself.

Bhakta—a devotee.

Bhakti-yoga—linking with the Supreme Lord by devotional service.

Brahmacarya—celibate student life; the first order of Vedic spiritual life.

Brahman—the Absolute Truth; especially the impersonal aspect of the Absolute.

Brāhmaṇa—one wise in the *Vedas* who can guide society; the first Vedic social order.

C

Caṇḍāla—a lowborn person accustomed to filthy habits such as dog-eating.

D

Dakṣiṇā—a disciple's gift to his spiritual master, collected by begging and given as a token of gratitude.

Dharma—eternal occupational duty; religious principles.

Dvi-parārdha—the duration of Brahmā's life.

E

Ekādaśī—a special fast day for increased remembrance of Kṛṣṇa, which comes on the eleventh day of both the waxing and waning moon.

G

Goloka (Kṛṣṇaloka)—the highest spiritual planet, containing Kṛṣṇa's personal abodes, Dvārakā, Mathurā and Vṛndāvana.
Gopīs—Kṛṣṇa's cowherd girl friends, His most confidential servitors.
Gṛhastha—regulated householder life; the second order of Vedic spiritual life.
Guru—a spiritual master.

H

Hare Kṛṣṇa mantra—*See: Mahā-mantra*

J

Jīva-tattva—the living entities, atomic parts of the Lord.
Jñāna—theoretical knowledge.

K

Kali-yuga (Age of Kali)—the present age, characterized by quarrel; it is last in the cycle of four and began five thousand years ago.
Karatālas—hand cymbals used in *kīrtana.*
Karma—fruitive action, for which there is always reaction, good or bad.
Karmī—a person satisfied with working hard for flickering sense gratification.
Kīrtana—chanting the glories of the Supreme Lord.
Kṛṣṇa-kathā—words spoken by Kṛṣṇa or about Kṛṣṇa.
Kṛṣṇaloka—*See:* Goloka
Kṣatriyas—a warrior or administrator; the second Vedic social order.

M

Mahā-mantra—the great chanting for deliverance:
Hare Kṛṣṇa, Hare Kṛṣṇa, Kṛṣṇa Kṛṣṇa, Hare Hare
Hare Rāma, Hare Rāma, Rāma Rāma, Hare Hare.

Mantra—a sound vibration that can deliver the mind from illusion.

Mathurā—Lord Kṛṣṇa's abode, surrounding Vṛndāvana, where He took birth and later returned to after performing His Vṛndāvana pastimes.

Māyā—illusion; forgetfulness of one's relationship with Kṛṣṇa.

Māyāvādīs—impersonal philosophers who say that the Lord cannot have a transcendental body.

Mṛdaṅga—a clay drum used for congregational chanting.

Mukti—liberation from birth and death.

Muni—a sage.

P

Paramparā—the chain of spiritual masters in disciplic succession.

Prasāda—food spiritualized by being offered to the Lord.

R

Ṛṣis—sages.

S

Sac-cid-ānanda-vigraha—the Lord's transcendental form, which is eternal, full of knowledge and bliss.

Sālokya—the liberation of residing on the same planet as the Lord.

Sāmīpya—the liberation of becoming a personal associate of the Lord.

Saṅkīrtana—public chanting of the names of God, the approved *yoga* process for this age.

Sannyāsa—renounced life; the fourth order of Vedic spiritual life.

Sārṣṭi—the liberation of having the same opulences as the Lord.

Sārūpya—the liberation of having a form similar to the Lord's.

Śāstras—revealed scriptures.

Satī rite—voluntary suicide by a widow at her husband's funeral.

Satyāgraha—fasting for political purposes.

Soma-rasa—a heavenly elixir available on the moon.

Śravaṇaṁ kīrtanaṁ viṣṇoḥ—the devotional processes of hearing and chanting about Lord Viṣṇu.

Śūdra—a laborer; the fourth of the Vedic social orders.

Svāmī—one who controls his mind and senses; title of one in the renounced order of life.

T

Tapasya—austerity; accepting some voluntary inconvenience for a higher purpose.

Tilaka—auspicious clay marks that sanctify a devotee's body as a temple of the Lord.

V

Vaikuṇṭha—the spiritual world.

Vaiṣṇava—a devotee of Lord Viṣṇu, Kṛṣṇa.

Vaiśyas—farmers and merchants; the third Vedic social order.

Vānaprastha—one who has retired from family life; the third order of Vedic spiritual life.

Varṇa—the four occupational divisions of society: the intellectual class, the administrative class, the mercantile class, and the laborer class.

Varṇāśrama—the Vedic social system of four social and four spiritual orders.

Vedas—the original revealed scriptures, first spoken by the Lord Himself.

Viṣṇu, Lord—Kṛṣṇa's expansion for the creation and maintenance of the material universes.

Vṛndāvana—Kṛṣṇa's personal abode, where He fully manifests His quality of sweetness.

Vyāsadeva—Kṛṣṇa's incarnation, at the end of Dvāpara-yuga, for compiling the *Vedas.*

Y

Yajña—sacrifice; work done for the satisfaction of Lord Viṣṇu.

Yogī—a transcendentalist who, in one way or another, is striving for union with the Supreme.

Yugas—ages in the life of a universe, occurring in a repeated cycle of four.

Sanskrit Pronunciation Guide

Vowels

अ a आ ā इ i ई ī उ u ऊ ū ऋ ṛ ॠ ṝ
ऌ ḷ ए e ऐ ai ओ o औ au

ं ṁ *(anusvāra)* ः ḥ *(visarga)*

Consonants

Gutturals:	क ka	ख kha	ग ga	घ gha	ङ ṅa
Palatals:	च ca	छ cha	ज ja	झ jha	ञ ña
Cerebrals:	ट ṭa	ठ ṭha	ड ḍa	ढ ḍha	ण ṇa
Dentals:	त ta	थ tha	द da	ध dha	न na
Labials:	प pa	फ pha	ब ba	भ bha	म ma
Semivowels:	य ya	र ra	ल la	व va	
Sibilants:	श śa	ष ṣa	स sa		
Aspirate:	ह ha	ऽ ' *(avagraha)* – the apostrophe			

The vowels above should be pronounced as follows:

a – like the *a* in org*a*n or the *u* in b*u*t.
ā – like the *a* in f*a*r but held twice as long as short *a*.
i – like the *i* in p*i*n.
ī – like the *i* in p*i*que but held twice as long as short *i*.
u – like the *u* in p*u*sh.
ū – like the *u* in r*u*le but held twice as long as short *u*.

ṛ – like the *ri* in *ri*m.
ṝ – like *ree* in *ree*d.
ḷ – like *l* followed by *ṛ* (*lṛ*).
e – like the *e* in th*ey*.
ai – like the *ai* in *ai*sle.
o – like the *o* in g*o*.
au – like the *ow* in h*ow*.
ṁ (*anusvāra*) – a resonant nasal like the *n* in the French word *bon*.
ḥ (*visarga*) – a final *h*-sound: *aḥ* is pronounced like *aha; iḥ* like *ihi.*

The consonants are pronounced as follows:

k – as in *k*ite
kh – as in Ec*kh*art
g – as in *g*ive
gh – as in di*g-h*ard
ṅ – as in si*ng*
c – as in *ch*air
ch – as in staun*ch-h*eart
j – as in *j*oy
jh – as in he*dgeh*og
ñ – as in ca*ny*on
ṭ – as in *t*ub
ṭh – as in ligh*t-h*eart
ḍ – as in *d*ove
ḍha- as in re*d-h*ot
ṇ – as r*na* (prepare to say the *r* and say *na*).

Cerebrals are pronounced with tongue to roof of mouth, but the following dentals are pronounced with tongue against teeth:

t – as in *t*ub but with tongue against teeth.
th – as in ligh*t-h*eart but with tongue against teeth.
d – as in *d*ove but with tongue against teeth.
dh – as in re*d-h*ot but with tongue against teeth.
n – as in *n*ut but with tongue between teeth.

p – as in *p*ine
ph – as in u*ph*ill (not *f*)
b – as in *b*ird
bh – as in ru*b-h*ard
m – as in *m*other
y – as in *y*es
r – as in *r*un
l – as in *l*ight
v – as in *v*ine
ś (palatal) – as in the *s* in the German word *sprechen*
ṣ (cerebral) – as the *sh* in *sh*ine
s – as in *s*un
h – as in *h*ome

There is no strong accentuation of syllables in Sanskrit, only a flowing of short and long (twice as long as the short) syllables.

Index of Sanskrit Verses

This index constitutes a complete listing of the first and third lines of each of the Sanskrit poetry verses of this volume of *Śrīmad-Bhāgavatam*, arranged in English alphabetical order. The first column gives the Sanskrit transliteration, and the second and third columns, respectively, list the chapter-verse reference and page number for each verse.

B

C

D

E

G

H

I

J

K

General Index

Numerals in boldface type indicate references to translations of the verses of *Śrīmad-Bhāgavatam.*

A

Ābrahma-bhuvanāl lokāḥ
quoted, 223
Absolute Truth
Ambarīṣa aware of, 169
features of, three listed, **169**, 170
mahātmā knows, 170
pure devotees know, 169
See also: Supreme Lord
Ācāryas (saintly teachers)
service to, recommended, 212
See also: Spiritual master, *all entries*
Activities
of Asamañjasa abominable, **248, 249**
in Deity worship, 109
of devotees inconceivable, 164, 165
five forbidden, in Kali-yuga, 182
material, devotee unattracted by, 107–108
Purañjaya named according to, **185, 186, 188, 189–190**
sinful, cow slaughter as, 34
spiritual vs. material, 108
of Vaiṣṇava misunderstood, 164–165
See also: Karma
Adhvaryu priest at Ambarīṣa's sacrifice, **105**
Aditi, **8**
Administrators. *See:* Kings; *Kṣatriyas;* Leaders, government
Age (time of life)
old. *See:* Old age
of retirement from family life, 28
Age of Kali. *See:* Kali-yuga
Agni, **46**
Agniveśya
brahminical dynasty from, **47**
other names of, **46**
Agricultural field tilled by proxy producer, woman impregnated by proxy progenitor compared to, 178
Ahaṁ tvāṁ sarva-pāpebhyo
quoted, 125
Air. *See:* Elements, material
Ajīgarta, **231**
Akāma defined, 106
Alambuṣā, **52**
Ambarīṣa, son of Māndhātā, **218**
Ambarīṣa Mahārāja
Absolute Truth known to, 169
aśvamedha sacrifice by, **103**
attachments shucked by, **110**
austerity by, **109**
brāhmaṇa guests satisfied by, **116**
brāhmaṇas consulted by, about breaking fast, **118**
brāhmaṇas heeded by, **101**, 102
brāhmaṇas worshiped by, **114**
citizenry under, 106
compared to mercantile man, 173
cows given in charity by, 116
curse ineffective on, **94–95**
Deity bathed & dressed by, **114**
in devotional service, **99, 101**, 104, **109, 169**, 173
Durvāsā angry at, **121–123**
Durvāsā appreciated, **160–166**
Durvāsā at feet of, **150, 151**
Durvāsā contrasted to, 139, 143
Durvāsā fed by, **163, 167**
Durvāsā's cause pleaded by, **152, 157–159**
Durvāsā's demon did not disturb, 124
as Durvāsā's friend, 168
as Durvāsā's host, **116**

E

Forest fire burning snake, Lord killing demon compared to, **125**, 126
Fortune, goddess of, as Nārāyaṇa's consort, **134**
Freedom
from birth, 41
from birth & death, 109
from material desires, 109, **258**
from material world, 41, **211**
from modes of nature, 255
Sagara achieved, **260–261**
for soul, 214, **235**
See also: Liberation

G

Gandharvas
Brahmā entertained by, **79**
Purukutsa killed, **220**
Gaṅgāsāgara, **240**
Ganges water
Aṁśumān's forefathers deliverable by, **259**
in Deity worship, 109
Garments changed by person, bodies changed by soul compared to, 23
Garuḍa, Saubhari Muni offended, 209
Garuḍa Purāṇa, quoted on Ambarīṣa-Durvāsā narrative, 147
Gautama, **103**
Gaya, **28**
Glowworms
Cyavana within, **62**
Sukanyā pierced, **59, 60, 62**
Goats, *śūdras* offer, to goddess Kālī, 182
Go-brāhmaṇa-hitāya ca
quoted, 139
God. *See:* Kṛṣṇa, Lord; Supreme Lord
God consciousness. *See:* Kṛṣṇa consciousness
Goddess Kālī, goat offerings to, 182
Goddess of fortune as Nārāyaṇa's consort, **134**
Godhead. *See:* Back to Godhead; Spiritual world; Supreme Lord
"Gods." *See:* Demigods
Gold
in Marutta's sacrifice, **50**
See also: Money; Opulence, material; Wealth
Goodness, mode of
Brahmā in, 252
Kapila's body completely in, **245**
Goodness in devotees only, 102, 123
Gopī-bhartuḥ pada-kamalayor dāsa-dāsānudāsaḥ
quoted, 137
Gopīs, Kṛṣṇa's bliss increased by, 138
Go-rakṣyam
defined, 182
See also: Cow protection
Gosvāmīs, the six
as servants of Kṛṣṇa's servants, 137
See also: Rūpa Gosvāmī
Gotra
defined, 26
See also: Dynasty
Government
of Ambarīṣa ideal, 102
material vs. spiritual, 102
Vedic vs. modern, 102
See also: Kings; Leaders, government; Society, human
Gṛhastha. See: Family; Household life; Marriage
Guṇas. See: Modes of material nature
Guru. See: Spiritual master

H

Haihayas, **241**
Happiness
in devotional service, **107**
of husband & wife, 64
of Lord & devotees, **138**
pure devotee understands, 141
See also: Bliss; Satisfaction
Happiness, material
devotee's consideration of, 107–108
nondevotee swept away by, 97
See also: Pleasure, material

M

N

Supreme Lord
devotional service to. *See:* Devotional service to the Supreme Lord
dharma as laws of, 154
direct servants of, 137
Durvāsā advised by, **144–145, 147**
Ekādaśī vow pleases, 112
as enjoyer, proprietor, friend, 101, 208
food offered to. *See:* Food, offered to Deity; *Prasāda*
form of, transcendental, **256,** 257
glories of, Ambarīṣa quoted on, **159**
happy with devotees, **138**
hearing about, by Ambarīṣa's citizenry, **105**
hearing about, by pure devotee, 105–106
in heart of all, 168, **253,** 254
Hiraṇyakaśipu killed by, 145
as Hṛṣīkeśa, 100
ignorance about, **252–255,** 257
ignorance dispelled by, 143–144
illusory energy of, mystifies even perfect persons, **133**
knowledge about, 100, **252–255**
knows everything, 125
Kumāras know, **255**
limitless, 138
lotus from, bore Brahmā, **7**
Māndhātā worshiped, **200**
Manu worshiped, for sons, **33**
mercy of. *See:* Mercy of the Supreme Lord
mission of, in material world, 138
names of. *See:* Names of the Supreme Lord
Nārada knows, 255
orders of, 130
as original person, **256,** 257
parts & parcels of, 23
peaceful, **256,** 257
power of, **132**
as proprietor, 101
protection by. *See:* Protection by the Supreme Lord
pure devotees of. *See:* Pure devotees of the Supreme Lord
sacrifice nondifferent from, **199**
sages know, **255**

Supreme Lord
as savior, **135**
seeing the, 254, **258**
Śiva controlled by, 132, 137, 148
via spiritual master, 137
as Supersoul, **6, 40, 188, 242**
surrender to. *See:* Surrender to the Supreme Lord
temple of. *See:* Temple of the Supreme Lord
time controlled by, 130
transcendental, **6–7,** 257
universe vanquished by, **130**
Vasiṣṭha blessed by, **16**
Vasiṣṭha prayed to, **16**
as Vāsudeva, 169
weapon of. *See:* Sudarśana *cakra*
worship of. *See:* Deity worship of the Supreme Lord; Worship of the Supreme Lord
See also: Absolute Truth; Kṛṣṇa, Lord; Nārāyaṇa, Lord; Supersoul; Viṣṇu, Lord
Supreme Lord, quotations from
on devotees controlling the Lord, **136**
on devotees never perishing, 112
on pure devotees, **139–143**
on spiritual abode by knowing the Lord, 41
Suras (godly persons). *See:* Demigods; Devotees of the Supreme Lord
Surrender to the Supreme Lord
by Brahmā & Co. **130**
dharma as, 154
as Lord's request, 138
Sūta Gosvāmī, quoted on Śukadeva & Parīkṣit, **5**
Svabhāva defined, 255
Svargāpavarga-narakeṣv
verse quoted, 106, 170

T

Tālajaṅghas, **241**
Tamo-guṇa. See: Ignorance, mode of
Tāṅdera caraṇa sevi bhakta-sane vāsa
quoted, 212

U

V